The Murder
of Julia Wallace

For my children, Christopher, Elizabeth, Sophie and Mary,
who have lived with the case as long as I have.

© James Murphy 2001

Published by The Bluecoat Press, Liverpool
Book design by March Design, Liverpool
Printed by The Cromwell Press, Trowbridge, Wiltshire

ISBN 1 872568 81 5

The Murder
of Julia Wallace

James Murphy

The Bluecoat Press

Acknowledgements

This book is the result of seven years of research. My starting point was the Wallace case file at Merseyside Police Headquarters and I am grateful to the former Chief Constable, Sir James Sharples, for granting me access to it and to Tony Mossman of Public Relations for the time he gave me. At the Crown Prosecution Service, Stuart Orr, Records Officer, allowed me to copy the Department of Public Prosecutions' Wallace file, and additionally sent me his wonderful, terse article, *Who Killed Julia Wallace?* from the CPS Journal.

I owe a huge debt to Douglas Birch, great nephew of Julia Dennis, who trusted me with several personal and important insights into the life of Julia and the Dennis family in general.

My thanks and appreciation go to my researchers, Dr Andrew Duncan, Trish Whelan, Fiona Rowland, Edward Lowe, TP Saxon, Elizabeth Murray and Frank Murphy, all of who laboured hard to lift the veils from the early lives of Julia and William Wallace. In North Yorkshire, Mr M Ashcroft of the County Records Office, and Mr PC Daw of the Library Service, Harrogate, provided additional background material.

In Liverpool, Dr James Burns, Head of Forensic Pathology at the University of Liverpool, took time to explain and elucidate the medical aspects of the case; Margaret Procter and Ruth Hobbins of the Merseyside Record Office, Janet Smith and David Stoker of the Liverpool Records Office and Harold Wolfe of the *Liverpool Daily Post and Echo*, set the scene in Liverpool. Laura Gomez recalled day to day life in the city in the thirties; BJ Harrison of Merseyside Historical and Transport Society provided the city's tramcar and bus routes for 1931 and James Allison Wildman, last survivor of the Wallace cast, talked of the events of the murder night as if they had occurred only yesterday.

My thanks also to Ian Kidd and Tom Lord, lifetime students of the Wallace case, who provided me with encouragement, assistance and advice; to Frank Cassidy at the *Barrow Evening Mail*, formerly the *North Western Daily Mail*, who opened up the archives; to Angus Adams of Forresters for his legal expertise; to Terry Storey for the illustrations and to those contributors from Liverpool and Cumbria who wish to remain anonymous.

But in the end, nothing would have been accomplished without the aid and abetment of my four children.

Contents

Introduction

In January 1931, Julia Wallace was found brutally murdered in the front parlour of her terraced home in the Anfield suburb of Liverpool. After a two-week investigation, Liverpool City Police, convinced that her death was little more than a common, though cleverly contrived, domestic murder, arrested her husband, William.

At his trial at the Spring Assizes, William Wallace was found guilty of wilful murder and was sentenced to death by hanging. However, the verdict of the jury was overturned by the Court of Criminal Appeal, on the grounds that the indictment was not proven and Wallace was released. The police sought no one else in connection with the death of Julia Wallace and when William Wallace died from a kidney complaint in 1933, Liverpool City Police file – 131GC, Julia Wallace,[1] was shelved and consigned to the archives, where it has been gathering dust ever since. However, the file remains open.

The Wallace case, as it is known, is unique: it is the only not proven murder case in English legal history. Not only is it an unsolved murder, it is a perfect murder, the 'nonpareil of all murder mysteries'.[2] And rarely a year goes by without a contribution being made to the voluminous literature on the case.

Did William Wallace brutally murder his wife on the night of Tuesday 20 January 1931? If he did not, then who did?

Since 1931, the Wallace case, and the questions it raises, has been re-examined and reconstructed, analysed and dissected, by a small army of writers, jurists and criminologists, in over forty publications and several radio and television broadcasts; it has even prompted questions in the House of Commons.[3] It stands next to the case of the Whitechapel murders of Jack the Ripper as one of the most documented and debated in the annals of crime. The Wallace case is 'more than a classic, it is *the* classic of criminology'.[4]

Yet, despite the probings and attention of this small army of investigators, it was not until 1969, thirty-eight years after the murder, that the scriptural book of Wallace, the book that answered the questions, was published: *The Killing of Julia Wallace* by Jonathan Goodman, which Wallace scholars today regard as the standard text on the subject.[5]

Goodman's study not only argued for, and conclusively proved, Wallace's innocence, but it also pointed the finger of suspicion at a Mr X as the most likely candidate for the role of Julia's murderer. Four years later, Robert Hussey in *Murderer Scot-Free*, gave added support to Goodman's thesis.[6]

In 1981, in a series of radio broadcasts marking the fiftieth anniversary of Julia Wallace's death, Roger Wilkes of Radio City, Merseyside, named Mr X as Richard Gordon Parry, the man who, in all probability, had murdered Mrs Wallace. Furthermore, Wilkes, like Goodman, was highly critical of the police. He alleged that there had been a conspiracy to cover up Parry's guilt, at the expense of Wallace's life, by officers of Liverpool City Police, acting in collusion with certain officials of Liverpool City Corporation. He developed this theme in his book, *Wallace: The Final Verdict*, first published in 1984.[7]

However, the accounts by Goodman, Hussey and Wilkes, despite their claims, have not established the identity of the killer. And they share a common characteristic with most of the major studies of the case, most notably those by Dorothy L Sayers, Yseult Bridges, Raymond Chandler, John Brophy, John Rowland, David Jessel and Colin Wilson:[8] they are factually flawed. And the flaws are so grave that none of the conclusions reached is tenable or justified: the basic geometry of the murder scene and its environs are beyond the grasp of many of the writers; vital evidence from the crime scene is overlooked, ignored and misrepresented, in order to promote a particular perspective, and supposition and speculation are paraded as fact to bolster flimsy conclusions.

Contrary to what the headlines in *The Daily Telegraph* announced on 21 January 1981, the Wallace case has not been solved, and the jury is still out. To date, there has not been a full and thorough examination of Julia Wallace's death, either by the police, or by the coterie of Wallace scholars, experts and aficionados.

In 1992 the Merseyside Police finally opened the dusty Wallace file to the public and the Department of Public Prosecutions also released its file. From these two, previously unavailable sources, it is now possible to reconstruct, for the first time, the events leading up to the murder, and the subsequent police investigation.

Furthermore, using the techniques and theories developed in America by the FBI's criminal personality profilers and refined by Professor David Canter in Britain, the evidence at the crime scenes will be explored and probed with the object of producing a profile of Julia's killer and, beyond a reasonable doubt, his name.

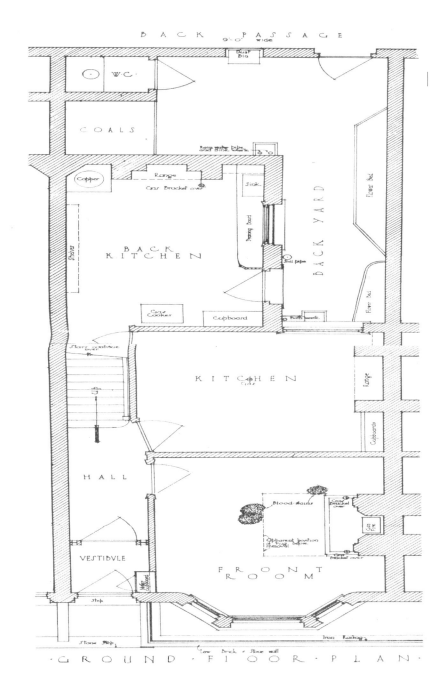

B A C K   P A S S A G E
9'-0" wide

Dust
Bin

W.C.

C O A L S

Copper

Range

Gas Bracket over

Sink

Draining Board

BACK
KITCHEN

Lamp under table
and Bible Board

B A C K   Y A R D

Flower Bed

Shelter

Gas
Cooker

Cupboard

Stairs cupboard
over

Up

Soil pipe

Roots sink

Flower Bed

K I T C H E N
Gas

Range

Cupboards

H A L L

Blood stains

Gas
Bracket
over

Gas
Fire

Gas
Bracket over

Approx. position
of body before
removal

VESTIBULE

Meter
Cupboard

F R O N T
R O O M

Step

Stone Step

Low Brick & Stone wall

Iron Railing

· G R O U N D · F L O O R · P L A N ·

The ground floor plan of 29 Wolverton Street.

8

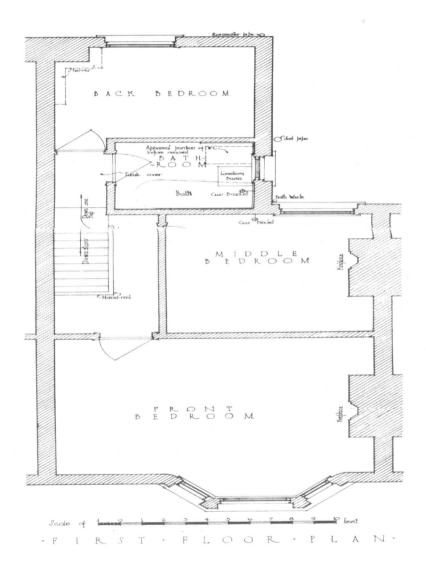

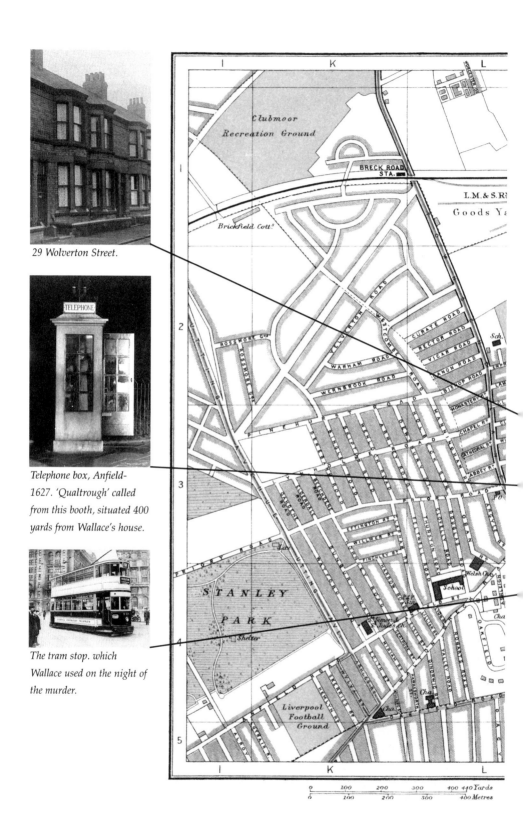

29 Wolverton Street.

Telephone box, Anfield-1627. 'Qualtrough' called from this booth, situated 400 yards from Wallace's house.

The tram stop. which Wallace used on the night of the murder.

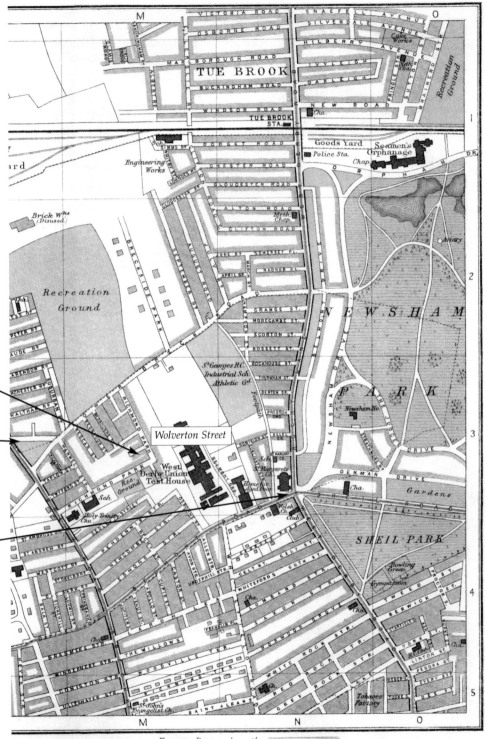

Wolverton Street

Bruntcliffe House, East Harlsey. The birthplace of Julia Dennis.

The Tin Tabernacle, the temporary church where William Wallace married Julia Dennis, in 1913.

The tombstone of Julia's parents, in the graveyard of St Oswald's Church, East Harlsey.

Julia Wallace, née Dennis, 1861 – 1931.   *William Wallace, 1878 – 1933.*

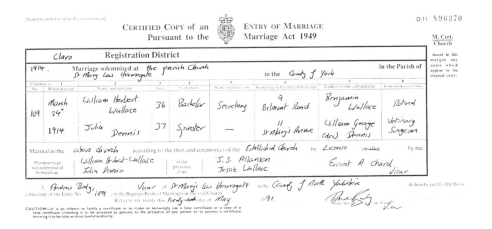

A copy of the marriage certificate of Julia Dennis and William Wallace.

Telephone box Anfield-1627. 'Qualtrough' called from this booth, situated 400 yards from Wallace's house.

2ⁿᵈ Class Championship.

1ˢᵗ Prize 10/- 2ⁿᵈ Prize 5/-

Mondays.

		NOV		DEC		JAN		FEB
		10	24	8	15	5	19	21
1	Chandler F.C.	X	2N	3D	4	5	6	7
2	Ellis T.	7L	1L	X	3	4	5	6
3	Lampitt E.	6W	7	1D	2	X	4	5
4	McCartney	5W	6	2	1	2	3	X
5	Moore T.	4L	X	6	2	1	2	3
6	Wallace W.H.	3L	4	5	X	7	1	2
7	Walsh J.	2W	5	4	6	6	X	1

Underlined take Black.

The chess match listings of the Championship players, which was publically displayed on the noticeboard of Cottle's City Café.

A tram, Wallace's form of transport on the night of the murder.

James Allison, the last surviving member of the Wallace case cast.

The death scene: the Wallaces' living room at 29 Wolverton Street, Anfield. Julia's body as it was found, slumped and face down before the fireplace.

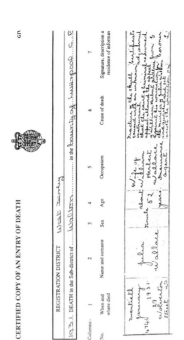

A copy of the death certificate of Julia Wallace.

The tombstone of Julia and William Wallace, in Anfield Cemetery.

Part One

Chapter 1

Prelude to Death

1

Friday 16 January, and it is just after dinnertime when John Paterson arrives at Holy Trinity Church at the corner of Breck Road and Richmond Park. He works for Condliff and Company, clockmakers, and taking out his pocket-watch, he notes that the church clock is two minutes fast. Entering the church, he slowly climbs the clock tower to reach the workings and he winds the clock before setting it right. He re-emerges into Breck Road, into the unsettled, wintry afternoon, to continue his rounds.

The following day fierce gales batter Liverpool, bringing little respite to its suffering inhabitants, ravaged by a flu epidemic and still recovering from the densest, most persistent fog in living memory. As the last, lingering wisps of the fog are carried off by the wind, low clouds and a withering rain descend, compounding the general misery.

As the gales abate, the rain continues as a keen drizzle into the evening, but some smiling faces are to be found in the welcoming pubs of Liverpool as a well-known phenomenon manifests itself: half the customers are celebrating, while the other half are laden with a disappointment as deep as the Depression.

Everton, at home to West Bromwich Albion, have won 2-1, the winning goal coming from Dixie Dean, and the team is still top of the Second Division, but arch rivals, Liverpool, have crashed 2-1 away to Huddersfield Town and have tumbled to fourteenth place in the First Division. As Evertonians drink to their good fortune, the disgruntled Liverpool supporters console themselves with the prospect of a better result at Anfield in a week's time.

The working-class suburb of Anfield is home to Liverpool Football Club; it is also home to Julia Wallace and her husband, William Herbert Wallace, at 29 Wolverton Street, Richmond Park, in the parish of Holy Trinity. And, like the Liverpool fans, Mr and Mrs Wallace are not celebrating on this Saturday night.

William Wallace has come down with flu, his second bout in six weeks. He has missed a morning's work, and has spent the day well wrapped up, his feet immersed in a mustard bath, sipping an occasional whisky and hot water and listening to the radio. Julia has developed a heavy, chesty cough and has taken to her bed.

2

William Wallace is six feet, two inches tall, slightly built and hunched at the shoulders. His receding hair is almost completely white and tops a gaunt face of sallowed complexion, set off by a pair of steel-rimmed spectacles and a greying moustache. He is conservative and reserved, both in manner and in dress, with a preference for sombre waist-coated suits, dark overcoats, black bowler hats and starched, winged collars attached to his white shirts, the traditional garb of the small-time businessman and clerk. His attire and demeanour give the impression that he is older than he actually is.

Julia Wallace is much shorter than her husband, five feet and three inches tall, of a similar slight build as William, but with a rounded, protruding stomach. Her once auburn hair is thinning and greying and she wears it off the face, pulled severely back into a plaited chignon at the nape of her neck, an unflattering style which accentuates her aquiline nose and narrow mouth. She dresses in loose-fitting, home-made clothes of uncompromising drabness and, except for shopping trips, visits to the doctor's and outings with her husband, she rarely leaves her home, having no intimate friends, and being shy and reserved, despite her Yorkshire upbringing. She, too, appears older than she says she is.

3

Sunday morning is damp and windy, and the church bells toll their beckoning call, tugging reluctant worshippers from warm beds to brave the assaults of the weather for salvation's sake. Julia and William ignore the summons and do not go out all day.

William Wallace's condition has improved somewhat, but not sufficiently so for him to venture into the frosty front parlour for violin practice, one of his usual Sunday pastimes. He tries to relax, to build up his strength, by reading and listening to the radio in the kitchen, and tending to Julia who, because of a restless night, coughing and wheezing, has remained in bed.

However, in the early afternoon, the quiet of the Wallace household is interrupted by a knock at the front door. Wallace answers the door to admit his sister-in-law, Amy Wallace, and his nephew, Edwin. Amy is married to Wallace's younger brother, Joseph, who works as a printer for the Malay Government in Kuala Lumpur. She chooses to live apart from her husband in Liverpool, in order to ensure a good education for her son. Amy and Edwin occupy a small flat in Ullet Road, off Smithdown Road, in the Sefton Park area of Liverpool. Edwin is hoping to enter the medical profession.

Since they are family, Amy and Edwin are shown into the kitchen, which is the warmest room in the house, and after stoking up the fire, Wallace brings Julia downstairs from her sick bed to join the family gathering. While they are not exactly friends, Julia and Amy do have a certain rapport and over tea, Julia tells her about the most recent of a series of burglaries which have plagued the Richmond Park area over the past few months, the work of the elusive 'Anfield Housebreaker'.

4

William Wallace met Julia Dennis in Harrogate, Yorkshire, and after a three-year courtship, they married at St Mary's Tin Tabernacle on 24 March, 1914.[1] William Wallace described himself as a thirty-six-year-old bachelor, employed as a secretary, the son of Benjamin Wallace, retired. Julia Dennis said she was thirty-seven years old, a spinster, the daughter of William George Dennis, veterinary surgeon, deceased.

Within a year of the marriage, the couple moved to Liverpool, where William took up the position of insurance collection agent in the Clubmoor area for the Prudential Assurance Company of Dale Street, in the city centre. At first they lived at 26 Pennsylvania Road, Clubmoor, but after four months they relocated half a mile away to their present home in Wolverton Street, Anfield.

Now, sixteen years later, aged fifty-two, William Wallace still works for the Prudential, in the same post as collection agent, walking the same Clubmoor district, visiting the same homes, in the same dreary streets, week in, week out, collecting insurance premiums.

5

The dawn chorus on Monday morning is the ring of hobnailed boots and wooden clogs on the cobblestones of the mean, gaslit streets converging on the Dock Road; thirty thousand dockers trudge to work on a six and a half mile front, tramping beneath the steel spans of the overhead railway, past the dozing policemen in their stone cubicles, and through the dock gates. The men congregate at the stands, cloth-capped, necks swathed in scarves, wrapped in heavy coats, bodies bent against the pelting rain and sleet, stamping their feet impatiently, waiting for the fresh-faced Dock Board clerks to call their names, to assign them work on one of the few boats tied up at the quays.[2]

Later in the morning the pavements are thronged with waif-like children on their way to school, bumping and boring past clerks, shop assistants and early shoppers, all oblivious to the weather. The streets echo to the hiss of steam lorries, the whoosh of trams, the growl of buses and the jingle of horse harnesses.

William Wallace decides he is fit enough to return to work. Before he leaves home at ten o'clock, he suggests that Julia should see the family physician, Dr Curwen. While he knocks on doors and collects premiums, Julia scurries through the wet streets to Anfield Road to the surgery, unaware that she has less than thirty-six hours to live.

6

From Holy Trinity Church on Breck Road, Richmond Park runs for four hundred yards before turning sharply at a right angle to run a further four hundred yards along the boundary wall of Belmont Road Workhouse[3] and into Lower Breck Road. At the right angle, Wolverton Street opens off to the left into two rows of thin-walled, red-bricked, terraced homes, most of which have yet to be converted from gas to the 'wonders of electricity'.[4]

Wolverton Street is closed to traffic and the top of the street is traversed by an entry behind which stands Campbell's Dancing Academy, whose entrance is in Richmond Park. The entry is just one of the many that criss-cross the area and which make the Richmond Park quarter a maze of narrow twists and turns, known only to its poor, but respectable, inhabitants.

The area swarms with children of all ages, but the Wallaces are childless, and live a rather introspective life with their cat in their three-bedroom home, which Julia cares for with the assistance of Sarah Jane Draper, who calls once a week to dust and clean. They eat in the kitchen, cook in the back kitchen or scullery, and entertain their infrequent visitors in the front parlour, which also doubles as a music room, wherein Julia plays the piano and William the violin. The front bedroom is used to store Julia's hats and handbags. They sleep in the middle bedroom, while the back one has been converted by William Wallace into a small chemistry laboratory – chemistry being a particular hobby, if not a vocation, of his.

Despite earning an above-average salary of almost six pounds per week,[5] including commission and bonuses from the Prudential, William Wallace does not own his own home. Like many houses in the district, 29 Wolverton Street is privately owned and the Wallaces pay their landlord, Samuel Evans of Anfield Road, a weekly rent of fourteen shillings and three pence.[6] The couple's income more than covers their outgoings and they are able to save. By January, 1931, they have accumulated two hundred and forty-two pounds in savings, approximating to a year's salary for William Wallace.

7

The rain and sleet continues into Monday night. The dockers have all gone home to their cubby-hole houses and the streets have emptied of children. The city centre offices have disgorged their staffs into the dark winter's night to crowd the bus and tram stops and the railway terminals for the journey home.

Samuel Beattie does not go directly home after work to the select residential area of Mossley Hill on Monday and Thursday nights. He is the manager for the cotton brokers, Messrs George Langley and Company of Orleans House, close to Exchange Station, the city's western commuter terminus. From the station it is but a short walk for Beattie down to 24B North John Street, where he descends a flight of steps into Cottle's City Café. At this time the café is closed to diners, but its doors are open to members of the Liverpool Central Chess Club. Samuel Beattie is the club's captain and William Wallace is a member.

The club meets twice a week on Mondays and Thursdays, and Beattie likes to arrive first to ensure that everything is in order before play commences. With the help of Gladys Harley, the café's waitress, Beattie arranges tables and chairs, sets up the chess boards and pieces and checks the results so far in the Second Class Championship, which has been in progress since November last. The club's noticeboard, displaying the championship playing order, hangs on the wall, diagonally opposite the café entrance. Adjacent to the board is a public telephone box with the number, Bank 3581, etched on the glass window.

It is after seven o'clock and Beattie is playing chess with a friend and fellow club member. The telephone rings. Gladys Harley answers it.

"Anfield is calling you," says the operator, as Gladys picks up the receiver.

Then a man with a deep voice speaks.

"Is Mr Wallace there?"

The man quickly goes on to explain that the call is in connection with the chess club.

"I'll bring the captain, Mr Beattie," replies Gladys.

"All right," says the man.

Gladys puts down the receiver and finds Beattie seated at a table.

"Is Mr Wallace here?" she asks, interrupting the chess game. "There's somebody on the telephone asking for Mr Wallace. Will you go and take the message for him? I don't know what he is talking about."

Beattie gets to his feet and walks over to the telephone box. He picks up the receiver and hears a man with a gruffish, strongly confident voice.

"Is Mr Wallace there? Will he be there?"

"I can't say," replies Beattie.

"Can you give me his address?"

"I'm afraid I cannot."

"Will you be sure to see him?"

"I don't know," says Beattie.

"Can you get in touch with him, as it is a matter of importance to Mr Wallace?"

"I'm not sure."

"I'm busy," says the man. "And I don't know if I can get him. It's my daughter's twenty-first and I want to do something for her which would be in the nature of business for Mr Wallace."

Even though Beattie has known Wallace for eight years he does not know what he does for a living.[7]

"If I can't get Mr Wallace himself, I can possibly get in touch with him through a friend," he offers.

"Will you ask him to call on me tomorrow night? You had better take my address."

"I'll take it," says Beattie, and takes out a used envelope and a pen from his coat pocket.

"My name is RM Qualtrough."

"Can you spell that, please?" Writing the name down, Beattie spells it back to the man. "RM Q-u-a-l-t-r-o-u-g-h."

"My address is 25 Menlove Gardens East, Mossley Hill."

"25 – Menlove – Gardens – East," repeats Beattie as he writes. "Mossley – Hill. Thank you. I'll pass on the message."

Beattie hangs up and returns to his chess game. The club is now beginning to fill up but Wallace is nowhere to be seen.

8

The night is cloudy and dark and the rain and sleet has subsided to a thin drizzle. At a quarter-past seven Wallace leaves 29 Wolverton Street by the back door. Usually when he goes out at night Julia walks down the yard with him to lock the door behind him, as it is his habit to return home through the front door.

Though averse to leaving Julia alone at night, particularly when she is ill, Wallace has, on the spur of the moment, decided to pay a long overdue visit to the chess club. He is an enthusiastic player rather than a good one and he only qualifies for the second class team. Chemistry, chess and reading, especially the works of the Stoic philosopher, Marcus Aurelius, are his three passions in life.

James Caird, a grocer by trade, is a near neighbour of William Wallace and they have known each other for almost fourteen years. Caird is also a member of the Central Chess Club, and on Monday night he arrives at the City Café at twenty-five to eight. He has no partner and watches the games in progress until seven-forty-five, when he notices Wallace enter the café. He approaches him and asks if he would like a friendly game.

"No," says Wallace. "I want to play my tournament games off."

He quickly arranges a game with Mr McCartney, which should have been played on 24 November. Club rules state that all games must commence by seven-forty-five, or else penalties will be imposed upon the players. Wallace and McCartney are soon engrossed in their match.

Caird wanders off, resuming his spectator's role, drifting from table to table in the crowded café, peering over shoulders at individual moves, until he arrives at Beattie's table.

"Good evening, Mr Beattie," he says.

Beattie glances up from the board.

"Good evening, Mr Caird," replies the club captain. Then he pauses for a moment as he remembers the telephone call. "Do you know Wallace's address? Will you be seeing him tonight because I have a telephone message for him?"

"Mr Wallace is here," says Caird. "He's playing on the table behind you."

Beattie looks over his shoulder and sees him.

"I'll go and speak to him." He excuses himself to his opponent and follows Caird to where Wallace is sitting, absorbed in the opening moves of his game. Beattie interrupts. "Good evening, Wallace. Someone has been on the telephone for you. A man called Qualtrough."

"Qualtrough?" asks Wallace, sitting back in his chair. "Qualtrough? I don't know him. Who is he?"

Beattie shrugs his shoulders.

"If you don't know him, I don't. But he left a message for you. He wants you to call on him tomorrow evening at seven-thirty. He says it's something in the nature of your business, to do with his daughter's twenty-first."

Wallace is perplexed.

"Qualtrough? I don't know anybody of that name. Where does he say he lives?"

Wallace takes out a pencil and a black Prudential memo book and Beattie pulls out the envelope on which he has noted Qualtrough's address.

"RM Qualtrough, 25 Menlove Gardens East, Mossley Hill," he recites.

Wallace begins to write in his book, murmuring to himself.

"RM Qualtrough, 25 Menlove Gardens West."

"Menlove Gardens East. East not West," reiterates Beattie.

"East," says Wallace and writes the word in block capital letters. "I don't know him. I don't know where it is. Menlove Avenue?"

"No, no," says Beattie. "Menlove Gardens. It's probably up by Menlove Avenue, though. In that area."

"I don't know where the place is but I suppose I'll find it," says Wallace, tucking away his pencil and memo book.

"Wait a minute," says Beattie. "I'll make enquiries from another member who lives in the neighbourhood." Caird and Wallace watch as Beattie approaches a club member named Deyes and engages him in conversation. "I can't help you any further," says Beattie when he returns. "You'd better look it up. It's a bad place to be knocking about in after dark."

"It's all right, Mr Beattie," replies Wallace. "I've got a tongue in my head. I can enquire."

"Perhaps you could get a tramcar to Penny Lane and then enquire," suggests Beattie, as he returns to his game.

"Oh, I belong to Liverpool," says Wallace, bringing the conversation to an end. "I suppose I'll find it."

McCartney, his opponent, suggests he take a tram from Spellow Lane to Smithdown Road and Wallace nods his assent.

And so the death sentence is passed on Julia Wallace.

9

It is after ten o'clock and most of the games are over. Wallace and some of the other members leave the café together and wait for a tramcar in North John Street. Wallace, Caird and Caird's friend, Betton, board a West Derby Road tram, but they do not sit together or speak to one another. Betton stays on the tram while Caird and Wallace alight at Belmont Road and walk home together.

Wallace is talkative, highly delighted at his win over McCartney, taking Caird through the endgame move by move. Then he changes the subject to that of RM Qualtrough.

"It's a funny name," comments Wallace. "I've never heard of it, have you?"

Caird avers and goes on to suggest that Wallace should take a bus along Queen's Drive to reach Menlove Avenue.

"I'll get a tram to town and another out again from town as I know the way," replies Wallace. "That's if I go at all. I'm not sure about going."

The two men part at Caird's front door in Letchworth Street. Wallace returns home, using the front door. Julia is still up, despite her cold, pottering around the kitchen. They eat a late supper before retiring.

Chapter 2
Murder

1

The lampmen walk and cycle through the streets and alleys turning off the gaslights, leaving it to the weak sun to penetrate and illumine the murk of the low clouds and keen drizzle on the morning of Tuesday 20 January 1931.

Wallace wears a grey trilby and dark grey mackintosh as he sets off for work at ten-thirty, catching a tramcar from Breck Road to Clubmoor. He knows the area well, the mean streets so typical of Liverpool, the forlorn terraces of the City Corporation and private landlords, the poor, brooding occupiers. On his weekly collection round he has almost six hundred calls to make, and he is often met at the door by a raggedy child pleading, 'me mam ain't home', or by a harassed, embarrassed woman bemoaning that, 'he ain't been paid yet' and asking Wallace to call for double the following week. And he always collects. Poor though the people may be, their pride will not allow the indignity of a pauper's funeral, or the burning shame of an enforced removal to the workhouse.

Julia is at home alone. An hour after her husband's departure, her routine is interrupted by a knock at the front door. It is Arthur Hoer, the window cleaner, who cleans windows along Wolverton Street. He asks for a bucket of warm water, which Julia provides. Arthur and his wife, Emily, wash windows in and around Wolverton Street until two o'clock, when Arthur quits to attend a meeting of the Markets Committee at the Municipal Offices in the city centre. As he leaves Wolverton Street, William Wallace arrives home for dinner, having completed his morning round. The rain has ceased, a stiff breeze has dispersed the clouds, and the afternoon is bright but chilly.

While the Wallaces eat their dinner, Charles Bliss, Arthur Hoer's brother-in-law, arrives in Wolverton Street to assist Emily. He is cleaning the top, back windows of a house a couple of doors up from the Wallace's at three-fifteen, when William Wallace leaves home to commence his afternoon round. His mackintosh is still damp from the morning drizzle.

Within minutes of his departure, Amy Wallace arrives at 29 Wolverton Street. She is calling to see how Julia's cold is progressing and she settles in for a chat with her sister-in-law. She refuses a cup of tea, saying she cannot stop long, but manages to extend a quick visit into an hour's stay. Julia tells her of the phone call that William received the previous night, and mentions the name Qualtrough, a name, she assures Amy, that neither she nor her husband knows.

Meanwhile, William Wallace is collecting insurance premiums in Maiden Lane. He is seen by a police constable, 206G James Rothwell, of Liverpool City Police, who is cycling towards the Anfield Bridewell.[1] He is acquainted with Wallace and is struck now by his demeanour; he appears to be crying, dabbing tears away from his eyes with the sleeve of his mackintosh. His face is haggard and drawn and PC Rothwell turns to have a second look at the Prudential man as he passes on his cycle, disturbed by Wallace's distraught appearance.

Just after four o'clock, Amy and Julia are interrupted by a knock at the front door. It is Neil Norbury, the baker's boy, delivering the bread. He comments that Julia does not look very well and she smiles at his concern, telling him that she has a slight touch of bronchitis. As four-thirty in the afternoon approaches, Amy Wallace decides it is time to go home; she puts on her coat and leaves, heading for the tram stop in Belmont Road.

While Julia is saying goodbye at the front door, Charles Bliss climbs over the back wall of 29 Wolverton Street, sets up his ladders, and cleans the top windows. He is on his ladder climbing over into number 31, where Florence Johnston lives, when Julia emerges from the back kitchen into the yard. "Where's Mr Hoer?" she asks.

"He had to go to town," replies Bliss, at which point Florence Johnston steps into her backyard to listen to what is going on.

"I had better pay you, then," says Julia, and she gives Bliss a shilling. He returns three pence in change.

At approximately five o'clock, Emily Hoer joins Bliss at the back of number 31, cleans the lower windows, then moves off to the Wallace's, where she wipes down the kitchen and back kitchen windows. It is dark now, but a fall of light from the kitchen and back bedroom aids Emily in her work. Usually Julia comes out for a chat but today there is no sign of her, which strikes Emily as odd, so odd in fact that she mentions it to her husband later that night.

2

William Wallace is on his last call of the day at 19 Eastman Road, Clubmoor, where he hands over to Margaret Martin details of how her daughter should surrender her insurance policy. Just before six o'clock he catches a bus at the junction of Queen's Drive and Townsend Lane, alights at the Cabbage Hall public house, and makes his way home down Taplow Street and along Redcar Street. He enters the house by the back door. Julia is in the kitchen and within minutes of his arrival, the two of them are sitting down to a meal of bread and scones, washed down with a cup of tea.

Wallace has decided to call on RM Qualtrough, of 25 Menlove Gardens East, Mossley Hill. After tea, he leaves Julia in the kitchen while he gathers and arranges some insurance papers which may be of use in the transaction. Completing that task, he moves upstairs to the bathroom, washes his hands and face, then changes his collar and brushes his hair in the middle bedroom.

At six-thirty, next door at number 27, Bertha Holme is serving tea to her husband, Walter, in the kitchen, when their quietude is disturbed by a noise at the front of the house.

"Is that a knock at the door?" asks Bertha.

Walter looks up from his tea and shakes his head.

"No. It's at the Wallace's."

David Jones pushes a *Liverpool Echo* through the Wallaces' letterbox and notices that Wolverton Street is dark and deserted. Within minutes, Allan Close, wearing his Collegiate College[2] uniform, arrives in Wolverton Street on his milk round. He knocks at number 29, pours some milk into the can, and leaves it on the doorstep. He goes next door to number 31, finds the door open and a milk jug just inside the lobby. He fills the jug with milk and raps on the door before returning to the Wallaces'. The front door is open and the can of milk has been taken indoors.

James Wildman passes Allan Close as he stands in front of the Wallace house; he posts an evening newspaper through the door of number 27 and carries on along the street and into Richmond Park.

Julia Wallace finally comes to the front door with the empty milk can and hands it over to Close.

"You had better hurry home out of the cold," she advises the young milk boy.

Allan Close takes the can. "Goodnight," he says and sets off to continue his round.

<h1 style="text-align:center">3</h1>

Wallace is dressed in a grey trilby and dark overcoat as he leaves home at approximately six-forty-five. His appointment with Mr Qualtrough is for seven-thirty.

He takes a number 26 tramcar to the junction of Tunnel Road and Smithdown Road, where he dismounts. Then he walks across the junction to the crowded tram stop at the corner of Tunnel Road and Smithdown Lane.[3]

A number 5 tramcar, destined for Penny Lane, pulls into the stop.[4] Conductor Thomas Phillips stands to one side of the platform to allow the passengers to board. Wallace is one of the last to approach the tram.

"Does this tram go anywhere near Menlove Gardens?" he enquires.

"No," replies the conductor. "You need a 5A, 5W or a number 7." Phillips pauses for a moment. "Hang on. You can get on this car and get a transfer ticket, or a penny ticket to Penny Lane."

Wallace boards the tram saying,

"I'm a stranger in the district and I have an important business call. I want Menlove Gardens East."

He takes a seat on the right of the tramcar next to the platform as the tram moves off across the junction and into Smithdown Road and Phillips steps inside to collect fares. Ticket Inspector Angus hops aboard the moving tramcar as it passes Earle Road. Phillips makes his way towards Wallace, collecting fares. He hands him a penny ticket.

"You won't forget, guard," says Wallace. "I want to go to Menlove Gardens East." Phillips nods and climbs upstairs to take fares while Inspector Angus checks tickets. "I want Menlove Gardens East," Wallace tells him, as he examines the proffered ticket.

"Change at Penny Lane," says Angus. "Then you want a 5A, 5W or a number 7."

Seconds later, Inspector Angus disembarks at Portman Road and notes that the time is ten minutes past seven.

Phillips descends from the upper deck and goes in search of new fares. Wallace turns to him.

"How far is it now?" he demands of the busy conductor. "Where do I have to change?"

"Penny Lane," says Phillips.

As the tramcar approaches Penny Lane terminus, Phillips looks out from the rear platform and sees a number 7 tram in the loop, destined for

Calderstones and Woolton.

"Menlove Gardens East," he announces. "Change here." He then points out the number 7 tram to Wallace. "If you hurry you will catch that car."

Wallace hurries from the tramcar but heads towards a waiting number 5 tram, rather than the number 7.

"Not that one," shouts Phillips, as he sees Wallace heading in the wrong direction. "The number 7, in the out loop." He points again and then notices another tramcar gliding down into the out loop, a number 5A, bound for Calderstones. He waves at the number 5A for Wallace's benefit. "Either that one, or the one in the loop."

He watches as Wallace strides towards the number 7 tram, then turns away as he is lost from view.

4

At approximately seven-fifteen, tramcar 5A, bound for Calderstones, leaves the Penny Lane terminus and runs into Allerton Road. Conductor Arthur Thompson moves through the car collecting fares. Wallace, seated on the left-hand side of the tram, asks to be put off at Menlove Gardens East. Thompson nods in acknowledgement.

The tramcar leaves Allerton Road for Menlove Avenue. As it nears Menlove Gardens West, Thompson beckons Wallace to the platform.

"This is Menlove Gardens West," he explains to Wallace. "Menlove Gardens is a triangular affair – three roads. There are two roads running off to the right. You will probably find it is one of them."

"Thank you," says Wallace. "I'm a complete stranger around here," he adds, as he dismounts from the tramcar.

Wallace stands at the corner of Menlove Avenue and Menlove Gardens West and checks his watch, noting that he has ten minutes until his appointment with Mr RM Qualtrough at seven-thirty. He walks up Menlove Gardens West to the junction with Menlove Gardens South, and continues until he reaches Menlove Gardens North, where he accosts a woman who tells him that Menlove Gardens East may be a continuation of Menlove Gardens West.

At the junction of Menlove Gardens West and Dudlow Road, Wallace meets Sidney Green who is on his way to Penny Lane to catch a tram.

"Do you know where Menlove Gardens East is?" enquires Wallace of Green.

Green shakes his head after considering the query for a moment.

"There is no such place to the best of my knowledge."

"I've been told to call at 25 Menlove Gardens East," continues Wallace. "I've walked up Menlove Gardens West and can only find Menlove Gardens North and South."

"You're in Menlove Gardens West," Green says.

"I know," Wallace pauses. "I will call at 25 Menlove Gardens West and see if that is the place. Goodnight."

Wallace knocks at the door of 25 Menlove Gardens West and it is opened by Mrs Kate Mather. "Does Mr Qualtrough live here?" he asks.

"There's no one of that name here," replies Mrs Mather.

"I'm looking for Menlove Gardens East," explains Wallace. "They tell me there isn't any."

"Sorry, I don't know the name."

"Are there any other gardens about here?"

"Who told you it was East?" asks Mrs Mather.

"I have had a message on the telephone," replies Wallace. "It's funny, isn't it? There is no East."

Wallace bids goodnight to Mrs Mather and continues his search into Menlove Gardens South and North but finds all the house numbers are even. He returns to Menlove Avenue and comes across a man waiting at a sheltered stop. The man answers Wallace's query about Menlove Gardens East by saying he is a stranger to the area.

5

Constable 220F James Serjeant, of Liverpool City Police, leaves Allerton Bridewell at seven-forty and walks up to the junction of Allerton Road and Green Lane.

Wallace has turned off Menlove Avenue and walked down Green Lane. He notices constable Serjeant at the junction and approaches him.

"Can you direct me to Menlove Gardens East?"

"There is no Menlove Gardens East," answers Serjeant. "But there is Menlove Gardens North, South and West."

To Serjeant, Wallace appears nervous and stutters as he speaks.

"I've been to Menlove Gardens West but the person I am looking for does not live there. I've also been to Menlove Gardens North and South but the numbers are all even. You see, I'm an insurance agent, and I'm looking for a Mr Qualtrough," explains Wallace. "He rang up the club and left a message for me with my colleague to call on him at 25 Menlove Gardens East."

"Have you tried 25 Menlove Avenue?" asks Serjeant.

"Whereabouts is it?"

"In the second or third block," replies Serjeant. "It's the third house in the second block," he adds after a moment's thought.

"Thank you," says Wallace. He begins to turn away, then stops. "Do you know where I can see a directory?"

"Yes," says Serjeant. He points towards Henley Road. "Down there at the post office. If you do not see one down there, then you can see one down at the police station." Serjeant nods in the direction of the bridewell.

"It's not yet eight o'clock?" asks Wallace, pulling out his pocket watch.

"It's a quarter to." Serjeant glances at his own watch and agrees to the time. Wallace sets off towards the post office.

The post office does not have a street directory and he is directed across Allerton Road to a newsagents and tobacconists, close to the Plaza Cinema, where an assistant, Nancy Collins, allows him to browse through the directory at the cigarette counter. After a few minutes the manageress, Lily Pinches, walks over to him to see if she can be of help.

Wallaces glances up from the directory.

"Do you know what I am looking for?" he asks.

"No," says Lily Pinches.

"I'm looking for 25 Menlove Gardens East."

"There's no East," says Lily Pinches. "There's only North, South and West." She searches through her account book. "I don't have a number 25 West."

"I've been to 25 West," says Wallace.

"Sorry," says Lily Pinches and Wallace walks out of the shop.

In Allerton Road, his search for Qualtrough over, Wallace catches a number 8 tramcar outside the Plaza Cinema, which takes him back to the junction of Smithdown Lane and Tunnel Road, from where he boards the number 27 tramcar for Belmont Road and home.[5] It has been a most disappointing and frustrating night for Mr William Herbert Wallace.

6

He reaches his front door at approximately eight-forty-five, inserts his key in the lock and turns it. The door will not open. He taps gently on the door, waits, but Julia does not come to answer it. He notices that there is no light from the transom window and he decides to try the back door.

He marches round the block and into the entry. The yard door unexpectedly opens and he gingerly walks up the yard to the scullery door. There is a dim glow from the scullery, but no light from the kitchen. Wallace tries the door but it will not yield. He knocks, but there is no reply.

Next door, at number 31, Florence Johnston is preparing to go out with her husband, John. She hears Wallace knocking on the scullery door.

Returning to the front door, Wallace tries the key again, but the door remains locked against him. He hurries to the back again and, as he reaches his own yard door, Mr and Mrs Johnston open their yard door and step into the entry.

"Good evening, Mr Wallace," says Mrs Johnston.

"Have you heard anything unusual tonight?" asks Wallace.

"No. Why, what has happened?" says Mrs Johnston.

"I have been out this evening since a quarter to seven," explains Wallace. "And on my return I find the front and back doors locked against me."

"Try again, Mr Wallace," advises John Johnston. "If it doesn't open, I'll get my key."

Wallace opens the yard door and walks up the yard towards the back kitchen door. He looks back at the Johnstons standing in the yard doorway.

"She won't be out," insists Wallace. "She has a bad cold."

The Johnstons watch as Wallace turns the door handle.

"It opens, now," he says, as he pushes open the door.

"We will wait here," says John Johnston. "Until you see if things are all right."

The Johnstons keep watch as Wallace enters the dimly lit back kitchen. They notice there is no light in the kitchen, but that there are dimmed lights in the bathroom and middle bedroom. Wallace lights the kitchen lamp with a match.

After a minute or two, John Johnston hears Wallace call out, and the light in the middle bedroom flares up. Then a match flickers briefly in the back bedroom. Silence.

No more flickering lights. The Johnstons wait. Suddenly, Wallace dashes from the scullery and into the yard, beckoning them towards him.

"Oh, come and see," he cries. "She's been killed!"

7

The front parlour is cramped and cluttered with furniture and knick-knacks. Immediately inside the door, along the wall common to kitchen and parlour, is a wide, ornate, mirrored sideboard, whose surface is crammed with bowls, vases, pots and framed pictures. An upholstered chair stands in front of it, close to the doorway.

Behind the door, two similar chairs, one in front of the other, are lodged against Julia's piano, and nearby a small circular table and William Wallace's music stand encroach upon the centre of the room. Opposite the piano is the fireplace, fitted with a Sunbeam gas fire and surrounded by a black slate mantelpiece. Above this is a large mirror, framed by a pair of matching gas brackets. The hearth is tiled and enclosed by a brass fender, against which lies a plain black hearth rug. To the left of the hearth, in the corner, next to the sideboard, sits a two-seater armchair, upon which rests William Wallace's violin case and to the right, jutting out from the opposite corner, is a chaise-longue. Behind the chaise-longue, a large, circular table holding an aspidistra, stands in the bay window. The window drapes are carefully drawn. The floor is covered by a thin woollen carpet.

8

"Oh, come and see," cries Wallace in distress. "She's been killed!"

Mr and Mrs Johnston are startled into action. They rush up the yard to the door and follow Wallace through the kitchen, into the hallway, and up to the open door of the parlour. They have been in the room, as guests, on three occasions and they are familiar with the general layout. But, as Wallace shuffles across the threshold and between the obstructing chairs, they are immediately aware of dramatic changes. Their eyes are drawn to a new centrepiece to the room – a bloody and horrific focal point – the shattered body of Julia Wallace.

Wallace stoops down over his dead wife. She lies on her stomach, diagonally across the hearth rug, her feet almost touching the right side of the brass fender. Her head is pointing towards the door, encircled by two chairs and the music stand. Her right arm is beneath her, while the left, bent at the elbow, rests on the floor.

Florence Johnston follows Wallace into the room and notices two spent matches in the doorway. Squeezing past the chair against the sideboard, she too bends over Mrs Wallace. In the glow of the light from the right-hand gas bracket, she can make out the sticky pools of blood enshrining her neighbour's head and the shards of skull bone protruding through the thinning hair.

Wallace grasps Julia's left hand for a moment, then slowly lets it go. Florence Johnston leans across the body and takes hold of the same hand.

"Oh, you poor darling," she gasps, and lets the hand fall.

"They've finished her," mumbles Wallace.

John Johnston steps nearer, up to the edge of the sideboard, for a closer look. He briefly surveys the body and the room and notes that the gas fire is unlit.

"Don't touch anything," he advises, "I'll fetch the police and a doctor."

Wallace turns to him.

"Yes, fetch a doctor," he says. "I'm afraid they've finished her."

9

Wallace and the Johnstons, a mournful trio, traipse back to the kitchen. The room is dominated by a square table covered with a plain, white cloth. Upon the tablecloth are two tea plates, a sugar bowl, a needlework basket, a clothes brush, and the evening's *Liverpool Echo*, open at the centre pages. Julia's handbag, partially obscured by a fold in the cloth, lies on the seat of an upright chair pushed hard up against the table. At the head of the table are two armchairs, half turned towards the black-leaded kitchen range.

To the right of the range, a recess holds a glass-fronted wall cabinet above a wooden floor cupboard upon which sits Wallace's radio, earphones and accumulator battery. A second recess, to the left of the range, is fitted with a shelved unit, seven feet high. Most of the shelves are lined with books, except for the lower, wider shelf, which contains Wallace's microscope, his chessmen, and a homemade, oblong cabinet packed with photographic materials. And it is to this cabinet that Wallace's attention is drawn as they enter the kitchen.

"See," he says, pointing to the broken door of the cabinet, which is lying on the floor in front of the unit, "they've wrenched that off."

"Is anything missing?" asks John Johnston.

Wallace reaches up to the top shelf of the unit and takes down a small, metal cash-box, which has been partially hidden between two piles of books. It is in the cash-box that he usually keeps the premium money which he has collected on his rounds. He opens the box and rummages through it.

"Oh, about four pounds," he replies. "But I can't say exactly until I've checked the books."

"Will you look upstairs to see if everything is all right before I go for the police and a doctor?" suggests John Johnston.

Wallace immediately leaves the kitchen and hurries upstairs, only to return seconds later.

"There's five pounds in a dish they have not taken," he announces.[6]

John Johnston leaves 29 Wolverton Street to fetch a doctor and the police.

Chapter 3
Julia Wallace

1

Two mysteries make up the Wallace case. The first and most obvious is who killed Julia Wallace? The second, less obvious, is, who *was* Julia Wallace?

Julia Wallace was the victim of a brutal and savage murder. Her killer was never brought to justice and questions of who killed her and for what reason remain unanswered. Much has been written about the killer's identity, but very little about the victim herself. Of all the protagonists in the Wallace case, she is the least known, the least understood. In fact, she is ignored, dismissed in the literature in two or three basic paragraphs, as if her life, and her being alive, are totally irrelevant. She appears as some ephemeral member of the cast, who glides in and out of the story on cue, an uncomfortable figure who generates uneasiness and uncertainty among the chroniclers of the Wallace case.

Thus, Julia Wallace, née Dennis, was born Julia Thorp, according to Colin Wilson; she was the only daughter of Mr and Mrs Dennis, writes David Jessel; Julia had an only sister, Amy, says Jonathan Goodman. Dorothy L Sayers, Robert Hussey and Colin Wilson have Julia marrying William Wallace in 1913; David Jessel has her aged twenty-two when first meeting Wallace, marrying him aged twenty-five, dying seventeen years later aged fifty-two.[1] Julia's year of birth is said to be 1877,[2] but no mention has ever been made in the literature of the day, month or place of her birth. Very little, if anything, is known of her life before she met William Herbert Wallace in Harrogate in 1911.

The more the Wallace literature is sifted and perused, the more apparent becomes the uncertainty over Julia, the more obvious the level of ignorance, and the more manifest the carelessness when dealing with her life history. However, the main points about Julia's life, which most writers agree upon, are that she was the daughter of William George Dennis, a veterinary surgeon, and his French-born wife, Aimée, and that she spoke French, played the piano, and died at the age of fifty-three.

Nowadays, police investigating a murder will check the antecedents of the victim, since such knowledge may have a bearing upon the murder. In 1931, the police were remiss in not examining Julia's background and all writers since have similarly been at fault. The police had eventually settled upon her husband, William, as her murderer and they simply accepted his account of her life story, supplemented with titbits from neighbours. The police did not seek confirmation of Wallace's version from Julia's sister, Amy, even though she made her presence known within days of the murder. Nor did they question her brother, George, who contacted them at the time of the investigation.[3] However, the only truth in the known account of Julia's life, is the fact that she played the piano and spoke some French: the remainder is pure fiction.

When Julia Dennis married William Herbert Wallace in Harrogate in March 1914, registering her age as thirty-seven, she was, in fact, almost fifty-three years of age. When she died in January 1931, supposedly at the age of fifty-three, she was in her seventieth year.

2

In 1824 William Dennis left his home town of Overdinsdale, four miles south-east of Darlington, and trekked south for ten miles to the village of East Harlsey in the North Riding of Yorkshire.[4] Aged twenty-eight and a farmer's son, he was looking for a tenancy and a wife. Within a year he had found both: a small farm on the outskirts of East Harlsey, and a young wife, Ann, aged nineteen, from Kirby-Wiske, a village close to the town of Northallerton, the administrative centre for that area.

East Harlsey lies seventeen miles north-east of Northallerton, on the western boundary of what is now the North Yorkshire Dales National Park. It is an ancient township, village and parish, set amid gently rolling hills, with the land given over to pasture and cultivation of wheat, oats, barley and beans. All the farmland at that time was owned by the Beaumont and Brown families.

Over the years, William Dennis worked hard and constantly improved his lot, graduating to larger holdings as they became available and gaining for himself the reputation as a competent man of the land. He and Ann had five children: Sarah, born in 1825; John, born in 1826; Jane, born in 1828; William George, born in 1834 and Thomas, born in 1837. Baby Thomas died at eleven weeks, the first of two tragedies to afflict the Dennis family that year, for Jane also passed away in October, aged nine.

In 1846, Sarah left home to marry into the Taylor family of East Harlsey, and the following year William Dennis was granted the tenancy of Morton Lodge Farm. Having three hundred and twenty-two acres, it was one of the more substantial farms in the area, and he employed twelve labourers. Three years later, his son John married Mary Ann Watson from Deighton, and he went to live with his wife's family at their smallholding in Deighton; Blackberry Farm. In 1851, John took up the tenancy of Bruntcliffe House Farm, adjacent to his father's land, and he worked its two hundred and fifty acres with the help of six men. William George, the younger son, then aged sixteen, worked at Morton Lodge Farm assisting his father.

William Dennis died in 1856 aged sixty. As the elder brother, John took over the tenancy of his father's farm, Morton Lodge, relinquishing Bruntcliffe House Farm to William George. Within a year of moving into Bruntcliffe House Farm, William George met, and fell in love with, Anne Teresa Smith, daughter of Nathaniel Smith, a farm labourer of East Harlsey.

William George Dennis, aged twenty-four, married Anne Teresa Smith, aged twenty, on 14 April 1859, at St Oswald's, the parish church of East Harlsey. They set up home at Bruntcliffe House Farm. Julia Dennis was born there on 28 April, 1861, and was christened at St Oswald's on 26 May.

3

Julia was the second child of the marriage. Anne Marie was firstborn, in 1860. Then came Julia, who was followed by Rhoda, in 1862; Amy, in 1864; George Smith, in 1867 and John Henry, in 1869. By all accounts William and Anne were a happy couple and the children were raised in a loving atmosphere. William George Dennis, like his father, was a hard worker and farmed his land with the aid of three labourers. He was well-liked in the area, a jovial sort, and he would spend some of his evenings in the local inn, the Cat and Bagpipes,[5] in company with other farmers and travelling stockmen. He was illiterate, having forsaken, as a youth, the opportunity for what then passed as an education, in favour of fully learning the trade of farmer. However, he insisted that his own children should grow up with the basics of an education and, with this in mind, he hired a young lady from Hull, Frances Mary Robinson, to act as governess to his young family. In addition, he employed Elizabeth Cowell, a local girl, as maidservant, to assist his wife in running the busy household.

But the idyllic life of the Dennis family was to be disrupted. In 1870, for reasons not known, William George Dennis relinquished the tenancy of Bruntcliffe House Farm to his brother-in-law, George Smith, and moved his family two miles away to the adjoining village of West Harlsey, where he took up residence at number 5 Farm House. He held the tenancy for Low

Moor, two hundred and thirty acres of the Earl of Harewood's vast estate.

West Harlsey, in the parish of Osmotherly, was not really a village, simply seven scattered farmhouses, each associated with a parcel of Harewood's land. The population did not exceed seventy souls, mostly farm workers, and compared with the close-knit community of East Harlsey, with more than four hundred inhabitants, West Harlsey must have seemed like the ends of the earth to the young Dennis children, cut off as they were from all they had known. And having barely settled into the new home, the family was struck by a terrible tragedy.

Anne Teresa Dennis, mother of six, died giving birth to her seventh child, a son, on 19 April 1871. Elizabeth Cowell, the family servant, attended at the death. The boy was christened Herbert William Dennis, on the day after Anne Dennis was buried in the graveyard of St Oswald's Church. One week later, Julia Dennis celebrated her tenth birthday.

4

The Dennis family was devastated. And it would appear that William George Dennis did not recover from his wife's premature death. His widowed mother, Ann, moved in with the family and tried to restore some stability to their shattered lives, but William George could not cope. In 1873, he once again moved his family, this time further afield, to the village of Romanby on the outskirts of Northallerton.

Nowadays, Romanby is a suburb of Northallerton, but it was once a small farming community quite distinct from its larger neighbour. But that had begun to change in 1841 with the advent of the railways. In that year, the London to Darlington railway line, the North Eastern Railway, had been completed. Northallerton, sixteen miles south of Darlington and thirty miles north of York, was an important junction; it also serviced a branch line of the Leeds-Stockton Railway. Romanby was the location of Northallerton's mainline station.

The Railway Hotel, built in 1849 by the North Eastern Railway Company, catered to the needs of the rail passengers, offering meals, drinks and lodgings for the night. It also provided a bar room for the locals and for the stockmen, whose job it was to load and offload the cattle and sheep in transit to and from the local markets. The hotel was a thriving and convivial place, the tenancy of which was highly prized. William George Dennis moved his family into the hotel when he took up the position of innkeeper. Perhaps this new post gave him a better income for the upkeep of his motherless children; perhaps running a very busy enterprise kept his mind from thoughts of his dead wife; perhaps the new job allowed him to further indulge his dependency upon drink, which seems to have arisen in the wake of Anne's demise.

Whatever the reason, or combination of reasons, for the relocation to the

Railway Hotel, Romanby, William George Dennis's stay was not a long one. On 19 February, 1875, he died at the hotel in the arms of his brother, John. He was forty years of age. The death certificate recorded jaundice and dropsy as the causes of death, both of which are associated with cirrhosis of the liver, brought on by alcohol abuse.

William George Dennis was laid to rest alongside his wife at East Harlsey. The Dennis children were orphans. What is more, with William's death, the tenancy of the Railway Hotel fell vacant and was soon taken up by Henry Clay; the Dennis children were also homeless. Julia Dennis was approaching her fourteenth birthday.

5

The National Census of 1881 shows that Ann Dennis, mother of the deceased, William George Dennis, was living at 162 Station Road, Northallerton. She was then seventy-eight years of age. Living with her were Amy Dennis, sixteen, a scholar; John Henry Dennis, aged twelve and Herbert William Dennis, aged nine. The whereabouts of the remaining Dennis children, Anne Marie, Julia, Rhoda and George Smith Dennis, is not recorded.

The Burgess Roll of 1910 for the Municipal Borough of Harrogate, Yorkshire, has Julia Dennis residing at 5 Dragon Parade.[6] Between the death of her father in 1875 and her registration in the Burgess Roll thirty-five years later, Julia Wallace seems to have disappeared. The only reference to her in public records is in 1892, where her address is given in Leeds, while her only contact with her family would appear to have been through a niece, Annie Theresa Dennis. But where else she lived, and how she lived, during those thirty-five years is a mystery.

Julia's father's will was proved at York in 1876 by his mother, Ann, and his brother, John, and the value of his estate was less than three hundred pounds. All his possessions were to be sold and the money thus realised to be invested for his children. The Clerk of the Court of Probate noted on the will that William George Dennis did not possess any land. However, that was not strictly true.

In 1855, he became leaseholder for land and property in East Rounton, North Yorkshire. The property was the Black Horse Inn and the associated house, barns, stable and outbuildings, together with several parcels of land amounting to seventeen acres. The lease was for one thousand years, for which Dennis paid an annual rent of one peppercorn to the owner of the property, Margaret Ware. To all intents and purposes, Dennis owned the land and property at East Rounton. It is probable that he inherited the lease from a relative. No members of the Dennis family ever lived at East Rounton, and the land and property were rented out, thereby providing a relatively good income for the family.

After the death of Julia's mother, the lease was amended in 1872 to include her grandmother, Ann, as a beneficiary and following upon her death in 1892, the lease came into the possession of her seven grandchildren. On the lease document, Julia Dennis is noted as living care of her tutor, Charles Henry Robinson, at 22 Cliffe Road, in the Hyde Park district of Leeds.

It is probable that she continued to live in Leeds for some years before moving to Harrogate, and that with her share of the yearly income from East Rounton she may well have been able to support herself without having to work. There is no doubt that she was well educated, and the possibility also exists that she may have become a governess in one of the large houses in the Leeds and Harrogate districts. But nothing is known for certain of her life between 1875 and 1910.

6

George Smith Dennis, Julia's younger brother, married Margaret Cowell, daughter of Elizabeth Cowell, the family servant, in Romanby in 1894. Their first daughter, Annie Theresa Dennis, was born in Romanby in the same year. Just after the First World War, Annie Theresa married Walter Hutton Birch and their son, Douglas Birch, went to live in the Manchester area.

Douglas Birch recalls that his mother lived in Romanby for several years as a young girl. Her father, George Smith Dennis, served with the British Forces during the Second Boer War and it was at this time that Annie Theresa, rather than living with her own family, found herself living with a succession of aunts. At first she moved to Leeds to live with her Aunt Amy, and later with her Aunt Rhoda. Then in 1908, she went to live with her Aunt Julia in Harrogate.

"Aunt Julia was her favourite," recalls Douglas Birch, "and she taught my mother music and French."[7]

Annie Theresa lived with Julia Dennis until 1910, when she rejoined her family who had by then settled in Redcar. A year later, Julia Dennis, still in Harrogate, moved to 11 St Mary's Avenue, and shortly thereafter met her future husband.

7

When Julia Dennis married William Herbert Wallace in 1914, no members of her family were present at the ceremony. When she was buried in 1931, none of her brothers and sisters attended the funeral, even though her sister Amy was in Liverpool within days of her murder.

William Herbert Wallace kept a diary throughout his marriage, and while those diaries are no longer extant, it would appear from researchers who had access to them before they disappeared, that no mention was ever made of Julia's immediate family. And from what he said of his wife to the police following her death, it would seem that he was unaware of the existence of any in-laws, except for Amy Dennis.

Whether William Wallace knew how old Julia truly was is not known. The tombstone on the grave wherein both Julia and William are interred says that she was aged fifty-two when she died. It is probable that Joseph Wallace had the tombstone emplaced after his brother had died and that he gave her age as he knew it. However, whether Wallace believed that was her true age, or gave it as such for Julia's sake while knowing her true age, cannot be ascertained.

Julia Wallace, née Dennis, was a woman of mystery. There can be no doubt that she was traumatised by the loss of both her parents when she was still a young girl, and that she compensated for this by glamorising them: her father, a tenant farmer and public house landlord, became a veterinary surgeon, while her mother, an untutored, country housewife, became Aimée, a French lady. Perhaps her fantasies about her parents estranged her from her family. The fact that no member of her family attended either her wedding, or her funeral, suggests some conflict.

In 1892, when Julia's address is given as care of Charles Henry Robinson, her tutor, in Leeds, she would have been thirty-one, a rather advanced age for a woman still to be undergoing private tuition. Whether Charles Robinson was any relation to Frances Mary Robinson, the Dennis's family tutor in West Harlsey, is not known. No other member of the Dennis family, from what has been discovered in family and public records, was privately educated as Julia was following the death of her father in 1875. Perhaps this fact contributed towards her separation and estrangement from them. There is also the possibility that she was living as wife with Charles Henry Robinson, which would have definitely alienated her from her family, given the mores and moral outlook of the period.

Julia was living alone in Harrogate in 1908, when she was joined by her niece, Annie Theresa. Jonathan Goodman writes that Julia worked in an estate agent's office in Harrogate and that she took in paying guests to supplement her income at 11 St Mary's Avenue, which she jointly owned with her sister, Amy.[8] However, she did not own 11 St Mary's Avenue, either by herself or jointly with Amy. The house was actually the property of the Pullan family, and it was divided up into what were then called apartments, and what today would be called bedsitters. Julia Dennis did not own a property.

She was probably in receipt of a seventh share of the yearly income from the land and property at East Rounton and she may well have given private lessons in music and French, though the Harrogate Directories of that time do not show her registered either as a private tutor, or as a music or language teacher.

Amy and Rhoda Dennis never married and lived in Hove, Sussex, until their deaths. Amy was ninety-nine when she died, Rhoda was ninety. George Smith Dennis settled in Redcar and worked until retirement as an assistant in a pharmacy. He died in 1954, aged eighty-seven. George Smith Dennis's youngest daughter, Florence, 'Majorie' as she was known to the family, died in February 1998, aged one hundred and one. Ann Dennis, Julia's grandmother, was eighty-nine when she died in 1892. Despite the relatively short lives of Julia's parents, longevity appears to characterise the distaff side of the family. Julia was approaching seventy when she was murdered, owning up to fifty-three, and probably would have lived for a considerable time longer had her life not been savagely cut short in 1931.

Was there a dark secret in Julia Dennis's past? Did someone, or something, reach out of the past to cause her death? What was she doing, and where was she living between 1875 and 1910? Why was she estranged from her family? Why did she lie about her age? Did her husband, or anyone outside her family, know her real age?

Perhaps the solution to her murder lies among the answers to these questions.

Chapter 4
The Police Arrive

1

John Johnston hurries down to Lower Breck Road, to the home of his general practitioner, Dr Dunlop, and informs him that he believes a woman has been murdered. The doctor advises him to report the matter to the police, as there is nothing he can do. Johnston runs on to the Anfield Bridewell, in Anfield Road.

On desk duty at the bridewell is PC 99G Saunders, and it is to him that John Johnston breathlessly makes his report of the murder of Julia Wallace. Within minutes, PC 191G Williams is dispatched to Wolverton Street and a phone call is made to CID headquarters in Dale Street, in the centre of Liverpool.

Meanwhile, at 29 Wolverton Street, Wallace and Mrs Johnston are in the kitchen. Wallace, pale and drawn, covers his face with his hands and quietly sobs for a few seconds.[1] Then they return to the front parlour. Wallace kneels beside the body of his wife, his back to the window, and both he and Mrs Johnston clasp her left hand for a few moments. Mrs Johnston notices that the body seems to be colder than it was on her first visit, ten minutes earlier.

Wallace stands then stoops over the body.

"They have finished her. Look at the brains," he remarks.

"Whatever have they used?" asks Florence Johnston, glancing around the room.

Wallace walks round his wife's body and stands between it and the sideboard, ready to leave the room. He looks down at the body again.

"Why, whatever was she doing with her mackintosh and my mackintosh?" he says.

Mrs Johnston glances down to where Wallace is staring.

"Is it your mackintosh?" she asks.

The mackintosh is almost completely hidden beneath the corpse. Wallace stoops and fingers it, examining it briefly.

"Yes, it is mine."

His fingers wander under the hearth rug, just under the edge, and he pats it, as if feeling for something. Then he straightens up and leads the way back out of the parlour and into the kitchen.

He slumps into an armchair, lights up a cigarette, and again covers up his face and sobs. Mrs Johnston, thinking he is about to break down, and at a loss as to what to do if he does, desperately looks round the room for something to occupy them both. She notices that what had once been a substantial fire in the range has almost burnt itself out.

"Well, we will have a fire," she announces, and walks off into the back kitchen to find some wood.

Mrs Johnston returns moments later with a small stack of wood and begins to lay it out on the dying coals. Wallace, having collected himself, gets to his feet to help her, stirring the dying embers to life with the poker. As the dry wood catches, he places several small nuggets of coal on top of it and they both watch as the fire takes.

Minutes later, at ten past nine, almost twenty-five minutes after Julia's body has been discovered, PC Williams raps loudly on the front door.

2

In response to the knock at the door, both Wallace and Mrs Johnston leave the kitchen and walk down the hallway to the front door. Mrs Johnston tries to open the door, fumbling at the lock, but is unable to do so. She steps aside to allow Wallace to open it. PC Williams is standing on the step.

"Come inside, officer," says Wallace, "something terrible has happened," and he leads the way into the parlour.

PC Williams surveys the murder scene, noting the position of the body lying diagonally across the hearth rug; the blood around the head and the staining on the floor and walls; the crumpled material beneath the body; the drawn curtains and the fact that the right-hand gas jet is lit.

He leans over the body and feels the right wrist but cannot detect a pulse.[2] He notes that the flesh is slightly warm.

"How did this happen?" he asks Wallace.

"I don't know," replies Wallace. He briefly explains his abortive trip to Menlove Gardens East to the policeman.

PC Williams closes the parlour door and, accompanied by Wallace, begins an inspection of the house, starting upstairs in the middle bedroom, where the gas light is lit.

"Was that light burning when you entered the house?" asks Williams.

"I changed in this room before leaving the house and probably I left the light on myself."

Williams notes a small ornamental jar on the mantelpiece from which protrudes a small bundle of pound notes. He picks up the jar and starts to take out the money.

"Here's some money which has not been touched," says Wallace.

Williams tells him to return both the notes and the jar to their original positions, which he does.

To the right of the mantelpiece is a curtained recess which Williams now approaches.

"My wife's clothes are kept there," says Wallace. "They haven't been touched. There appears to have been no one here."

Williams pulls aside the curtain and flashes his torch onto the hanging garments. Satisfied that all is in order, he lets it fall and follows Wallace into the back bedroom, which is fitted out as a small chemistry laboratory. Williams glances briefly into the room.

"Everything seems all right here," comments Wallace, before leading the way to the bathroom where a low light is burning.

"Is this light usually left burning?" asks Williams, as he surveys the room and notes that everything appears to be in order.

"We usually have a low light here," replies Wallace and they move off to the front bedroom.

The room is in darkness but, even in the torchlight, it is plain to Williams that the room is in a state of disorder. He can make out a wardrobe, a dressing table and a bed. The bedclothes are strewn half on, half off, the bed, and two pillows are lying in the fireplace. Two handbags and three hats of Julia's are also on the bed. The door of the wardrobe and the dressing table drawers are shut.

Wallace and Williams go downstairs and into the kitchen where Mrs Johnston is sitting. The policeman makes a note of the broken door from the cabinet lying in front of the bookshelf. Wallace then indicates the small cash-box on the top shelf.

"There was about four pounds in the box," he declares. "Now it has gone."

Wallace then pulls out his wife's partially hidden handbag from the seat of one of the chairs at the table. He opens it and takes out a one pound note and some silver, muttering to himself about the money as he does so. When making his record later, PC Williams is unable to remember exactly what Wallace says.

Williams glances round the kitchen again before asking Wallace to follow him back to the parlour. Both men stand in the doorway looking down at the body. Wallace moves into the room, close to the sideboard, stepping round the body, and lights the left-hand gas jet. Then they both return to the kitchen, Williams closing the parlour door behind him. In the kitchen, he examines the heavy drapes covering the windows.

"Did you notice any lights in the house when you entered?" he asks Wallace.

"With the exception of the lights upstairs, the house was in darkness. There was no light on in the kitchen."

Williams parts the drapes and examines the window.

"When you first came up the yard, did you notice any light shining through the curtains?"

"The curtains would prevent the light from escaping," replies Wallace.

"I'll try them," says Williams, moving towards the kitchen door.

"It's no use now," Wallace points out. "You've disturbed them."

Williams nods agreement and for the next five minutes or so checks through the kitchen until there is a knock at the front door. He opens it to admit Police Sergeant Breslin, his immediate superior in G Division.

Breslin asks to be taken to the murder scene and Williams shows him the way, accompanied by Wallace. The three men grimly survey the murder room. It is only now that Williams realises that the crumpled material beneath Julia's battered body is, in fact, a mackintosh.

"This looks like a macintosh," he exclaims, pointing down at the garment, so that both Wallace and Breslin can see it.

Wallace is standing near the doorway.

"It's an old one of mine," he informs them, then glances over his shoulder into the hallway. "It usually hangs here," he adds, indicating a row of hooks.

The conversation is interrupted by another knock at the front door. John Edward Whitely MacFall, Professor of Forensic Medicine at Liverpool University, has arrived to conduct the medical examination of the corpse. It is ten minutes to ten, approximately an hour since Julia's body was discovered.

3

MacFall insists that he works alone and undisturbed and herds Wallace, Breslin and Williams into the kitchen to join Mrs Johnston.

In the front parlour he makes a general inspection of the murder scene, noticing the position of the body and the fact that it is fully clothed. Next he turns his attention to the body itself: he notes that the head is badly battered on the left side, above and in front of the ear, where there is a large open wound which he measures at half an inch by three inches. From this wound, bone and brain tissue protrude. At the back of the head there is a great depression in the skull with several wounds which are partially hidden by the matted hair. The hair is disarranged and loose, drawn out from the head, and a pad of hair, the chignon, is almost free from the head hair.

He examines Julia's hands which, though bloodstained, bear no evidence of defensive injuries such as cuts and bruises. The fingernails are clean. The hands are both cold but the body is still warm, and he records that post-mortem rigidity is present in the neck and the upper part of the left arm. There is a small amount of serum exudation from the huge pool of blood which runs from the leading edge of the hearth rug and onto the floor and in which can be seen bone and brain tissue. He lifts the head but can find no trace of brain tissue beneath it, and he concludes that the last smashing blows to the head were made when it was on the floor. He briefly examines the mackintosh which is bundled up beneath the right shoulder of the body and he notices that, besides being heavily bloodstained, it is partly burnt at the front and sides.

Finally, he traces the line of blood splashes, from the sideboard to the mantelpiece and to the wall to the left of the fireplace, which, in two or three places, have reached a height of seven feet. He also finds some blood splashes between the door and the wall against which the piano stands. The blood marks show three distinct patterns: soda-water bottle spots, round spots and diagonal spots. MacFall concludes that the focal point of the attack upon Julia Wallace is in the corner of the room, to the left of the fireplace.

As he begins to sketch the dispositions of the bloodstains in his notebook, there is a knock at the front door. It is now five past ten, and PC Williams answers the knock to admit Detective Superintendent Hubert Moore, the head of Liverpool CID and Detective Sergeant Fothergill. Williams shows Moore[3] directly into the front parlour.

After exchanging greetings with MacFall, Moore begins a quick inspection of the murder scene, questioning the professor from time to time, to check if his initial impressions agree with those of the medical examiner. MacFall tells Moore that the assailant's clothing would be heavily bloodstained. After a few minutes, Moore joins PC Williams and Sergeant Fothergill in the hallway, where Williams recites Wallace's account of the events leading up to the discovery of Julia's body and tells him of his search of the house. Then Moore enters the kitchen where Wallace and the Johnstons are seated in front of the fire.

"Julia would go mad if she could see all this," sighs Wallace, as Moore enters the room.

"Mr Wallace," says Moore, "did you see anybody hanging about when you returned home?"

"No," replies Wallace, shaking his head, "nobody."

Then Moore turns to Mrs Johnston.

"Did you hear any unusual noises in the house?"

"None," says Florence Johnston.

"And what about this mackintosh, Mr Wallace?" demands Moore.

"Oh, it's mine," acknowledges Wallace.

Moore returns to the hallway and climbs the stairs for a brief tour of the premises, checking the windows for signs of forcible entry. He is aware of the activities of the elusive burglar, the 'Anfield Housebreaker', who has plagued the area over the past six months, and his first thoughts are that Mrs Wallace is a victim of a burglary that went sadly wrong.

As he comes downstairs, Detective Sergeant Harry Bailey arrives, and Moore directs him to the front parlour before driving off to the Anfield Bridewell, where there is a telephone. When he was first informed of the murder, he had called his seven divisional inspectors and placed them on standby. Now he briefs the Anfield inspector and his men before individually telephoning the other six divisional inspectors with details of the killing. He orders a city-wide search for suspicious characters and anyone with bloodstained clothing. He calls Harry Cooke, the official photographer for the Liverpool City Police, ordering him to go to Wolverton Street as soon as possible. Next he telephones the Fire Brigade and asks them to supply a set of flood-lights to Wolverton Street.

4

In Moore's absence, Superintendent Broughton and Assistant Chief Constable Glover have arrived on the premises. Sergeant Bailey has made a detailed examination of doors, locks and windows, again looking for signs of a forcible entry into the house. In the kitchen, Bailey takes possession of Julia's handbag. In one compartment he finds a half crown piece; in another some loose change to the value of one pound, five shillings and ten and a half pence.

Moore's return coincides with the arrival of Detective Inspector Gold. After a brief consultation with Superintendent Broughton and the Assistant Chief Constable, Moore and Gold enter the front parlour where MacFall is still seated, making notes, and periodically checking the progression of rigor mortis though the body. Again Moore scrutinises the murder scene and then once more tours the house, finishing up at the front door where he carefully examines the lock. Then he returns to the kitchen with Inspector Gold. Wallace, who is stroking the family cat, exchanges greetings with Gold. He collects insurance premiums from him; the two men have known each other for almost ten years.

"Mr Wallace," says Moore. "How did you find the house on your return?"

Wallace begins a second recitation of the events.

"I was called by telephone to a business appointment at 25 Menlove Gardens East at seven-thirty tonight. I went there but could not find the address. I hurried home. I tried the key in the front door but it would not act. I went around to the back door but I could not open it. I returned to the front door, again tried the key which would not act, went around to the back door which opened easily. I met Mr and Mrs Johnston and asked them to wait while I came in. I found my wife murdered in the parlour and this, just as you see it," and Wallace points to the broken door of the small cabinet lying on the floor. Then he indicates the cash-box on the shelf. "About four pounds has been stolen from that box, which includes a one pound Treasury note; three, ten shilling Treasury notes; about thirty or forty shillings in silver; a postal order for four shillings and six pence from WL Springer of 41 New Road, and a cheque on the Midland Bank, Dale Street, for five pounds seventeen shillings, payable to me and crossed. That was my company's money. That is all missing except for the four stamps which I have."[4]

Moore makes brief notes of Wallace's statement. On the floor, close to the bookshelves, to the right of the range, Moore spots a half crown piece and two, one shilling pieces.

"Where did you find the cash-box?" he asks.

"Where it is now," replies Wallace, pointing to the top shelf.

Moore removes the cash-box from the shelf and places it on the table. The hinge on the lid is broken and he lifts off the lid. He takes out the top tray to reveal three small compartments, two of which are empty. The third contains an American one dollar note.

"I cannot understand why a thief should go to all this trouble of fixing the lid on and putting the box back on the shelf where he had found it." He glances over at Wallace, but he does not reply. "Right," says Moore, as he finishes reassembling the cash-box. "Will you accompany me upstairs, please?"

Moore leads the way up to the back bedroom, Wallace's laboratory.

"Have a good look in the room, Mr Wallace, and see if anything is missing."

As Wallace inspects the room, Moore notices a scattering of tools, including a hammer, on the work bench, some photographic materials and a case containing a number of bottles of chemical reagents.

"I cannot say that anything is missing," states Wallace finally.

Moore moves on to the middle bedroom where he immediately realises that nothing has been disturbed. His attention focuses on the ornamental jar on the mantelpiece and he notices the protruding bank notes. He directs Wallace to the front bedroom. The disorder in the room is apparent, just as PC Williams has described it.

"Has the room been used recently?" asks Moore. "Was the bedding like that today?"

"I cannot say," replies Wallace. "I don't think I have been in this room for a fortnight."

Moore checks through the clothing in the wardrobe and in the drawers of the dressing table. His trained eye tells him that nothing has been disturbed.

The two men go downstairs. Moore asks Wallace to wait in the kitchen and he then goes back into the parlour. As he enters, Professor MacFall leaves.

5

The time is now eleven o'clock, and MacFall is carrying out a painstaking search of the house, looking for bloodstains. His only success is a tiny, circular clot of blood, which he finds at the front and slightly to the right on the rim of the lavatory pan. He quickly sketches and measures the clot. Then he notes that a thin, grimy white towel, perfectly dry, hangs over the side of the bath, which is itself dry. Only the nail brush on the edge of the bath, its bristles damp, shows any sign of recent use. Having finished his note-taking, MacFall calls downstairs for an officer to bring up Superintendent Moore.

After a short consultation in the bathroom with MacFall, Moore returns downstairs to the hallway. He still has not resolved the problem of the front door lock, of why Wallace could not open the door with his key upon his return, of why there were problems opening the door when PC Williams first arrived. He calls Inspector Gold from the parlour and Wallace from the kitchen, and then, under their scrutiny, he thoroughly examines the lock. Then he asks Wallace for his key. Moore tries the key in the lock and finds that when it is turned beyond a certain point, the lock slips and re-locks itself.

Moore opens the door and steps outside, closing the door after him. He inserts the key in the lock and after a moment or two, he opens the door and re-enters the house.

"I could open the door all right, but the lock is defective," he reports to Gold.

"It was not like that this morning," states Wallace.

Moore pockets the key and beckons Wallace to follow him into the front parlour to join Sergeant Bailey, leaving Gold by the front door. Once again, he examines the room. What strikes his attention is the position of the body, the extent of the blood spillage to the left of it, and the disposition of the brain tissue to the right, hemmed in by the doorway and the cramped furniture. Moore concludes that anyone entering the room to light the gas jets would have to step over blood if he approached to the left of the corpse, or step over brain tissue if he approached to the right. He turns to Wallace.

"Were the blinds drawn when you first entered the room?"

"Yes," affirms Wallace. "I lit a match and put the gas on."

"Did you not scream or shout?"

"No. I thought she might have been in a fit. I lit the gas to go to her assistance but, of course, I found that she was dead."

Wallace is sent back to the kitchen while Moore continues his examination of the room. He now focuses upon the mackintosh which is lying under the right side of the corpse. Again he summons Wallace from the kitchen. Wallace stands in the doorway with Inspector Gold looking over his shoulder. Moore points down at the mackintosh.

"Is this your mackintosh?" he asks. Wallace makes no reply. "Had Mrs Wallace a mackintosh like this?" When Wallace fails to make a reply to this second question, Moore turns to Sergeant Bailey. "Take it up and let's have a look at it."[5]

Sergeant Bailey stoops over the body, gently pushes at the right shoulder, and pulls the mackintosh free. He holds up the garment with the inside towards him, the outside towards Wallace, who is still standing in the doorway.

Superintendent Moore takes hold of the right sleeve and stretches it out. Both Moore and Bailey notice the heavy bloodstaining, and the burn marks on the left hand side which extend around to the centre of the skirt at the back.

"This is a gent's," says Moore, after completing his inspection.

Wallace now steps into the room and takes hold of the garment, briefly examining it.

"If there's two patches on the inside, it is mine," he asserts. He then locates the two patches. "It's mine. I wore it this morning, but the day turned out so fine I wore my fawn coat this afternoon. Of course it wasn't burnt like this when I wore it."

"Where did you leave it?" asks Moore.

"Hanging up in the hall at half past one," replies Wallace, pointing to the hat stand.

For the last time Wallace is sent back to the kitchen. Minutes later, he is asked by Inspector Gold to accompany him and Sergeant Bailey to Anfield Bridewell to make a statement.

6

As Wallace leaves the house with Inspector Gold and Sergeant Bailey, his sister-in-law, Amy Wallace, arrives with her son, Edwin. Earlier in the evening, Florence Johnston has sent her daughter to inform Amy of the tragedy.

Amy Wallace stands in the hallway offering her condolences to Wallace. She insists that he spends the night at her home once he has finished at Anfield Bridewell. Wallace says he wishes to sleep in his own home. Moore interrupts to tell him that it will be impossible for him to stay in his own home for the foreseeable future, and agrees with Amy that it would be better for him to stay with her. Wallace reluctantly agrees. Amy and Edwin hasten home to prepare a room for Wallace, who is driven off in a police car at a quarter to twelve.

Harry Cooke, the police photographer, arrives, laden with the tools of his trade. Moore shows him into the front parlour and informs him that he requires two views of the body, one shot from the doorway, the other from the bay window. Cooke begins to assemble his camera and flash, and then realises that the shot from the doorway will be impossible, as the door cannot be fully opened because of the two, obstructing chairs behind it, next to the piano. Moore orders a constable to take the door off its hinges.

With the door removed, Cooke takes his picture and then sets up his camera again in the bay window. As he does so, somebody removes the chair from in front of the sideboard and places it down at its side. Cooke does not notice, nor does Moore, and the photograph is taken.

7

On the way to the bridewell, Wallace informs Inspector Gold that on the previous night he had been given a telephone message at the chess club by Captain Beattie, from a man named Qualtrough, asking him to go to Menlove Gardens East. He exclaims that that was why he had been absent from home earlier in the evening, when Julia died.

In the interview room at Anfield Bridewell, a few minutes before midnight, Sergeant Bailey takes down Wallace's voluntary statement, a process which takes twenty minutes. When it is completed, Gold reads it back to Wallace, who signs it. Then Gold begins to question him.

"Did you see anyone loitering about when you left the house?" he begins.

"I saw no suspicious persons about when I left the house to go to Allerton," replies Wallace.

"Tell me exactly which way you went to the tram and back."

"I left by the back door, then up the entry to Richmond Park by the new Institute to Sedley Street, and then to Newcombe Street, Castlewood Road and to Belmont Road and St Margaret's Church, where I got on a tram to Allerton and back. I got off the tram at Shiel Road and West Derby Road and went home by the same route, except that I went to the front door."

"Did you see or speak to anyone on the way to the tram and back?"

"I saw no one about the entries or streets near home. The first persons I spoke to were the Johnstons."

"Did you think there was someone in the house when you got back?"

"I think there was someone in the house when I went to the front door, because I could not open it and I could not open the back door."

"Did you hear anyone moving about the house?"

Wallace shakes his head.

"No. I heard no noise in the house."

Gold consults the statement.

"Was the yard door bolted when you got back?"

"It wasn't bolted but closed."

"Was anyone likely to call when you were out?"

"Only the paper boy from Cabbage Hall."

"And what time would that have been?"

Wallace pauses before replying, as if gathering his thoughts.

"I'm not sure whether he had delivered the paper before I left or not."

Gold glances through the statement again.

"Tell me exactly what was stolen from the cash-box."

Wallace once more lists the contents of the cash-box which have been stolen.

"Did your wife have any money in the house?"

"I think she had some," replies Wallace, "but I don't know where she kept it."

Once again Gold checks through the statement.

"Do you know anybody named Qualtrough?"

"No. I know no one of that name."

"Do you know anyone who would be likely to send you a message at the chess club?"

"No," says Wallace. "I cannot think of anyone."

"Would your wife admit anyone to the house who called on business while you were away?"

"No. She would not admit anyone unless she knew them personally. If anyone did call, she would show them into the front parlour."

"Do you know of anyone besides the paper boy who would be likely to call, either to see you or your wife?"

"I cannot call to mind anyone likely to call and I don't know that she had any friends unknown to me."

"Who gave you the message at the chess club?"

"Captain Beattie."

"Do you know anyone who knew you were going to the chess club?" asks Gold. "Had you told anyone you were going?"

"No. I hadn't told anyone I was going. And I can't think of anyone who knew I was going."

Inspector Gold deposits Wallace's statement on the desk.

"Mr Wallace," he begins. "We have to examine you for traces of blood. Do you object to such a search?"

Wallace does not raise an objection, and Gold begins the inspection of his clothing, hands, face and shoes. No blood traces are found, either on him, or his clothing.

Police Constable James Rothwell has heard of the murder and he reports to the bridewell to give an account to the inspector of his sighting of Wallace that afternoon, in a distressed state, as he made his collection round. He makes a statement and signs it.

Chapter 5

Investigation and Arrest

1

News of the murder has spread throughout the Richmond Park area, and a small crowd has gathered at the front door. Moore orders his uniformed officers to disperse the onlookers, to make way for the Fire Brigade truck which arrives with the two electric lamps. By now, the house is congested with policemen of all ranks, and to facilitate his search of the house and its environs with the floodlights, Moore re-assigns most of his officers to house-to-house enquiries, leaving himself space in which to function.

He works steadily and methodically with the aid of the two lights, from eleven-thirty to four o'clock in the morning. He illuminates the floors and walls, from the parlour door to the kitchen, then up the stairs to the landing and into the bedrooms and bathroom, where the bath, sink and toilet bowl come under particular scrutiny. Except for the small clot in the lavatory pan, there are no other bloodstains in the house outside the front parlour.

Next he rigs up one of the lamps by the front door and carefully inspects the door for signs of forcible entry. He then repeats the exercise with the back door. He finds nothing suspicious about either door. Finally, he examines all the downstairs windows for anything unusual but, again, the results are negative. There are no signs of forcible entry, no signs that the 'Anfield Housebreaker' has been at work. Nothing that could possibly resemble the murder weapon comes to light, either.

At ten minutes to twelve, Dr Hugh Pierce, the Police Medical Officer, arrives at the scene. He joins MacFall in the front parlour and together they examine the corpse. Pierce examines the wounds to the left side of the head, and notes that rigor mortis has set in along the upper part of the left arm and in the neck. For the next hour, he and MacFall inspect the body every quarter of an hour, to note the progression of the rigor and, like MacFall, Pierce does not take notes of his observations. MacFall shows Pierce the small blood clot in the lavatory pan before gathering it up onto a piece of paper, which he folds away into an envelope.

By one o'clock in the morning, Pierce observes that the rigor has extended to the right arm and leg, and he forms the opinion that death had taken place some six hours before his arrival at the house, giving the time of death as six o'clock in the evening of 20 January. Professor MacFall concurs.

At one-fifteen, Sergeant Bailey returns to Wolverton Street and, under instructions from MacFall and Pierce, he supervises the removal of Julia's body to the Princess Dock mortuary, leaving behind on the hearth rug a piece of matted hair.

2

The body arrives at the mortuary just before two o'clock and is immediately wheeled into the autopsy room. Two assistants deposit the corpse on a mortuary slab, and under the watchful eye of Sergeant Bailey, they strip off its clothing in preparation for the autopsy. Bailey records that Julia is wearing her wedding ring and a small brooch at her throat. As the assistants remove her skirt, Bailey observes two burn marks upon the front and side of the garment, but cannot detect any burning or scorching on the underskirt. He takes possession of the skirt. Beneath the underskirt, Julia is wearing what appears to be a home-made nappy, held in place by a large safety pin. As this is removed, a pocket is exposed and Bailey finds a one pound note and a ten-shilling note in the pocket. He gathers up the clothing and the money and leaves the room at two o'clock to return to the bridewell, where he temporarily stores Julia's clothing and effects. Wallace is still sitting in the interview room, chain-smoking, and drinking tea, as he awaits the return of Superintendent Moore.

Just after four o'clock in the morning, Moore returns to the bridewell, his search of 29 Wolverton Street complete: the house is locked and two uniformed officers stand guard at the front and back entrances. Moore confers with Inspector Gold, who gives him a copy of Wallace's statement. After reading it, Moore leads the way into the interview room. Wallace rises to his feet.

"Is there nothing more you would like to tell us?" asks Moore. Wallace shakes his head. "Are you sure?" he persists.

"What about?" asks Wallace.

Moore conducts a whispered conversation with Gold and then turns again to Wallace.

"You're staying with your sister-in-law tonight?" Wallace nods. "Inspector Gold will take you." As Gold leaves the room to make arrangements for a car, Moore approaches Wallace. "Mr Wallace," he says firmly. "You will report to Dale Street Detective Office later today. At ten o'clock, please."

"Yes," replies Wallace.

Wallace leaves the bridewell with Gold and a police driver. Moore sends Bailey home to get some sleep and at five o'clock, he too goes home. He is aware that his work is only just beginning.

3

Amy and Edwin Wallace live at 83 Ullet Road, just off Smithdown Road. They are both up when William Wallace arrives with Inspector Gold. Moore has instructed Gold to take statements from Amy and Edwin and he immediately sets about his task. Neither of them can tell Inspector Gold anything of significance relating to the night of the murder; they simply talk in general about William and Julia being a reasonably happy couple. Amy briefly relates details of her visit to see Julia on the Monday afternoon, and of leaving her alive and well at about four-thirty. As an afterthought, Amy adds that William Wallace relied upon his wife a great deal, with the implication that he took her for granted. Gold takes notes of what he has been told before he leaves Ullet Road and then goes home to bed. He will only sleep a couple of hours before his ten o'clock appointment with Wallace.

As the city sleeps, police officers, plain-clothed and uniformed, continue their hunt for anyone with bloodstained clothing, and they check out any individual acting in an unusual or suspicious manner. The homes of known criminals, doss houses and cheap lodging houses, the Salvation Army Hostel, cafés, shebeens, brothels, railway terminals, bus and tram depots, the ferry terminals at the Pier Head and New Brighton, are all methodically searched. Tramps and derelicts, in doorways, on park benches, huddled in their newspapers against the cold, are rudely awakened from their meths-induced slumber to answer questions beneath the probing flashlights of the inquisitive police.

The search will continue throughout Wednesday and Thursday, and thousands of men will be questioned and interrogated. Hundreds of statements will be taken from men and women who believe they saw something on the night of the murder which may be relevant to the investigation. Many hoax and crank letters and telephone calls will be received, logged and investigated, some coming from as far afield as Blackpool and London. Many man-hours will be spent following up every possible lead, however minor, however bogus; but nothing directly relating to the murder of Julia Wallace will come to light.[1]

4

Dale Street Detective Office is a scene of frenetic activity when William Wallace reports at ten o'clock, as instructed, on Wednesday morning. He is shown into an interview room where Inspector Gold is waiting. Even though the murder has not been reported in the morning's *Daily Post and Mercury*, news of it has spread like a contagion and covers most of the Liverpool suburbs, its epicentre at Richmond Park, where the activities of the police are being monitored by the locals, the curious and the tardy press corps.

Superintendent Moore arrives at Dale Street. He hurries to his office, past the harried telephonists, whose switchboard is overloading with the huge volumes of incoming calls, only to find his desk awash with reports and messages from his night-duty officers. He seats himself at his desk and opens a new file, 1341GC: Julia Wallace, Murder.

He checks that Wallace has reported in, and learns that Inspector Gold has already organised officers to go to 31 and 27 Wolverton Street to take the statements from the Johnstons and the Holmes and to Orleans House to speak to Samuel Beattie.

He then sketches out what he has learnt so far, from Inspector Gold, from his conversations with Wallace and from his statement, from his own observations and impressions at the crime scene, and from the verbal reports of Dr Pierce and Professor MacFall.

Once he has the events leading up to the crime organised in his mind, he sets to work, to check it all through. There were no signs of a forcible entry to the house; Wallace was absent from home on what appears to be a bogus errand; the house was robbed. Keeping in the back of his mind the policeman's rule of thumb that the majority of murdered wives die at the hands of their husbands, his initial, working theory, is that Mrs Wallace admitted someone to her home in her husband's absence, and that this person robbed and killed her.[2]

Moore's first task is to check through Wallace's story and he sends Sergeant Bailey in search of Qualtrough, any and all Qualtroughs who can be found in the Liverpool area. He dispatches officers to Cottle's City Café to speak to anyone who can be of help with the Qualtrough telephone call. A team is organised to search for a murder weapon: Moore does not know what the killer used to bludgeon Mrs Wallace to death, but he is certain that the weapon is not in the house. He orders his men to make a blanket search in the immediate vicinity of the Wallace home, and he calls for the help of the Sanitation Department to investigate the drains, sewers, dust-bins and middens of the area.

Harry Cooke is contacted again, and Moore tells him to report to the Princess Dock mortuary. Next, he telephones the main Liverpool Telephone Exchange in Victoria Street, which runs parallel to Dale Street, and speaks to a supervisor. Moore is told that it will be impossible to trace the call. As he hangs up, he is handed a message by his secretary – an anonymous caller alleges that Wallace is having an affair with Julia's maid. Moore passes along this piece of information to Gold in the interview room, and instructs him to interrogate Wallace for details about the maid.

When confronted about the maid, Wallace is unsure of himself in his reply. He tells Gold that neither he nor Julia has ever employed a maid, adding that they do employ a part-time cleaner, whose name he cannot remember. Gold sends back the reply, and yet another constable is dispatched by Moore to question the Wallaces's neighbours about a cleaning woman or maid.

Just before eleven o'clock, Moore and Gold, accompanied by several officers, set off for Wolverton Street, where they are met by the Chief Constable, Lionel Everett, the City Analyst, William Roberts and Dr Hugh Pierce. Moore speaks briefly to the press, outlining the basic facts of the case. As Gold enters the house, the policeman on duty at the front door informs him that a Sarah Jane Draper called at the house earlier in the morning, claiming to be Julia's char lady, and demanding admittance. The policeman turned her away, but not before noting both her name and address. Gold orders her to be brought to the Dale Street office.

Inside the house, Superintendent Moore conducts Everett and Roberts on a tour of the house, during which he takes the time to re-examine, in daylight, the front and back doors, their locks, and the ground floor windows, pointing out to his superior the absence of any signs of forcible entry. He explains to Everett that his conclusion is that the killer gained entrance to the house either by subterfuge, or with a key, and that in all probability it was not the elusive 'Anfield Housebreaker', who always targets empty homes. In the kitchen, the cash-box and the broken cabinet are inspected, together with Julia's handbag and Moore orders Gold to begin labelling and collecting evidence.

Moore leads the way into the front parlour where he briefly describes to Everett the position in which the body was found, and how the mackintosh was partially concealed beneath it. Roberts examines the garment and notes the heavy bloodstaining inside and outside on the right side, running up to the inner side of the sleeve. On the left cuff and over the left pocket further staining is obvious.

The bottom right-hand side of the mackintosh is badly burnt away and Roberts spots charred fragments of material on both the floor and the hearth rug. As Moore and Everett continue their discussions, Roberts begins a fruitless search in the parlour, hallway and kitchen for additional fragments, before dusting the house for fingerprints.

Meanwhile Gold has ordered two constables to dismantle the lavatory seat and pan in the bathroom, while another pair of officers are disconnecting the Sunbeam gas fire in the front parlour, prior to its removal. With the assistance of another officer, Gold gathers up the cash-box, Wallace's diaries, and Julia's handbag from the kitchen. They proceed into the front parlour to collect the mackintosh, the piece of matted hair, the hearth rug, and several other items which have been splashed and spotted with blood.

5

Harry Cooke arrives at the Princess Dock mortuary just before midday. He has to wait while Amy Wallace formally identifies the body of Julia Wallace, née Dennis. When she has gone, the mortuary assistants prepare the body for Professor MacFall, and Cooke is able to take three photographs of the body on the dissecting table before MacFall sets to work.

I found the body to be that of a lightly built woman of about fifty-five years of age. Her abdomen was prominent and had no linea ablicantes.[3] The external genital orifice was quite clean with no evidence of blood. There was a small recent bruise mark on the inside of the left upper arm. There were no other external marks of violence on the trunk or limbs. The hair was matted with blood and brain tissue. I removed the hair. Two inches above the zygoma was a large lacerated wound, two inches by three inches, from which brain and bone was protruding. On the back of the head, towards the left side, were ten diagonal, apparently incised, wounds. On removal of the scalp, the left frontal bone was seen, driven into the front of the brain corresponding to the external wound. The whole of the left side of the back of the skull was driven inwards and broken into pieces. The fracturing extended into the middle and rear fossal, fracturing the base of the skull and breaking up part of the cerebellum. The tenterium cerebelli was burst. The left lateral synus was broken across, also the left meningeal artery. The appearance was as if a terrific force with a hard instrument had driven in the skull in eleven places. The edges of the wounds were not sharp. The body was generally healthy and carried on the functions in a normal way. There was no evidence of menstruation.

Death was due to fracture of the skull by someone striking the deceased eleven times upon the head with terrific force with a hard instrument. From my findings, in my opinion, one blow was harder and more severe than the rest. This one blow produced the front, open wound, and caused death, which took place in less than one minute.

The lungs, heart, kidney and spleen were normal. The stomach contained about four ounces of semi-fluid food, consisting of currants, raisins and unmasticated lumps of carbohydrate. The small bowel was normal, the caecum ascending and transverse colon were enormously and chronically distended (typical constipated bowel). Uterus virginal and clean. The vagina clean and no evidence of bleeding. The right ovary normal, left ovary three and a half by two and a half inches fibroid.[4]

Next, Professor MacFall turns his attention to the blood clot which was found in the lavatory pan. He establishes that it is human blood by the Kastle-Meyer, Teichmann and Guaiacum tests and under the microscope he sees that it contains both red and white corpuscles but no epithelial cells. It is human blood, he concludes, but not menstrual blood. He passes on the notes of his findings to Florence Brook, his secretary, who begins to type them up into report form.

6

At Dale Street Detective Office, Wallace has been informed that there are no signs of forcible entry into his home and that, in all probability, Julia's killer gained entrance either with a key, or by a subterfuge, with the added possibility that Julia knew him and admitted him willingly. Later, Wallace is allowed out for lunch. Julia's sister, Amy Dennis, has arrived in Liverpool, and he meets her for the only time, in company with Amy Wallace.

Moore has perused Amy Wallace's statement and notes that a baker's boy made a delivery at 29 Wolverton Street on the Tuesday afternoon. Upon Wallace's return to the interview room, Moore ascertains the boy's name and place of work, and he sends out an officer to find him. Then he speaks again briefly to the press, outlining the events leading up to the murder, and appealing for witnesses to come forward. Charles Bliss and Mr and Mrs Hoer, the window cleaners, are among the first to respond.

Inspector Gold is busy sorting through the evidence he has collected, together with that brought in by Sergeant Bailey, when he is informed that Sarah Draper has arrived.

"I have known the Wallaces for nine months," Mrs Draper tells Inspector Gold. "And I have been going to their house every Wednesday morning to do the cleaning since I have known them."

"When was the last time you were there?" enquires Gold.

"A fortnight ago today, that was the seventh of January. I used to clean the house right through. Mrs Wallace used to help me. I didn't go on the fourteenth. I have not been for two weeks because I lost my husband."

Inspector Gold elicits from the char lady that she knows the house and its contents very well. Bailey and Gold drive her out to Wolverton Street and allow her to roam around the premises with Gold in attendance to ensure that she touches nothing. In the meantime, Bailey is labelling and bagging the remaining pieces of evidence.

"I used to clean the front bedroom," says Mrs Draper, looking in at the disturbed bed. "And the bed was always kept made, with blankets, sheets and pillows. Mrs Wallace used to have her hats spread out on it. I have never seen the bed in the state it is now."

Downstairs in the kitchen, Mrs Draper reports that one of the pokers from the fireplace is missing.

"There used to be two small steel pokers, one about a foot long, that is there now. The other was about nine inches, this one is missing. It had a small knob on it. Both pokers were in the fireplace in the kitchen when I was last here."

Inspector Gold takes notes, and then shows Mrs Draper into the front parlour. She has a good look round the room.

"There was a straight piece of iron in the parlour fireplace," says Sarah Draper, pointing to the hearth. "It was about a foot long and about as thick as an ordinary candle. That is missing. It was used for cleaning under the gas fire."

"Do you remember particularly when you last saw it there?"

"The last time I was in the parlour was Wednesday 31 December, and the bar of iron was in the fireplace then. I used it that morning, under the gas fire, to find a screw that had come off the gas bracket."

"Is there anything else missing?" asks Gold, and Mrs Draper shakes her head.

At the front door, Gold asks her if she has ever had any problems with the lock, and she says not. But she volunteers the information that the catch on the back door, the door from the backyard to the scullery, is defective.

"When the knob was turned either from the inside or the outside, it would not bring the bolt back from the lock socket," she continues. "This happened pretty regularly and on many occasions I have had to ask Mrs Wallace to open the door for me and she used to do it by gripping the spindle close to the door. There did not seem to be any spring in the lock."

Gold thanks Mrs Draper for her help and arranges for her to be taken to the mortuary to speak to Professor MacFall. Gold and Bailey then drive off to Dale Street, where Gold reports the absence of the poker and iron bar to Superintendant Moore, who sends out word to his officers to be on the look out for the missing implements.

The pair are cataloguing evidence when Bailey comes to the Treasury notes in the jar, which he removed earlier in the day from the mantelpiece in the middle bedroom. As he spreads out the four, one pound notes, he notices that one of them is smeared with blood. The notes are sealed in an envelope and carefully labelled, awaiting forensic examination. He immediately informs Gold of his find and the information is passed on to Moore. The three detectives contemplate this new find: would the killer, a thief, his hands bloodied following the murder, have handled the notes and then left them behind? The only other person known to have been near the notes, is Wallace, says Gold. Could he have smeared the bank note with blood? All three agree that the robbery was a bungled, amateurish affair.

Later that evening, Police Constable James Serjeant reports for duty at Allerton Bridewell, and parades with the other members of the night shift before going on duty. He has read the account of the murder in the *Liverpool Echo*, and when he hears his name called by his inspector, he immediately guesses why. He remembers speaking to a tall, thin man on the previous evening, who was looking for Menlove Gardens East. He has no doubt that he spoke to William Herbert Wallace. Serjeant volunteers what he knows to the CID officers at the bridewell.

7

It is Wednesday evening, just after seven o'clock, and inside the Holy Trinity church hall, in Richmond Park, two young boys, both members of the Boys Brigade, are playing a desultory game of table tennis. James Allison Wildman, aged sixteen, tells his opponent, Douglas Metcalfe, that he walked past the Wallace house on the night of the murder at approximately twenty-five minutes to seven. He did not see Mrs Wallace, although he did see a milk boy standing on the step wearing a Collegiate College cap. Metcalfe concludes that the milk boy was Allan Close.

Having finished their game, Wildman and Metcalfe part company, Wildman going home, Metcalfe walking up Richmond Park and into Breck Road, where he meets up with Elsie Wright and Kenneth Caird outside the library, next door to Holy Trinity Church. All three youngsters make evening deliveries in and around Wolverton Street. Elsie Wright, a pert thirteen-year-old, works for the Close Dairy, delivering milk with Allan Close, the son of the proprietor. She is the centre of attention: she has been very near to the scene of the murder. She reports that she and Allan Close tried to deliver milk at 29 Wolverton Street earlier in the evening, but were told by the policeman who answered the door not to make any more deliveries until further notice.

"Did you deliver the milk there last night?" asks Douglas Metcalfe.

"No," says Elsie Wright. "Wolverton Street is part of Allan's round not mine."

She goes on to tell him that Allan Close had said he had delivered the milk to the Wallace house at about a quarter to seven on the night of the murder.

Metcalfe, an intelligent and self-assured young man, remembers that the report in that evening's *Liverpool Echo* had said that the baker's boy, Neil Norbury, was the last person to see Mrs Wallace alive at about four-thirty in the evening. Metcalfe informs his friends that Allan Close is probably the last person.

Within minutes, Allan Close joins his fellow workers.[5] Metcalfe ascertains from Close that he did indeed deliver milk at the Wallace house the previous evening, and that he saw and spoke to Mrs Wallace between six-thirty and a quarter to seven. Metcalfe suggests that he should go to the house and report the matter to the police.

Led by Metcalfe and Wright, Close arrives at 29 Wolverton Street. He knocks on the door and after explaining to the policeman the reason for his second visit that night, he is admitted to the murder house. Inside, he makes his statement, saying he delivered the milk to Mrs Wallace between six-thirty and six forty-five on the Tuesday night. Upon leaving the house, he refuses to speak to his friends to relate what has gone on, and he runs home with his lips sealed. The following day he will sign his typed statement at Anfield Bridewell.

William Wallace spends the night at Wolverton Street: Amy Dennis is staying with Amy Wallace before returning to Hove the following day, so there is no room at the flat for him. Amy Dennis has made a very brief statement to the police and before she leaves for home, she will write Wallace a curt note, requesting that he send on to her Julia's fur coat.

8

On Thursday morning, the Liverpool City Coroner, Dr C Mort, formally opens the inquest into the death of Julia Wallace. After hearing evidence of identification from Amy Wallace, the inquest is adjourned pending further inquiries. A report is sent to the Chief Constable and it is passed to his assistant, Glover, who in turn informs Bernard Pearce at the Office of the Director of Public Prosecutions, in Whitehall, London.

William Wallace once again reports to Dale Street Detective Office at ten o'clock and is seen by Inspector Gold.

"I think I have some important information for you," he informs Gold.

"Do you wish to make a further statement?"

"Yes," replies Wallace, as he then proceeds to volunteer his second statement, which Gold writes down in longhand.

Wallace gives the police the names of fourteen men who would be admitted to the house by Mrs Wallace in his absence. When he has completed his statement, he reads and signs it. Later in the day he will sign a typed copy.

Superintendent Moore is busy in his office, collating the rising mound of reports and statements, and co-ordinating and extending the investigation. He learns of the noticeboard in Cottle's City Café, adjacent to the telephone box, upon which is displayed the chess club's playing lists: Wallace was due to play at the club on the Monday night; anyone, particularly Qualtrough, entering the café for a meal could have seen it.

Then, he reads the statement of Gladys Harley, waitress at the café, the one who first answered the Qualtrough telephone call. Harley states that when she answered the call, the operator said, "Anfield calling". Moore immediately contacts the Anfield Exchange. He tells the supervisor that he wants the names of the telephone operators who were on duty on the night of Monday, 19 January. After a few minutes, he is given their names. Moore asks if it would be possible to trace a call that was placed via the exchange. The supervisor tells him probably not, as the exchange is a manual one, but that he is welcome to speak to the operators that evening when they come on duty.

Press coverage of the murder, both local and national, is detailed and regular, and the public is gripped by the news as it unfolds. Already rumours are rife about Wallace, about Julia, and about their relationships with one another and their friends, and accusations are being fed steadily into the rumour mill. Sidney Green, who has been following the newspaper reports, calls at the detective office. He relates his encounter on the Tuesday night with a man who could only have been Wallace. He makes a statement and leaves. Police officers contact the friends of Allan Close: Elsie Wright, Douglas Metcalfe and Kenneth Caird, and they are interviewed at Anfield Bridewell. It is now known that Allan Close is the last person, outside of the Wallace household, to have seen Julia Wallace alive.

Superintendent Moore calls a case conference of his senior officers in the afternoon. Sergeant Bailey's team is interviewing all fourteen Qualtrough families in Liverpool. With the interviews and checking almost complete, the murderous RM Qualtrough[6] remains an enigma. Details of Wallace's movements on the Monday and Tuesday nights are being checked, and confirmation by witnesses is positive. In particular, two tram conductors, Phillips and Thompson, have come forward, and they have identified Wallace as the man who boarded their trams on the Tuesday night.

The police are working on the theory that Wallace was lured from his home by the prospect of business with Qualtrough, who knew from the playing list that he would be at the chess club to receive his message and that, in Wallace's absence, Qualtrough entered the house, robbed it, and murdered his wife. Inspector Gold offers an alternative theory, one which has been voiced by several of his officers: the robbery was amateurish, almost as if it had been staged. Could the real objective of the attack on the Wallace household have been murder, the murder of Mrs Wallace, and the deed dressed up to look like a robbery which had gone wrong?

Moore agrees with Gold's notion, but he is disturbed by Professor MacFall's report on the murder scene, which confirms a niggling doubt in his own mind: why was there no blood outside of the immediate vicinity of the body, except for the tiny clot in the lavatory pan? Considering the amount of blood spilled in the violent attack, Moore argues, surely the assailant should have been covered in blood, surely he should have left traces throughout the house? And yet there were none. What is more, there were no blood traces on any of Wallace's clothing. He makes a mental note to speak to MacFall about this.

Moore distributes Wallace's second statement among his officers, together with the notion that the murder weapon could be the missing iron bar, and a plan of action is set in motion to interview all the men supplied by Wallace. Particular attention will be given to three men, Parry, Marsden and Young. According to Wallace, they each knew the location of the cash-box in the kitchen.

Wallace attends the police station after his afternoon collection round. Moore orders close surveillance of him to begin forthwith. Wallace has mentioned that some of his clients have been hostile and abusive towards him on his rounds, and Moore does not want any incidents. The surveillance will also afford him the opportunity to observe Wallace's behaviour.

Later in the evening, as Moore is preparing to go home, a supervisor at the Anfield Exchange telephones him to say that three of the operators at the exchange remember putting through a call to Cottle's City Café on the Monday night. Moore is overjoyed. He arranges, for the sake of propriety, for the three women to make their statements the following morning at the main Telephone Exchange in the General Post Office building in Victoria Street, just around the corner from Dale Street.

9

Wallace leaves Dale Street Detective Office at ten fifteen, at the end of his second day of assisting the police in their inquiries. A plain clothes policeman is in close attendance. He is returning to his sister-in-law's flat in Ullet Road, Sefton Park, and the nearest tram stop for him is at the corner of North John Street and Lord Street. Wallace stands at the kerb with his back to Lord Street, looking down along North John Street.

At twenty-minutes past ten, James Caird and Samuel Beattie, in company with two other chess club members, leave Cottle's City Café after the usual Thursday night meeting, and walk along North John Street towards the tram stop in Lord Street. As they near the corner, Caird recognises the hunched figure of Wallace ahead.

"Mr Beattie!" exclaims Caird. "Look who's here!"

Caird approaches Wallace and greets him. Beattie and the other two members join in. No one notices the policeman huddled in the doorway of an office building, eavesdropping on the conversation. Wallace turns to Beattie.

"That telephone message. Can you remember what time you actually received that message? It may be very important."

"About seven o'clock or shortly after," replies Beattie.

"I'd like to get nearer than that if you can remember," urges Wallace.

"I'm afraid I can't."

"There are a lot of strange things in connection with the murder," continues Wallace. "I have just left the police office, and the police have cleared me."

"Oh! Have they?" says Beattie. "I'm pleased to hear it."

"Yes, they've cleared me," reiterates Wallace. "There are many strange features about the case. I hope the police catch him. I would like to meet him as there are some things I would like to ask him."

"You know the police have been in touch with me over this business," says Beattie. "I would advise you not to discuss it with anyone other than the police, because any simple thing you might say might be distorted."

"I thought the police would have been in communication with you," says Wallace.

"Have you made arrangements for the funeral?" enquires Caird, as the conversation begins to flag.

"I think it will be on Saturday, but I don't want any fuss."

Wallace bids goodnight to his friends as a number 8 tram pulls in at the stop. He boards the tram and is followed by the policeman.

10

On Friday morning, Superintendent Moore receives a statement from David Jones. A copy of Tuesday night's *Liverpool Echo* has been found in the Wallaces' kitchen. Jones, a newsagent, had delivered the newspaper to 29 Wolverton Street at six thirty on the night of the murder. On Thursday night he was stopped on his rounds by a policeman, and had confirmed the delivery to the officer, who then told him to report to Anfield Bridewell to make a statement. According to Jones, when he made his delivery, 29 Wolverton Street was in darkness, there was no sound from within, and he neither saw, nor heard, anyone in the street.

Inspector Gold and Sergeant Bailey report for duty, and as soon as Wallace arrives, they drive him to his home, under the probing eyes of the press corps. He is told to search the house to see if anything is missing, particularly from downstairs.

They start upstairs. There is nothing missing from the bedroom which Wallace has converted into a laboratory. In the middle bedroom, where he slept with Julia, again there is nothing missing. The front bedroom is still in a mess, and after picking his way through the disorder, and finding Julia's fur coat in the wardrobe and her Post Office Savings Bank book and her jewellery in the chest of drawers, Wallace affirms that everything is where it should be.

He makes a thorough search in the downstairs room. He uncovers Julia's Prudential Insurance policy in the kitchen, and assures Gold that it is the only one she had. When he is finished, he informs Gold and Bailey that all he can find missing is a small axe, used for chopping up wood.

"I haven't seen it for about twelve months," he declares.

Gold and Bailey begin a search for the missing axe and, under the stairs, in a basket full of old clothes, Inspector Gold finds it.

"Are you sure there is nothing else missing, Mr Wallace?" presses Inspector Gold.

"Nothing that I can see."

"Mrs Draper has stated that there is a poker about nine inches long missing from the kitchen fireplace, and a piece of iron about a foot long missing from the fireplace in the parlour," prompts Gold.

"She must have thrown the poker away with the ashes," Wallace concludes. "I do not know anything about the piece of iron in the parlour."

Wallace is left alone in the kitchen while the two officers make notes of the proceedings. Then they go through the house again, collecting evidence. Moore removes a suit from the wardrobe in the middle bedroom: he knows that it is the one which Wallace was wearing on the night of the murder, and it will be re-examined for blood traces. A grubby white towel and a nail-brush are taken from the bathroom.

Meanwhile, back in the city centre, a team of Moore's officers is interviewing the three operators from the Anfield Exchange at the main telephone exchange in Victoria Street. Their information will cause a sensation.

At seven-fifteen on Monday 19 January, Louisa Alfreds, who had been on duty since four-thirty that afternoon, received a call from a public telephone box, Anfield 1627, and a man's voice asked to be connected to Bank 3581, Cottle's City Café. Alfreds made the connection.

Two minutes later, Lily Kelly, sitting next to Louisa at the switchboard, also received a call from Anfield 1627. A man's voice complained that he had pressed button A but had not been connected. Kelly asked what number the man had been trying to get and the reply was Bank 3581. Kelly informed

Alfreds of this, then advised the caller to press button B to regain his three pennies.[7] Then she tried, but failed, to connect the caller to Bank 3581.

Kelly then waved over her immediate supervisor, Annie Robertson, and explained the situation. Robertson, noting that the red light on the switchboard indicated that the caller's money had been returned, finally made the connection from Anfield 1627 to Bank 3581. As the connection was made, both Kelly and Alfreds listened in to hear the caller inquire, "Is that the City Café?" Then they both unplugged. Because it had been put through free of charge, a note of the call and the time it was finally put through was made in the log book: twenty minutes past seven. Supervisor Robertson shows the police the note, to which has been appended the initials NR, signifying no reply.

Within minutes of taking the three operators' statements, the police discover that Anfield 1627 is a telephone kiosk located at the junction of Rochester Road and Breck Road[8] - four hundred yards from the home of William Herbert Wallace.

11

Superintendent Moore is in his office reading the report from the detective who shadowed Wallace on Thursday night. He is disturbed and suspicious as he notes the details of Wallace's conversation with Beattie at the tram stop. When he is informed of the location of the kiosk from where Qualtrough made the telephone call, he is stunned, then elated. He adds this to his growing belief that murder, and not robbery, was the main objective of the mysterious RM Qualtrough. The robbery was so amateurish as to appear staged: the thief did not touch Julia's handbag in the kitchen and missed her jewellery, fur coat and the money upstairs in the bedrooms, in addition to the brooch and ring she was wearing when murdered. Moore begins to focus his suspicions on Wallace.

At Tuebrook Bridewell, Richard Gordon Parry is being interviewed by Sergeant Breslin about his movements on the night of the murder and his knowledge of the Wallace household. He is co-operative and supplies details without prompting of all he knows. When the statement is completed and signed, it is rushed over to Dale Street for the attention of Superintendent Moore.

When Gold returns with Bailey and Wallace to Dale Street, Moore brings Gold up to date on the latest developments. Both men concur that there is a big question mark hanging over Wallace. Their vague intuitions of his guilt are now hardening in the light of the two recent pieces of information: the location of the telephone kiosk, and what they now interpret as his attempts to influence Beattie. Is RM Qualtrough in reality William Herbert Wallace? Moore is eager to speak to Wallace about his encounter with Beattie. However, he decides to delay for the time being.

Once more, Moore and Gold peruse the details of Wallace's movements on the night of the murder, from the moment he left home at six-forty-five, until he returned home to find his wife's body. They decide to question him again about his journey. Was he engaged in an elaborate charade, constructing a contentious time factor by establishing himself over two miles away from home through his persistent questions and demands upon the two tram conductors?

Inspector Gold speaks first and asks Wallace to repeat the details of his tram journeys, from Smithdown Lane to Penny Lane, then from Penny Lane to Menlove Gardens West. Sergeant Bailey records his account, has it typed up into statement form, and hands it to Wallace to sign. This is Wallace's third statement.

At six thirty in the evening, Gold leads him into Moore's office. The Superintendent comes straight to the point without any preamble.

"You saw Mr Beattie of the chess club last night?"

"Yes," confirms Wallace. "While I was waiting for a tramcar in Lord Street."

"You asked him about the telephone call and what time he received it?"

"Yes."

"You told him the time was important?"

"Yes."

"In what way was it important?" probes Moore, gently.

"I had some ideas of my own. We all have ideas. It was indiscreet of me," replies Wallace. He then lapses into silence.

"What were your ideas?"

"I can't say why I asked him, I admit it was an indiscretion on my part. I cannot say anything further."

Moore lets the matter rest there for the moment and dismisses Wallace, but the interview has done nothing to alleviate his growing suspicions. He next turns his attention to Richard Parry's statement and arranges for two officers to start checking out his movements the following day.

12

It is Saturday morning, and a withering drizzle descends upon the city. At Anfield Cemetery, William Wallace, accompanied by Amy and Edwin, bury Julia under the observant eyes of Constable Thomas Hudson. The ceremony is brief and there are few flowers. Wallace is unable to control his emotions and weeps copiously.

At Dale Street Detective Office, Moore receives a statement from Professor MacFall and Doctor Pierce. They have considered the possibility of Julia's killer not being covered in her blood, and both agree that the killer could have struck her at such an angle that the blood flew away from him and that only his left hand, which made contact with the body, would have become bloodstained. This theory would account for the lack of bloodstains outside the murder room. The killer then washed his left hand in the bathroom upstairs, and in so doing, left the tiny blood clot in the lavatory pan.

Moore and Gold have also been contemplating the notion that Wallace wore his own mackintosh, the one found beneath Julia's body, when he bludgeoned her to death, to avoid contaminating himself with her blood. Wallace's suit, the one he wore on the night of the murder, has been re-examined at the police laboratory, and no bloodstaining has been found. Moore now has two possible means, in the light of MacFall's statement, to account for the lack of staining on Wallace's clothing. He cannot be eliminated from the investigation because of a lack of bloodstaining on his clothes.

A little later in the day, a Mr Hall is shown into Moore's office. He is clutching a letter which he says he was going to post to Moore, but decided it would be better to deliver it personally. It is from his daughter, Lily, who is ill in bed. In it, she says that she saw Wallace on the night of the murder, just after eight-thirty, talking to another man in Richmond Park.

Moore checks through Wallace's statements but can find no mention of this incident. He arranges with Mr Hall to call on his daughter the following day to take a statement.

Samuel Beattie calls in to see Inspector Gold. He makes a statement in which he describes his encounter with Wallace on the Thursday night after he had left the chess club. The details coincide with those given by the police officer who had Wallace under surveillance that night.

13

Early Sunday morning, Inspector Gold calls at 9 Letchworth Street to speak to the bed-ridden Lily Hall. She claims that on the night of the murder, at approximately eight-thirty-five, she saw William Wallace deep in conversation with another man at the mouth of the alleyway between 79 and 81 Richmond Park, the alley that runs through the middle of Wolverton Street. Lily Hall could plainly make out Wallace, but not his companion, whom she describes as being six inches shorter than him, of stocky build and wearing a cap and a dark overcoat.

Back at the detective office, Gold and Moore once more scrutinise Wallace's statements and those of all the other witnesses. Lily Hall's statement adds to the clouds of suspicion gathering over Wallace. If her statement is true, Gold argues, it makes Wallace a liar on two counts: he stated quite clearly that he had not spoken to anyone on his way home and that he had become suspicious when he could not find Menlove Gardens East and had hurried directly home. Gold arranges for an advertisement the next day in the local press asking for the unknown man, whom Hall saw talking to Wallace, to come forward.

They conclude that if Wallace is the murderer, then on the Monday night he must have made the Qualtrough telephone call himself, from the call box close to his home, prior to boarding the tramcar to the chess club and that, on the Tuesday night, he must have killed Julia just after Allan Close had delivered the milk.

The detectives can envisage no difficulties with the Monday night. The problem is the Tuesday night, a problem of time: Close claimed that he saw Mrs Wallace sometime between six-thirty and six-forty-five; Wallace maintained that he left home at six-forty-five and arrived at the tramcar stop at Smithdown Lane at six minutes past seven, a journey of two miles, which took twenty-one minutes. Could he have killed Julia immediately after the milk boy's delivery, cleaned up, staged the robbery, and made it to the tramcar stop by six minutes past seven?

Moore and Gold agree that six minutes past seven is a fixed point in the time frame, as there can be no doubt that the evidence of the tram conductor, Thomas Phillips, is accurate. They conclude that they will need a far more accurate time from the milk boy, and that they will have to determine whether Wallace's journey to the tramcar stop at Smithdown Lane can be made in less than twenty-one minutes. If Close's timing can be pushed closer to six-thirty, and if Wallace's journey time of twenty-one minutes can be considerably reduced, allowing him to leave later than six-forty-five, then he could have had the time in which to kill his wife.

Gold and Moore call on Allan Croxton Close at 51 Sedley Street. Close delivers milk from his father's dairy to homes in and around the Richmond Park area. He usually delivers on his bicycle, but on the night of 20 January, it was being repaired and he made his rounds on foot. The two detectives take Close on his round, re-enacting the events of the night of the murder.

Close was part of the way through his round when he passed Holy Trinity Church on Breck Road. He noted the time at twenty-five minutes past six by the church clock. This clock, Moore now knows, is accurate, having been reset on the Friday before the murder by John Paterson of Condliff and Company, who has given a statement to that effect to the police. Timing Close from the clock, Gold and Moore follow him into Sedley Street, to the dairy, where he had picked up several cans of fresh milk before setting off to Letchworth Street to deliver to his only customer there. Then Close proceeds into Richmond Park, where he had made a second delivery, before going down the alleyway into Wolverton Street and calling at number 29.

According to Close, he had left a can of milk on the front doorstep of the Wallace home and knocked at the door, before moving off to make a delivery next door at number 31. The delivery completed, he had returned to number 29, had noted that the can had been taken in, and had waited for Mrs Wallace to return the empty can. Close and Mrs Wallace had exchanged greetings before he had moved off into Redford Street.

Moore checks his stop watch. It has taken Allan Close six minutes to walk this part of his round and make his deliveries, from Holy Trinity Church to Sedley Street, to Letchworth Street, to Richmond Park, and finally to Wolverton Street. As the Holy Trinity Church clock was correct and he passed the church at twenty-five minutes past six, then Close, the last person outside the Wallace household to see Julia alive, must have seen her at six-thirty-one.

14

Monday 26 January sees the birth of the 'Anfield Harriers'. Superintendent Moore has called in his most experienced officers, the Chief Constable and the Assistant Prosecuting Solicitor for Liverpool, Mr JR Bishop. Moore outlines his scheme: that night and the next, pairs of detectives will follow the route that Wallace maintains he took on the night of the murder, from the back door of 29 Wolverton Street, down to St Margaret's Church on foot, then by tramcar to the number 5 stop at Smithdown Lane. The journeys are to be timed, and the detectives are to begin the time trials, or the 'tram tests', as they will become known, at approximately six-forty-five; the time Wallace claimed he left home on the night of the murder.

Moore has the tests conducted in secrecy, so as not to alert anyone connected with the case, in particular Wallace and the press, as to where his suspicions are directed. Later, during Wallace's committal, Sydney Scholfield Allen, his counsel, will dub the detectives involved in the tests, the Anfield Harriers. The local press and the public will join in the barracking, and the detectives, already known as 'Jacks', will be further burdened with the sobriquet of 'Spring-heeled Jacks'.[9]

Moore dispatches his officers to continue their enquiries, ordering them to report back in the early evening for the first of the tram tests. He spends most of the day in conference, presenting his notes and detailing progress in the investigation to JR Bishop and the Chief Constable and his assistant. Moore informs the men of his growing suspicions about William Herbert Wallace and JR Bishop forwards a précis of the facts, and all statements by witnesses, to the Director of Public Prosecutions in Whitehall. The press is kept informed and there are hints that a development is due in the case. Liverpool is in the grip of a murder fever not seen since the poisoning of James Maybrick and the arrest of his wife, Florence.[10]

15

Inspector Gold and JR Bishop are the first of three pairs of 'Harriers' on the tram tests on the Monday night. They leave the back of 29 Wolverton Street at six-forty-five and follow Wallace's route to Belmont Road, where they turn left, down to St Margaret's Church at the corner of Belmont Road and Rocky Lane.

At six-forty-nine, Sergeants Bailey and Fothergill leave the back of

Wolverton Street and walk up to Belmont Road, where they turn right and catch a number 26 tramcar at the request stop. They travel in this tramcar down to St Margaret's Church, where Inspector Gold and Mr Bishop board. The four men journey down to the junction of Smithdown Lane and Tunnel Road, where they alight and walk across to the stop at Smithdown Lane. The time is four minutes past seven.

Detective Constables Gilroy and Christie leave Wolverton Street at six-fifty-three and follow in the footsteps of Wallace down to the same tramcar stop, and arrive there at ten minutes past seven.

Gold and Bishop have completed Wallace's journey in nineteen minutes; Bailey and Fothergill, who have taken a different route from Wallace, reach the tramcar stop in fifteen minutes; Gilroy and Christie have taken seventeen minutes. Superintendent Moore is pleased with the tests.

Later that evening, confirmation arrives at Dale Street that the alibis of Parry, Marsden and Young, the three former Prudential agents named by Wallace as knowing the location of his cash-box, have been confirmed. Nevertheless, Moore, with his suspicion of Wallace hardening, and determined to eliminate all other possible suspects, insists that forensic tests for bloodstains be carried out on the clothing of Parry, and upon the interior of his car.

In addition, statements are taken from James Caird and Thomas McCartney at Cottle's City Café, about the events at the chess club on Monday 19 January, in particular Wallace's reaction to the Qualtrough message and the address at Menlove Gardens East. Caird, as well as detailing his own movements on the night of the murder, also provides confirmation of what occurred between Wallace and Beattie on the Thursday night.

16

On Tuesday morning, Moore calls another case conference. Bishop reports that he has telephoned Bernard Pearce at the office of the Director of Public Prosecutions and arranged an appointment for Wednesday morning. The Chief Constable delegates Inspector Gold to accompany Bishop to London with the police file, and the two men set off by train in the afternoon, a fact that is reported in the evening's *Liverpool Echo.*

Three more pairs of 'Harriers' re-enact Wallace's journey to the tramcar stop at Smithdown Lane on Tuesday night. Sergeant Bailey and Detective Constable Oliver complete the trip in twenty minutes; Sergeant Fothergill and Detective Constable Prendergast in eighteen minutes and Sergeant Hill and Detective Constable Gilroy in seventeen minutes.

At six o'clock, at Dale Street Detective Office, Superintendent Moore is interrupted in his work by the unexpected arrival of William Wallace: he wishes to go to Wolverton Street for a change of clothing and Moore has the only key. The police presence has been removed from the house, but with the removal of the bath and sink, the toilet and all the waste pipes, the house is uninhabitable, and Wallace is still residing at Amy Wallace's flat.

Moore hands over the key, but he forestalls Wallace's exit with a series of questions.

"Did you speak to anyone on the way home on the night of the murder after leaving the tramcar?"

"No," replies Wallace.

"Are you quite sure?"

"Yes, I am sure."

"A lady who has known you for some years stated that she saw you at eight-thirty-five speaking to a man on the footway in Richmond Park, by the entry near Letchworth Street."

"I was not so alarmed that I would not raise my hat or speak to anybody but I did not." Wallace pauses for a few seconds. "I am positively certain."

"Okay, Mr Wallace, you may go," says Moore, as he makes notes of his replies.

Later that night, with all the reports in from the Anfield Harriers, Moore works out an average time of eighteen minutes for Wallace's journey. From the fixed time point at six minutes past seven, Moore calculates that Wallace could have left home on the night of the murder at twelve minutes to seven. Next, he turns to his notes of the time trial conducted with Allan Close: the boy delivered the milk to Mrs Wallace at six-thirty-one. Wallace, therefore, could have been alone with his wife from six-thirty-one until six-forty-eight, Moore concludes, ample time in which to kill her, clean up, and stage the robbery before leaving home …

17

Gold and Bishop return from London late on Wednesday night with little encouragement from the Director of Public Prosecutions to proceed against Wallace. They report this fact to Moore and the Chief Constable at the Thursday morning conference. Moore brings everyone up to date on his conclusions following the second series of tram tests, and the men spend the remainder of the day discussing and dissecting the case against William Herbert Wallace.

Forensic tests have shown that Richard Parry's car and clothing are free from bloodstains and he has finally been eliminated from the investigation. Only Wallace remains in the frame, says Moore, and he outlines the case against him.

On Monday 19 January, Wallace left his home just after seven o'clock and made his way under cover of darkness to the telephone kiosk at the corner of Rochester Road and Breck Road. From there he made the Qualtrough telephone call to his chess club, and then boarded a tramcar into town. Only Wallace knew that he was going to the chess club that night. At the club he received the message from Samuel Beattie, made a fuss about his name and address, and involved several club members in discussions as to the whereabouts of Qualtrough's home, in order to impress both the name and address upon their minds.

The following night, Tuesday 20 January, immediately after the milk delivery, Wallace dressed in his mackintosh, brutally murdered his wife with the iron bar from the grate in the front parlour. He then removed all traces of her blood from his person, staged a robbery, disposed of the murder weapon, and hurriedly made his way to the tramcar stop at Smithdown Lane, where he established himself with the tram conductor, Thomas Phillips, and the ticket inspector, Edward Angus, by his persistent questions about Menlove Gardens. Wallace's wanderings around the Menlove Avenue area were simply an elaborate sham.

No motive for Wallace wanting to kill his wife has been ascertained by Moore and his officers despite their extensive enquiries, but several suggestions have been put forward, some coming from anonymous callers: Wallace was having an affair with his sister-in-law, Amy Wallace, or, with Sarah Draper, the char lady, and Julia, having found out, was murdered to avoid the inevitable scandal; Julia was a licentious woman, whom Wallace murdered for all the heartache she had caused him; Wallace could not father the child Julia wanted, and she derided him, challenging his manhood to such an extent that he responded with murder.

All such motives have been dismissed as highly improbable, as has a financial motive: Wallace had one hundred and fifty-two pounds in his bank account, while Julia, whose life had been insured for a mere twenty pounds, had ninety pounds in a Post Office Savings Account and her jewellery and fur coat would not have realised more than a hundred pounds.

Lionel Everett, the Chief Constable, believes that Moore has a substantial case against Wallace, but the lack of encouragement from the Director of Public Prosecutions is disheartening for Moore and his officers. What more, asks Everett, is needed to prosecute the case? What more can Superintendent Moore uncover to stir the Director into action?

Inspector Gold is sent to interview Wallace at his temporary abode in Ullet Road. He is to question him once again about his journey to the chess club on the Monday night; to find out if he knows Lily Hall and to obtain from him a possible explanation for the lack of signs of forcible entry to his home on the night of the murder, whether a key, for example, could have been used to gain entrance.

At his sister-in-law's flat, Wallace provides answers to all Gold's questions. The inspector writes up his answers in the form of a statement, which Wallace signs, and Gold carries it back to his superiors at Dale Street. This, his fourth statement, provides no glaring contradictions, or any additional information which can be of help to the police. Moore, Gold, Everett and Bishop continue their conference into the early hours of the morning, but there is nothing they can add to the case against Wallace.

18

For the next three days, Superintendent Moore and Inspector Gold check through every statement on file, including those made by the cranks, to see if anything has been overlooked. More advertisements are placed in the local press in order to encourage the man seen by Lily Hall talking to Wallace to come forward. Bishop again contacts Bernard Pearce at the Office of the Director of Public Prosecutions, with a far more substantial account of the case against Wallace, and he keeps in touch daily by telephone with Pearce, offering advice and making arguments in favour of arrest and prosecution. In the meantime, Wallace is kept under surveillance.

On Monday 2 February, the Director of Public Prosecutions relents, and agrees that there is a case for Wallace to answer. Bernard Pearce telephones Bishop with the news, and he in turn informs Everett, Glover and Moore.

Bishop writes up his brief for the committal, and a warrant is sworn for the arrest of William Herbert Wallace, aged fifty-two, of 29 Wolverton Street, Anfield, in the city of Liverpool, temporarily residing at 83 Ullet Road, Sefton Park. The charge is the wilful murder of Julia Wallace on the night of 20 January 1931.

At seven o'clock on the Monday night, Superintendents Moore and Thomas accompany Inspector Gold to 83 Ullet Road. They are admitted to the flat by Edwin Wallace, who leads them into the sitting room where his uncle is seated at the table writing a letter.

"You know who I am?" says Inspector Gold, as Wallace rises to his feet.

"Yes," says Wallace.

"William Herbert Wallace," intones Gold. "It is my duty to arrest you on the charge of wilful murder of your wife, Julia Wallace, on the night of 20 January 1931, at 29 Wolverton Street." Gold produces both the warrant and his notebook from his pocket. "It is also my duty to caution you that anything you may say will taken down in writing and may be used in evidence against you. Do you understand?"

Wallace is stunned and ashen-faced. He looks directly at Gold as he replies.

"What can I say in answer to this charge of which I am absolutely innocent?"

The three policeman escort Wallace out to their car and drive him in silence to Liverpool's Bridewell in Cheapside, just off Dale Street. In an interview room in the presence of Superintendent Moore, Gold once more cautions Wallace before charging him again with the murder of his wife. Wallace makes no reply. Moore and Gold then hand him over into the custody of Superintendent Gill, Governor of the bridewell. No mention is made of a solicitor.

Part Two

Chapter 6

William Herbert Wallace

1

William Herbert Wallace was born in Millom, Cumbria, on 29 August, 1878. His life story is fairly well documented, though, as with his wife, there are times when he completely disappears from view.

His parents, Benjamin and Margery, both came from Coniston in the Lake District, a town then renowned for its copper mining.[1] Benjamin Wallace did not work as a miner but was a printer and part-time agent for the Prudential Assurance Company, with whom his son was to find employment one day. The family was of Scottish stock, probably descendants of itinerant Scottish miners who had migrated south of the border to work the copper lodes. Possibly their roots lay in the Highland Rebellion, descendants of the remnants of the Scottish army which the Duke of Cumberland vengefully pursued north, following the Battle of Preston Pans; local tradition has the Highland stragglers finding shelter and refuge in and around the Lake District with sympathetic households.

By 1876 the Wallaces had moved to Millom, where prosperity and good fortune had landed with the opening of the Hodbarrow mine, which produced some of the finest hematite ore ever mined in the world.[2] The town was booming and all trades were in demand, and Benjamin made a decent living working his trade of printer. The birth of William Wallace was followed by that of his brother, Joseph, and sister, Jessie. Though there were two years between the brothers, they were very close, both emotionally and physically, so much so that they were often mistaken for twins.

When William was ten years of age, the family began a series of moves, first of all to Blackpool, where he was struck down with typhoid fever, and then to Dalton-in-Furness, the ancient capital of the Furness peninsular, across the Duddon estuary from Millom. In Dalton, the Wallaces resided at 27 Victoria Street, and the children attended the local Board School in Broughton Road.

After William left school, aged fourteen, the family moved across the peninsular to Walney Island, part of Barrow-in-Furness, to live at 89 Dominion Street and it was here that he first gained employment, as an apprentice draper's assistant at Messrs Tenants, of 72-74 Cavendish Street, Barrow.

According to JT Ferguson, who, like Wallace, was one of a group of young shop assistants who enjoyed the outdoor life, Wallace was an active participant in nature rambles through the ruins of Furness Abbey and camping expeditions along the coast of Walney Island. He was a keen follower of local sports, particularly cricket and soccer, and was generally well liked within the group.

He was a distinctly cultured youth with a scientific mind, … keen on botany and natural history … while the rest of us liked popular novels … I can still hear him now saying to us, 'you will regret reading that kind of book; you should study something of value to the mind'.[3]

At the turn of the century, Barrow was set on a course which was to make it pre-eminent in the design and building of British warships, particularly submarines. However, the town, in reality a conglomerate of small villages, had not outgrown its origins, and remained a collection of close-knit, parochial communities on the tip of the peninsular.

Wallace had been an avid reader at school, and throughout his apprenticeship he continued his reading, concentrating his attention upon the newly developing sciences, and the writings of the Greek and Roman philosophers. He was always open to new ideas and experiences, always willing to experiment. Whether it was his reading, or the insularity of the town where he lived and worked which prompted him and drove him on, he seemed determined, at an early age, to try and better himself, rather than resign himself, like so many of his acquaintances, to the confines and limited horizons of the Furness peninsular.

2

As soon as he had completed his apprenticeship at Tennants in 1898, Wallace took the unprecedented step of moving to Manchester, where he was engaged as a draper's assistant with Messrs Whiteway Laidlaw and Company, outfitters to Her Majesty's Armed Forces and the Colonial, Indian and Foreign Services.

Wallace lived and worked in Manchester for five years. Meantime, his brother had married Amy Blackwell from Dalton-in-Furness, and as soon as he had completed his apprenticeship as a printer, he set sail with his bride for Shanghai, where he took up the position of printer in the government service. No doubt spurred on by the letters from Joseph, he resolved to leave Manchester and when a vacancy arose in the Calcutta branch of Messrs Whiteway Laidlaw and Company, he applied and was accepted.

On 30 October 1903, William Wallace set sail from Tilbury for India, as a second class saloon passenger on board *SS Rewa*. He was aged twenty-five. If, on the journey to Calcutta, the City of Palaces, his expectations were high, and he was looking forward with relish and determination to the challenge of India, no doubt imbued with popular misconceptions of the prospects awaiting resolute young men in that country, then he was to be greatly disappointed. This was the first, and perhaps the most indelible, of several disappointments which were to litter his life.

3

The tradition of the English Charter Companies commenced in the sixteenth century when Edward VI issued Royal Charters to various groups of English merchant venturers to search for trade and profit throughout the world for the benefit of Britain and the directors of such companies as the Muscovy, Levant, Gold Coast and Gambia, which laid the foundations for the future British Empire. By the turn of the nineteenth century the most formidable representatives of this tradition were the Hudson Bay Company and the East India Company, both of which held monopoly trading rights throughout their respective domains, Canada and the Indian sub-continent.

By 1833, the East India Company, having traded on the sub-continent for almost 200 years, was a shadow of a mercantile concern, having surrendered its monopoly of the India and China trades and it had become an instrument of British supremacy in India, which it administered through its three former trading estates, the Presidencies of Bombay, Madras and Bengal. With trade, finally came thoughts of Empire. Following the annexation of the Sindh in 1843, a purely imperialist move, the last vestiges of the company's trading philosophy disappeared from India, and over the next ten years, the sometimes rascally, though more often brave and adventurous, traders of the company left India.

They were replaced by a more zealous, evangelical, earnest breed of English men and women, who saw Britain as the centre of world science, industry and culture, with a mission to civilise the world. This new administrative hierarchy, the harbinger of nascent British Imperialism, was determined to bring to the Indian heathens the benefits of British civilisation, and the religious and moral teachings of Christianity, all of which had been denied them previously by the rapscallions of the East India Company.

Following the Indian Mutiny of 1857, India was governed directly by the British Parliament through the India Office. There was a resolve within the British establishment not to let the conditions and opportunities which had given rise to the mutiny, and resulted in the deaths of hundreds of British civilians and troops, re-emerge and prevail. India, through the Viceroy, his staff, and the army, was ruled with a rod of iron.

British society in the sub-continent became inward-looking, rigid and hierarchical, where before it had been extrovert and extravagant. There was a place for everybody, and everybody knew his place, and had to remain therein. This system was reinforced, and to some extent enforced, by the structure and strictures within the Indian community itself, with the divisions of caste and religion. There was no opportunity for change, advancement, or upward mobility.

The pressures and movements for social change which were then occurring in Britain were resisted and brusquely pushed aside by the British community in India and such impulses only sought to render the ex-patriots more rigid and unyielding, and their social positions more clearly demarcated. The British in India were more British, and saw themselves as such, than their compatriots at home, and they were resolved to uphold British law and tradition, however archaic, whatever the costs.

4

The term 'in trade' was pejoratively applied by polite society to the men of commerce in India; the grubby money men who had once ruled, or rather misruled, as the East India Company, and who had allowed the mutiny to occur. While the directors and managers of the commercial houses and other enterprises were tolerated by the ruling élite, they were certainly not welcomed and were looked down upon contemptuously, while their employees were disdainfully dismissed as being beyond the social pale.[4]

Messrs Whiteway Laidlaw and Company was a commercial enterprise, not of the top drawer but of the second division. The major outfitter and supplier to the brass of the army and the various British Government agencies was the Army and Navy Stores. Whiteway Laidlaw and Company served the needs of the junior officers and the middle and lower ranks of the Civil Service, who could not afford to equip themselves at the Army and Navy Stores.

Wallace was one of several draper's assistants working at the Calcutta branch of Whiteway Laidlaw and Company, 'Rightaway and Paid For', as it was referred to by its customers. He was assigned a bed in the dormitory above the shop on Chowringhee Street, and there he lived and worked in the oppressive heat of Calcutta for two years. Not only was Wallace 'in trade', but he was in bottom drawer trade. He was of the lower level of the British hierarchy, on a par with the rank and file of the army and the administration.

Not for him the deference and preferment accorded by the locals to the sahibs: the sports and social clubs, the dinners and galas, the social circuit, the cool hill-stations in the heat of summer, the never-ending stream of servants and wallahs to cater to their every whim. For Wallace, during the day, it was work in the emporium, at the beck and call of everyone who crossed the threshold and at night a lonely bed in a sweaty dormitory.

His room overlooked the Maidan, a vast open space of greenery dominated by Fort William, a well-ordered pleasure garden for the British hierarchy, with golf-links, tennis courts, cricket pitches and picnic grounds. From his window he no doubt witnessed the athletic prowess of the officers and gentlemen at play, and the evening paseo of the great and good of Calcutta society, for whom he and his fellow workers were, 'only just acceptable as Britons at all'.[5]

There was no room, no time and no opportunity, for reading, for discussion, for parading ideas and thoughts; in fact such activities were frowned upon and considered disloyal, particularly if they conflicted in any way with the status quo. Wallace arrived in Calcutta and was firmly put in his place, and was constantly enjoined, on a daily basis through his job, to remain there.

If he had anticipated that his move to India was to be one of liberation, improvement and advancement following his years in Barrow and Manchester, then he would have been profoundly disappointed and frustrated. For a man of some intelligence, Wallace's India experience must have been oppressive, miserable and demeaning. To compound his misery, a kidney complaint, for which he had received treatment in both Barrow and Manchester, began to bother him again, necessitating several visits to the British Hospital.

During his time in Calcutta, he had kept up a correspondence with Joseph in Shanghai, where he was still working as a government printer. Conditions in Shanghai were much better than those prevailing in India under the British Raj, for Shanghai was an international city, where British rule had yet to dominate, and the atmosphere was more liberal and less structured. Whiteway Laidlaw and Company had a branch in Shanghai and Wallace sought a transfer.

He arrived in China in 1905. However, his kidney ailment had progressively worsened and within weeks of his arrival, he was so much weakened by it that he was unable to perform a full day's work. His manager relieved him of his serving duties and placed him in charge of window dressing and displays. He kept up regular contacts with his brother, hoping to use his inside knowledge as a means to advance himself, but his days in Shanghai were numbered. Having found the city a place of opportunity where he could live happily, Wallace was now thwarted by illness; his doctors advised his return to England for further treatment of the kidney ailment.

5

In February 1907, having resigned his position with Whiteway Laidlaw, he set sail from Shanghai as a third class passenger on *SS Gucisenan*, out of Yokohama, bound for Southampton via Bremen. He arrived in England on 19 March and within a month, he underwent an operation at Guy's Hospital for the removal of his left kidney.

After leaving hospital, and presumably undergoing a period of convalescence, Wallace drops out of sight and does not reappear in the public records until 1910, when he was working in Harrogate, North Yorkshire, for TH Mattison, election agent for the Liberal Party, Ripon Division. The Party's offices were at 5 Raglan Street, Harrogate, and upon succeeding Mattison in the post of election agent in 1911, Wallace lived in the flat above, number 5A.

Jonathan Goodman writes that after convalescence and a long period of unemployment, Wallace was re-employed for a time at Whiteway Laidlaw and Company in Manchester, before moving on to Harrogate.[6] It would appear that his mother was dead, since his father was living alone in Harrogate at 9 Belmont Road at the time, and his sister, Jessie, was employed as a nurse, possibly in the immediate vicinity. What had inspired the family to congregate in Harrogate is not known. Upon arrival there, Wallace was, at first, a voluntary worker for the Liberal Party prior to his appointment as agent, and what he did for a living is also unknown.

What has been established is that later the same year, Julia Dennis moved from her flat in Norfolk House, 5 Dragon Parade, Harrogate, to 11 St Mary's Avenue, which ran parallel to Belmont Road and that sometime the following year she met William Herbert Wallace. They were married on 24 March 1914 and after a brief honeymoon, Wallace and his father moved into Julia's apartment.

With the outbreak of the Great War and the cessation of party political activity in Britain, Wallace lost his position as agent for the Liberal Party. And it was through his father and his long-standing connection with the Prudential Assurance Company that he landed the position of collection agent for the Prudential in Liverpool. But within weeks of moving to the city with Julia, he was back in Harrogate for his father's funeral. He had died in Knaresborough Infirmary, where he had been nursed by his daughter, Jessie.

6

Wallace saw neither active nor volunteer service during the Great War, and he made no mention of the War years in any of his accounts of his early life. He continued his reading, both in science and philosophy, while earning his living as a collection agent, and the War seemed to have brought no interruptions to his or Julia's routines. His interest in science blossomed to such an extent that he converted the back bedroom of Wolverton Street into a laboratory, where he conducted experiments in chemistry and biology.

Jonathan Goodman claims that Wallace began studying chemistry at Liverpool Technical College in the city centre in the early twenties, and that he was eventually appointed as a part-time, assistant lecturer in chemistry at the college, while continuing his job with the Prudential.[7] It would appear that Wallace, now in his mid-forties, had finally risen above his roots, and had achieved a definite advancement up the social scale. He had driven himself forward from an early age, and now he had been rewarded with the teaching post.

However, he held the post of part-time lecturer for five years only. He did not reveal why he relinquished it, or why he continued with the mundane and uninspiring job with Prudential, rather than pursuing an academic career.

Julia made no great financial demands on him and they led a very simple, frugal existence, which could have been adequately maintained with his Prudential salary while he studied for the necessary academic qualifications which would have brought him a full-time position. It was not as if his interest in science was a passing fancy; it was an abiding passion which he kept alive throughout his life. Two or three years before Julia's death, he invested eighty pounds, a third of a year's salary, in a microscope, to aid him in his scientific studies and even as late as a fortnight before her death, he prepared a scheme of study and exercises with which he hoped to break out of the workaday routine with the Prudential and to make something of a success for himself. That is, he was still yearning for something better, something other than what he had so far achieved.

7

During 1928 and 1929 Wallace suffered recurrent problems with his health. Besides his kidney complaint, he endured frequent, severe headaches and pain above and behind the left eye. He was depressed and unsettled, nervy and temperamental, as he confided to his diary.[8] His reading and his thoughts centred around death and the dead. In June 1930, following several bouts of illness, he was admitted to the Royal Southern Hospital in Liverpool and spent a month under the care of Dr Unsworth, receiving treatment for the kidney complaint which was to kill him in 1933.

Throughout these years, whenever Wallace recovered from a bout of illness, it would appear from the entries in his diaries, that Julia then took to her bed. Between 1928 and 1930 the diary entries show a tit for tat relationship between Julia and William Wallace when it came to illness, so that whenever he was recovering from an illness, she was preparing herself for her turn in bed, and vice versa. Wallace bemoans in his diary on 29 March 1928 that Julia had been an invalid, 'for years, a great worry'.

Wallace always maintained that his relationship with his wife was warm, close and loving and that her death robbed him of an irreplaceable friend and companion. The entries in his diaries would appear to contradict this. While there is no overt criticism of Julia, an undercurrent of frustration and despair, arising from her many illnesses, from her failure to understand and appreciate his interests, permeates his writing. There is mention of times when he fell out with Julia and she with him. But besides the record of their various illnesses, there is no hint in his writings of the love and affection which he claimed they shared.

Jonathan Goodman quotes an entry from 7 January 1931, in which Wallaces describes with delight the effects of the frost and fog which had settled across the city: 'After dinner, I persuaded Julia to go to Stanley Park. A gradual thaw seems to be settling in now'.

Goodman assumes the thaw refers to a change in the weather.[9] It could equally refer to a thaw in the relationship between Mr and Mrs Wallace.

The Johnstons, at 31 Wolverton Street, referred to their neighbours as a happy and loving couple, though in all the years they lived next door to them, they only ever visited the Wallace home three times.

James Caird, a long-time friend of Wallace, also described the Wallaces as a loving couple though he, like the Johnstons, rarely called on them. Amy Wallace was restrained in her description of the relationship between Julia and William Wallace, making little reference to any state of happiness between them, but asserting that Wallace was condescending towards Julia and tended to treat her as the little woman about the house, unable to grapple with the new ideas and abstract concepts which he found exciting and worthy of interest.

The Wallaces kept very much to themselves. Their most frequent contacts outside their small circle of relatives and friends, was the family physician, Dr Curwen, and some of Wallace's business colleagues. A Mrs Wilson lived with them for a period of three weeks in 1923, when she nursed Wallace through a bout of pneumonia. She described them as a very peculiar couple, claiming that:

Their attitude towards each other appeared to be strained and that the feeling of sympathy and confidence which one usually found existing between man and wife appeared to be entirely absent. They were not the happy and devoted couple some people thought.

She stated that Mrs Wallace …

… was peculiar in her manner and dirty …

While Mr Wallace …

… appeared to have suffered a keen disappointment in life.[10]

Alfred Mather, who had worked with Wallace at the Prudential, described him as, "the most cool, calculating, despondent and soured man" he had ever met, a man with an evil temper, who considered his job as an insurance agent beneath him. On a visit to 29 Wolverton Street, Mather met Julia, and she made a lasting impression upon him. She was very offhand and Mather found her to be, "a proud and peculiar woman" who believed she had lowered herself by marrying Wallace.[11]

The number of illnesses which struck the Wallaces meant that Dr Curwen was a very frequent caller at 29 Wolverton Street. He claimed that on one occasion when Wallace was ill in bed, Mrs Wallace implied that he was malingering. "He wants to stay at home", she said. On another occasion, when Julia was ill, Dr Curwen reported that William appeared indifferent to her state of health.

When Wallace was released from hospital in July 1930, Dr Curwen informed him that his condition was serious and that he should take care of himself. Dr Curwen later reported to the police that Wallace treated the matter of his illness with apathy, saying that he would, "just have to carry on", regardless of his condition.[12]

During the investigation of Julia's death, several reports were made by the police, which were later brought out at the trial, of Wallace's demeanour in the aftermath of his wife's murder and his general attitude towards her death, which, to the police, suggested an indifference bordering on callousness.

Wallace claimed that he was a Stoic, and in his *John Bull* articles he made great play of his Stoical stance in the aftermath of his wife's murder.[13] His philosophical outlook might explain certain aspects of his behaviour.

His favourite reading was *Meditations* by Marcus Aurelius, the second century Roman Emperor and Stoic Philosopher.[14] The Stoic School of Philosophy was founded in the third century BC by the Greek sage, Zeno of Citium, in response to the despair and anomie which swept the Greek world following the collapse of the Alexandrian Empire. Basically, Stoicism is a philosophy of consolation, and Zeno's teachings consisted in advising his pupils on how to attain personal salvation in a world which was falling apart: Be indifferent to external influences.

The Stoics believed in predestination: everything which occurs is fixed by god, the universal reason, according to his preconceived plan for the cosmos. Nothing happens fortuitously: what occurs must occur; it is ordained to take place, and man is powerless to alter god's design.

Since god is directing the activities of the cosmos, it must be for his purpose, towards his ultimate goal, which must be good, so that everything that happens is the result of necessary actions by god to attain his goal.

It is pointless, argued the Stoics, to attach any significance to any one part of god's evolving plan, to despair, for example, over war and famine, earthquakes and floods, murder and social upheaval, for it is to miss the essential point that god's design is evolving and developing, and is worked out throughout the entire cosmos, which is interrelated and inter-directed. The cosmos must be viewed as a whole.

The catastrophes, large and small, which afflict mankind, are necessary aspects of god's overall design for the cosmos which he is directing towards the good goal. Thus, at any time in history, the world man inhabits must be the best of all possible worlds and it will eventually improve as god's purpose unfolds and moves forward to its ultimate goal.

Only when man understands this can he truly be free. The man who struggles to change matters, who becomes frustrated and despairing when he fails, when he is overtaken by events, is a man in chains, destined to battle against fate. Men who are indifferent to external influences and forces, who accept their god-given fate, are virtuous, their wills being in agreement with god; they are independent of the world and can achieve personal salvation by accepting what god, rather than man or nature, has in store for them.

Thus a true Stoic is indifferent to all around him, to his own fate and that of everybody else. He accepts what occurs in life, in the universe, in the cosmos, because it necessarily has to occur, a stage from which other stages will follow in god's plan.

Wallace did not always adhere to the precepts and tenets of Stoicism and resign himself with indifference to his fate throughout his lifetime. He struggled to improve and educate himself, to overcome his various illnesses, to move forward beyond the place which nature and society had set for him. And when he failed in his endeavours, he became frustrated and depressed, angry and disappointed, behaviour witnessed by friends, family and others, and by the entries in his diary.

However, sometimes he did maintain a Stoical front which Zeno would have applauded: the indifference he showed towards his own illness, as noted by Dr Curwen; his indifference towards his wife's death, as reported by the police during their investigation; the resignation he exhibited during his trial and appeal, sitting, standing, and listening to the evidence against himself without apparent concern or emotion.

It is worth noting that one of the main criticisms of Stoic philosophy, and part of the reason why Stoicism was eventually superseded by Christianity, was that men of conscience did not accept that it was correct to cultivate indifference to the exclusion of all other virtues, to dismiss death and disaster with a shrug of the shoulders.

If a friend dies, it would appear callous ... to suggest that indifference is the proper way to react ... Moreover, it seems to follow from Stoic theory that acts which would normally be regarded as immoral are right if performed indifferently. Murder committed from a sense of indifference would seem to be proper if we follow out the implications of Stoic theory.[15]

Did William Herbert Wallace take his Stoicism to extremes?

Chapter 7
Trial, Appeal, Release

1

On the morning following his arrest, Wallace appeared before Stipendiary Magistrate, Stuart Deacon, at the Police Court in Dale Street. Prosecuting solicitor JR Bishop[1] outlined the police case and Wallace was remanded in custody to Walton Gaol, Liverpool's main prison in the northern suburb of

Walton. Being a prisoner on remand, he was dressed in a dark blue uniform and, as it was a capital charge, he was confined to the prison hospital under the watchful eye of the senior medical officer, Mr W Davies Higson, and his staff.

The police were confident that Wallace had a case to answer; but then there arrived at Dale Street headquarters a medical report from Mr W Johnston of the Royal Southern Hospital, where he had been treated for his kidney complaint in 1930. Johnston indicated that Wallace might be insane, and Moore and Gold envisioned him possibly pleading insanity under the McNaughten Rules.[2] They passed the report and the question of his sanity to Bishop and the medical authorities at Walton Gaol.

Wallace was again remanded in custody on 10 February. At the committal proceedings, which commenced on 19 February and lasted until 4 March, he was represented for the first time by his barrister, Scholfield Allen, who took issue with the prosecuting solicitor, Bishop, over the number of errors of fact in the police case, which, he argued, were prejudicial to Wallace. After a spirited defence by Scholfield Allen, Wallace was nevertheless committed to stand trial at the next Assizes.[3]

Wallace had chosen Hector Munro as his solicitor from the firm of Herbert J Davis, Brethen and Munro, whose offices were in the same Prudential Building in Dale Street as the headquarters of the Prudential Assurance Company. Coincidentally, Munro was also a member of the chess club in Cottle's City Café:

I didn't actually know Wallace, but he knew me by sight. And I suppose when he was charged with murder, he felt that I'd be the person who could deal with the case for him.[4]

Having read the police case against Wallace, Munro realised at once that time factors formed an important part of the case, particularly the timing of Allan Close's milk delivery at six-thirty on the night of the murder. Munro spoke to Elsie Wright and Kenneth Caird, who, in turn, brought to his attention Douglas Metcalfe, who finally introduced him to James Wildman.

The day before the committal proceedings began against Wallace, Munro interviewed Wildman, who stated that he had seen a boy, who could only have been Close, on the doorstep of 29 Wolverton Street at approximately six-thirty-five. Wildman's time would be the starting point of Wallace's defence. The police took a statement from Wildman on 2 March, the day before the proceedings finished, but decided his evidence, recalled for the first time forty days after the murder, might not have been reliable.[5]

Munro was also responsible for initiating the WH Wallace Defence Fund: having calculated his own fees, that of defence counsel and expert witnesses, and having arrived at a cost of approximately one thousand pounds for the defence, with Wallace's contribution from his savings of only one hundred and fifty pounds, there was a shortfall of almost nine hundred pounds.

Munro contacted his employers about setting up the fund. The Prudential agreed, and made a substantial contribution, as did individual members of the Prudential Staff Union and the union itself.

The overwhelming majority of the Liverpool populace favoured a guilty verdict, and since the jury was to be picked from Liverpudlians, a verdict of guilty was confidently expected. Nevertheless, high public interest in the case was maintained throughout the remand and committal proceedings and did not flag, in fact it soared, in the interim as the trial date approached.

Two years previously in Liverpool, in February 1929, Joseph Clark, charged with the murder of Mrs Alice Fontaine, had disappointed the public by pleading guilty to the murder, the trial lasting just under five minutes, one of the shortest murder trials in history.[6] The public was, in a sense, determined to have its day in court with Wallace, and an event on a par with the trial of Florence Maybrick in July 1889 was eagerly anticipated.

Maybrick was charged with murdering her husband, James, a prominent cotton broker in Liverpool, by poisoning him with arsenic. She had taken a lover after the birth of their second child, and it was this, plus the fact that she was an American, which fuelled the salacious imagination of the public, and led to crowd scenes in and around the courtroom which bordered on hysteria. However, the public was to be greatly disappointed, if not bored, by the Wallace trial.

2

The trial of William Herbert Wallace was heard before Mr Justice Wright in St George's Hall in the centre of Liverpool, during the Liverpool Spring Assizes of 1931. Edward Hemmerde KC, the Liverpool Recorder, led for the Crown, and Roland Oliver KC for the defence. The trial began at 10 o'clock on Wednesday 22 April and all the evidence was heard within three days.

On Saturday 25 April, Hemmerde and Oliver addressed the jury, Mr Justice Wright summed up, and the jury was sent to make its deliberations at twenty past one in the afternoon. An hour and five minutes later, the jury returned to give its verdict of guilty to the charge of wilful murder against William Herbert Wallace. Mr Justice Wright sentenced him to death.

For all the public's anticipation and expectation of scandalous events and revelations in the Wallace household, the trial proved mundane and ordinary fare. With the exception of Hemmerde's allegation that Wallace, wearing only his raincoat, was virtually naked when he murdered his wife, the trial uncovered nothing to titillate the popular imagination.

However, it was notable for three things: Hemmerde's opening address to the court, Mr Justice Wright's admirable summing up and the biggest red herring in British legal history.

It took Hemmerde two hours to outline the prosecution's case to the jury, and there can be little doubt that the case was decided there and then. His speech was a veritable tour de force, and he kept the jury and the gallery spellbound as he outlined and insinuated the case against Wallace.[7] For reasons unknown, argued Hemmerde, Wallace decided to murder his wife, and conceived a devious plan: he sent the Qualtrough telephone call to himself at the chess club on the Monday night; before setting out in search of Qualtrough the following night, he murdered his wife and staged the robbery; his journey to Menlove Gardens and the search for Qualtrough were diversionary shams; he caused a commotion on his return home so that the Johnstons would witness his entry into the house, to be at hand when the gruesome discovery of Julia Wallaces's body was made.

For the defence, Oliver argued that Qualtrough was a thief who, knowing Wallace would be at his chess club on the Monday night, had planned to lure him from his home on Tuesday night in order to steal his insurance takings; that in the course of the theft he killed Mrs Wallace; that Wallace could not have had the time in which to kill her and that anyway, he was a loving husband who had no motive whatsoever to murder his wife.

The witnesses for the Crown were put through their paces by Hemmerde and cross-examined by Oliver in turn. For the events of the Monday night the arguments centred on the telephone call and Wallace's presence at the chess club: whether Wallace himself had made the call; or whether Qualtrough had made it, having ascertained from the playing list on the club's noticeboard that Wallace would attend the club.

The events of Tuesday night, from the search for Qualtrough in Menlove Gardens, to the murder itself, were not examined as thoroughly as they should have been and there were many areas where the prosecution, and to some extent the defence, might have benefited by better preparation, more attention to detail, and more informed research, particularly regarding the actual crime scene and the journey to Menlove Avenue.

Oliver presented his witnesses for the defence first of all with a view to highlighting Wallace's fine character, which the prosecution had impugned by arguing that his demeanour following the discovery of his wife's body, had been callous and indifferent.

He followed with the question of the time factor; whether Allan Close, the milk boy, saw Mrs Wallace alive at six-thirty or twenty-two minutes to seven. This was an important aspect of Oliver's case, as it ate into the time that Wallace had available in which to kill his wife, stage the robbery, and travel down to the tram stop at Smithdown Lane by six minutes past seven.

There can be no doubt that Oliver had the better of the exchanges with the prosecution witnesses. Allan Close became confused, sulked, and at one point refused to answer questions. Inspector Gold was made to read aloud selected passages from Wallace's diaries which described the good relationship between the Wallaces; Lily Hall was unintelligible; Professor MacFall was often bombastic and contradictory in his assertions about the actual killing of Mrs Wallace, the evidence of the time of death, and the bloodstaining and blood clot found in the toilet.

In contrast, the defence witnesses, such as James Wildman, gave their evidence clearly and concisely, without equivocation and Hemmerde was unable to make any inroads into Oliver's case. There was reasonable doubt, and Oliver had brought it to the attention of the jury by his clever presentation. He insisted, quite rightly, that the Crown had failed to produce one piece of direct proof that Wallace had instigated the Qualtrough plan in order to kill his wife. The impression upon the jury, however, was not as marked as it should have been.

Altogether, forty-eight men, women and children were called to the stand as witnesses during the trial. The transcript of their testimony, Wallace's included, covers three hundred and thirteen pages of A4 typescript. Five of the witnesses dealt with the medical aspects of the case, particularly the bloodstaining, and their testimony alone accounts for one hundred and twenty-one pages and most of that dealt with the tiny clot of blood, which Professor MacFall uncovered on the inside rim of the toilet bowl some hours after the murder.

This small clot was the only blood found outside the murder room.[8] It was alleged by the prosecution that Julia's killer, following his murderous assault, went upstairs to the bathroom to wash and clean up and that, while doing so, a tiny droplet fell from him and into the bowl.

The scientists established that it was human, but not menstrual blood. Much was made of how the clot happened there, its dimensions, its shape, the height from which it might have fallen, whether it coagulated before, or after, falling onto the rim, and how long it had been in place prior to discovery. There was much disagreement among the expert scientific witnesses on all these matters and the jury fell into a stupor as the arguments raged and confusion reigned.

Both Oliver and Hemmerde allowed themselves to be diverted and led into irrelevancy by the arguments over the clot, causing them to ignore and overlook far more pertinent issues which did have a direct bearing upon the case. What relevance the blood clot had to the question of whether or not William Wallace murdered his wife was never explained to the jury, nor to Mr Justice Wright. Even if it could have been proven that the killer had brought the blood clot from the parlour to the bathroom, that would not, of itself, have brought the police or the prosecution any closer to his identity. The whole question of the blood clot was irrelevant, a red herring.

3

Mr Justice Wright dispatched the jury to its deliberations after a masterly summing up, which was both erudite and fair.

Then again, the question is not, who did this crime? the question is, did the prisoner do it? Or rather, to put it more accurately – is it proved to your reasonable satisfaction, and beyond all reasonable doubt, that the prisoner did it?[9]

In his summation, Mr Justice Wright made it abundantly clear to the jury that he thought there was sufficient reasonable doubt about the Crown's case to merit Wallace's acquittal. But, a judge directs a jury on matters of law, and the jury is bound to follow his direction. He cannot direct the jury on matters of facts and his opinions are not legally binding upon the jury.

In the exchanges with the witnesses, and in the presentation of his case, Oliver outshone Hemmerde and produced, for all to see and hear, reasonable grounds for an acquittal. However, it was Hemmerde's opening address to the jury which carried the day. That all of his witnesses did not come right up to proof, that some of them qualified or retreated from their positions under Oliver's excellent cross-examination, had no effect upon the jury; nor did the judge's summing up. The Liverpool public was not to be denied: a verdict of guilty was what was wanted and its representatives on the jury provided it.

4

Wallace sat passively through most of the proceedings and even under questioning he appeared calm and in control. The only emotion he showed was after the verdict of guilty had been brought. In a shaky voice he replied to the clerk of the Assizes:

I am not guilty. That is all. I cannot say anything more.[10]

Mr Justice Wright then donned the black cap.

William Herbert Wallace, the jury, after a very careful hearing, have found you guilty of the murder of your wife. For the crime of murder by the law of this country there is only one sentence, and that sentence I now pass upon you. The sentence of the court upon you is that you be taken from this place to a lawful prison and thence to a place of execution, and that you be there hanged by the neck until you be dead, and that your body be afterwards buried within the precincts of the prison in which you shall have been last confined before your execution and may the Lord have mercy on your soul.[11]

Wallace was taken down to the holding cells below the court, and kept there until the crowds in and around St George's Hall had dispersed. Then he was transported in a Black Maria back to Walton Gaol, given a bath, a meal and a full medical, before being taken to the condemned cell next to the execution shed at Walton. He remained there until his appeal was granted in May.

5

The date for Wallace's execution was set for Tuesday 12 May. While he languished in the condemned cell at Walton, his solicitor, Hector Munro, and Roland Oliver, assisted again by his junior from the trial, Sydney Scholfield

Allen, feverishly put together the grounds for appeal within days of the verdict.

Ten points, one of them with fourteen sub-divisions, were enunciated as the grounds for appeal and the appeal was lodged with the Director of Public Prosecutions on Thursday 30 April. The date for the hearing before the Court of Criminal Appeal was set for Monday 18 May, six days after the proposed execution date and so the death sentence was respited, which no doubt Wallace was relieved to hear.

However, the precedents for a successful appeal were not good. The Court of Criminal Appeal, which sat in the Royal Courts of Justice in the Strand, was instituted in 1907 for the purpose of hearing appeals against convictions and on only two occasions had it allowed appeals against conviction for murder.[12]

On Saturday 16 May, Wallace was taken by train to London and lodged in the condemned cell at Pentonville Prison. The following Monday he was carried by a Black Maria to the Strand and brought before the bench, where sat the Lord Chief Justice of England, Lord Hewart of Bury, assisted by Mr Justice Branson and Mr Justice Hawke. As at the trial, Wallace was represented by Roland Oliver KC, who this time spoke first, while Edward Hemmerde KC led for the Crown.

Oliver argued that the jury's verdict was unreasonable, that it could not be supported, having regard to the evidence at the trial and that Mr Justice Wright should have withdrawn it from the jury and released Wallace. He attacked Mr Justice Wright for not directing the jury to ignore several mis-statements by Hemmerde in his opening speech: though challenged at the time as being wrong, nevertheless, said Oliver, the mis-statements had made a lasting impression upon the jury, which the judge should have determined to remove. Further, Oliver challenged the verdict over the errors that Bishop, Prosecuting Solicitor at the Police Court, had made in his presentation, which were wildly inaccurate and widely circulated in Liverpool and which, maintained Oliver, could have been highly prejudicial to Wallace, since the jury was picked from Liverpudlians.

Throughout Monday, Oliver kept up his attack: he challenged the notion of Wallace's indifference to the fate of his wife and the allegation that he wore the mackintosh; he stated that the police had tried to suppress the evidence of James Allison and that it was obvious that Qualtrough knew that Wallace would be at the chess club by reading the playing list. What Oliver had done in court during the trial, he repeated in greater detail for the benefit of the Appeal Judges.

On Tuesday morning Hemmerde rose to speak. He granted that there was no direct evidence that Wallace had made the Qualtrough telephone call, but insisted that the overwhelming circumstantial evidence could only point to Wallace as the murderer. After he had finished his brief recapitulation of the case, Oliver spoke again, stressing once more that the prosecution had failed to produce anything that could be construed as direct proof of Wallace's guilt.

At half past three on the Tuesday afternoon, Oliver was finally finished, and he sat down exhausted. The three Appeal Judges, rather than delivering their verdict directly to the court, rose and left the chamber for consultation. It was obviously an exceptional case.

At quarter past four, the court reassembled, and in the following fifteen minutes the Lord Chief Justice delivered the findings of the bench.

Section Four of the Criminal Appeal Act of 1907 provides that the Court of Criminal Appeal shall allow the appeal if they think that the verdict of the jury should be set aside on the grounds that it cannot be supported having regard to the evidence. The conclusion at which we have arrived is that the case against the appellant, which we have carefully and anxiously considered and discussed, was not proved with that certainty which is necessary in order to justify a verdict of guilty, and therefore it is our duty to take the course indicated by the section of the Statute to which I have referred. The result is that the appeal will be allowed and this conviction is quashed.[13]

The Scottish verdict: the case against William Herbert Wallace had not been proven.

6

Wallace was released almost immediately. With his brother, Joseph, who had come over to England from Malaya for the trial, he jumped into a taxi outside the Law Courts and took off for an unknown destination.

Wallace would not harm a fly, and those of us who knew him are immensely glad he has been set free, for we never believed he was capable of such an act of murder.[14]

Two weeks later, Wallace sat next to Joseph on the steps of Langham House, a guest house in the square of Broughton-in-Furness in the Lake District, to watch a school parade. It was a beautiful spring day, and the parading children, shepherded by their teachers, glanced over at the two brothers, so alike that no one could be sure which of the two was the man who had cheated death.[15]

Wallace returned to Wolverton Street and his collections in the Clubmoor area, despite the offer of an office job with the Prudential. While the majority of his customers were prepared to accept him and carry on as before, there were others who resented him, and made their feelings known. He complained to his employers and was taken into the Prudential offices in Dale Street, where he worked behind a desk until his death.

However, his home in Wolverton Street became the centre of attraction for the local mischief-makers and he was taunted and abused in the streets of Richmond Park as he went to and from work.

Find all the neighbours up against me. They are the rottenest crowd I ever struck. Mean and paltry brained.[16]

According to Goodman, towards the end of June, Wallace had finally had enough. Through Hector Munro he purchased a small bungalow in Meadowside Road, Bromborough, on the other side of the River Mersey, into which he moved before the end of the year.[17] From there he commuted daily to the Prudential offices in Dale Street.

Meanwhile, on Thursday 21 May, the inquest into the death of Julia Wallace was resumed. It was a formality which lasted only a couple of minutes.

The Coroner, G Cecil Mort, said that he had received notice from the Registrar of the Court of Criminal Appeal that a conviction had been quashed regarding the murder of one Julia Wallace. In accordance with that notice and section 20 of the Coroner's Amendment Act, he formally closed the inquest, without giving a verdict.

The Liverpool Police stated officially today that they would not re-open the investigation into the circumstances of Mrs Wallace's death.[18]

Wallace's story was ghosted in the *John Bull* magazine. Under the banner headline of *The Man They Did Not Hang*, he began to confide his belief, as he did in his diaries, that Richard Gordon Parry was his wife's killer, and that he lived in dread of meeting him. He did not name him, but hinted strongly that Parry had been intent upon – and here Wallace went awry with the truth – robbing Wallace of his monthly collection round.

Several articles and stories, in a variety of publications, libelled Wallace and he sued. It was the money which he received from out of court settlements which enabled him to purchase his bungalow in Bromborough. The most serious libel occurred in the May 1932 edition of *True Detective Mysteries*. But before the matter could be brought to the courts, Wallace died.

He entered Clatterbridge Hospital on 9 February 1933, with a recurrence of his kidney problem. He was treated with drugs, more to ease his pain than to cure his problem, but on 25 February he sank into a coma from which he did not recover, and he died in the early hours of the following day. The causes of death were uraemia and pyelonephritis.[19]

He was buried in the same plot as his wife in Anfield Cemetery, on 1 March 1933. Someone, probably his brother Joseph, had a tombstone erected above the grave.[20]

Chapter 8
The Case Against Richard Gordon Parry

1

If William Wallace did not kill his wife, then who did? Apparently Richard Gordon Parry did. Rowland, Goodman, Hussey and Wilkes all believe that Parry had a case to answer, but that for various reasons he was not tested by the police. Among the reasons cited by the writers are the police themselves, who, as the investigation unfolded, either through incompetence, or chicanery, did not see matters in the same way as they did. But is there a case against Parry? Were the police right to charge Wallace? Or should they have had Parry in the dock?

According to Roger Wilkes, it was John Rowland in his book, *The Wallace Case*, who first hinted at the existence of a police suspect other than William Wallace. However, Wilkes is incorrect. It was generally known at the time of the police investigation that Richard Gordon Parry was under scrutiny, as were several other men. Later, at the trial, during the cross-examination of Joseph Crewe, Wallace's supervisor at the Prudential, Parry was named by Roland Oliver KC and his name appears in the trial transcript. The trial judge, Mr Justice Wright, asked the press not to publish Parry's name in their reports, and this request was complied with.[1] Dorothy L Sayers, among others, is aware of this in her 1936 article on the case, and while she does not name Parry, she refers to an unnamed man who was under suspicion together with Wallace.[2]

After his release, Wallace hinted, in a series of articles in 1932 for the *John Bull* magazine, that he knew who killed his wife and these suspicions, and the dread of meeting his wife's killer and perhaps, like his wife, falling victim to him, he committed to his diary without naming the man. Word of his suspicions whirled around Liverpool following the *John Bull* articles, and Parry's name was bandied about as the man whom Wallace suspected. A year later, Parry himself took the unprecedented step of countering Wallace's claims in an article in the *Empire News* newspaper.[3]

It was Jonathan Goodman who first put together the case against Richard Gordon Parry after he had conclusively proved Wallace's innocence.[4] His starting point was Wallace's second statement to the police, in which he named Parry and thirteen other men, each of whom would have been admitted to the house by Julia Wallace in his absence. Statements were taken from the men by the police in the days following the murder.

However, Wallace had a great deal to say about Richard Gordon Parry in his second statement, and even though Parry was cleared by the police of having any involvement in the crime, it was Wallace's statement which laid the scent giving rise eventually to the belief that Parry was Julia's killer. Wallace accused Parry of being a thief.[5]

Parry had also been employed by the Prudential Assurance Company. In the winter of 1928, Wallace was taken ill and confined to his bed. Parry substituted for him on his collection round in Clubmoor. When he called at Wolverton Street, on completion of the round, to pay over the money, Wallace noticed several small book-keeping errors and corresponding monetary deficits. When these were pointed out to Parry some days later, he apologised for them and repaid the missing money.

But, according to Wallace, this was not the first time that Parry had been challenged about missing cash. He had failed to pay over money from his own collection round to his superintendent, Joseph Crewe. The deficit amounted to thirty pounds, according to Wallace, and Crewe had bearded Parry in his own home about the discrepancy, which he admitted, and which his father had made good. At the trial, Crewe admitted that the discrepancy of thirty pounds, mentioned by Wallace, was in fact substantially less.[6] Despite these shortcomings, Parry had been allowed to continue to work at the Prudential as a collection agent for some months afterwards, until, as Wallace said, he resigned to improve his position.

The financial irregularities uncovered by both Wallace and Crewe probably forced Parry into resigning his post. After leaving the Prudential, he went to work for the Gresham Insurance Company and, at the time of Julia's murder, he was aged twenty-two and employed by the Standard Life Assurance Company. He lived at home with his parents.

Parry had frequently called at the Wallace home and was familiar with their domestic arrangements. He knew all the details of Wallace's collection round and where he kept the premium money.[7] He was also a member of the Mersey Amateur Dramatic Society, and in November 1930 he was cast in *John Glayde's Honour*, which was rehearsing at the City Café, where Wallace played chess.[8] He saw Wallace there on three occasions. The two men had met up with each other several times since Parry had left the Prudential, but in his second statement, Wallace made no mention of any animosity on Parry's part. In fact, the meetings had been brief but amicable.

Goodman's thesis is that Parry held a grudge against Wallace, holding him responsible for branding him a thief, thus forcing him to resign from the Prudential. In addition, because of his visits to the City Café for rehearsals, Parry would be aware of Wallace's commitment to play in the chess tournament from the list on the noticeboard, and would thus know when he could receive the bogus Qualtrough message. Goodman learnt that Parry was always short of money and that, knowing Wallace as he did, he devised the Qualtrough plan to lure him from home in order to steal the insurance money from the cash-box. Parry murdered Julia Wallace, not as part of his scheme, but in a panic when she discovered him stealing the cash.

Goodman also found that Parry had been in trouble with the police, both before and after the murder and that, in addition to several juvenile cautions, Parry had been charged with a variety of very serious offences. He had served three months with hard labour for stealing a car in Aldershot in 1934, he had been bound over for a year in 1935 for embezzlement and he had been charged in 1936 with causing grievous bodily harm and indecently assaulting a young girl in Rainhill, on the outskirts of Liverpool.

In 1966, Goodman traced Parry to London, and together with the writer, Richard Whittington-Egan, he interviewed him on the doorstep of his home.

While he readily admitted his criminal past, he would not be drawn on the Wallace case, not even if Goodman and Whittington-Egan offered him two thousand pounds. However, he did claim that he had been on very intimate terms with Julia Wallace, often spending afternoons at her home without Wallace's knowledge, being entertained in the front parlour – the music room – with the implication that these musical sojourns were something more than that. As Whittington-Egan later observed when recalling the meeting with Parry, he was convinced that he had met Julia's killer.[9]

Because Parry was alive at the time Goodman's book, *The Killing of Julia Wallace*, went to print, he could not be named for legal reasons, and he was referred to in the text as Mr X. Goodman was also able to point out that Parry's alibi for the night of the murder was highly suspect.

> *When interviewed by the police (less than forty-eight hours after the murder) he said that he had spent an innocent Tuesday evening in the company of friends, one of whom he named. Separately interviewed, the friends confirmed that this was so. But two years later it was admitted that this was a mistake. If the police had investigated properly they would have discovered that it was quite impossible for them to have been together.*[10]

To overcome the legal difficulties in naming Parry as Julia Wallace's killer, Goodman penned a fictionalised account of the Wallace case in 1978, *The Last Sentence*, in which Parry is thinly disguised as the villain, George Palermo.[11] Goodman expounds his views that Parry-Palermo, short of money, sets out to rob the Wallace household, and in the course of the robbery, is forced to kill Mrs Wallace in order to protect himself from being branded a thief and ending up in prison.

In 1972, the American writer, Robert F Hussey, investigated the Wallace case, and he, too, concluded that Parry, Mr Z this time, murdered Julia Wallace while attempting to rob the Wallace household with the aid of an accomplice.

Parry died in North Wales in April 1980, and later in the same year, radio journalist, Roger Wilkes, joined the fray in pursuit of Parry, having stumbled across the case after a chat with his producer, Michael Green.[12] Wilkes was News Editor of Radio City, Merseyside's independent radio station, and through his contacts and researches, and having spoken to Jonathan Goodman, he claimed that:

> *The name of Julia Wallace's killer was given to me nearly half a century after the case.*[13]

Unlike Goodman and Hussey, who believe that Parry killed Julia only when he was caught in the act of robbing the cash-box, Wilkes believes that Julia's murder was premeditated, that Parry deliberately set out to vengefully silence the only witness to his theft and to implicate Wallace.

In a radio broadcast from Radio City, marking the fiftieth anniversary of Julia's death, Wilkes documented the Wallace case, from the Qualtrough telephone call, to the murder, to Wallace's arrest, trial, conviction and subsequent release. The programme was followed by a studio discussion of the case with the participation of Jonathan Goodman and several other Wallace experts and Richard Gordon Parry was paraded as Julia's killer.[14]

During the studio discussion, it was announced that the friend who had given Parry his alibi for the night of the murder, the friend whom Goodman had not named, was Parry's girlfriend at the time, a Miss Lily Lloyd. Wilkes had contacted Miss Lloyd before the broadcast, but she had refused to be interviewed about Parry, saying that her past, and in particular her association with Parry, was not open to a public airing.

However, Wilkes was able to say that in 1933, two years after Julia's murder, Lily Lloyd had contacted Wallace's solicitor, Hector Munro, offering to swear an affidavit to the effect that she had given Parry an alibi for the time of the murder in her statement to the police of 27 January 1931, and that her statement was untrue: she had lied to cover up for him. Apparently Miss Lloyd was playing the piano at the Clubmoor Cinema at the time of Julia's murder, and Parry could not have been with her.

During the phone-in following the studio discussion, Wilkes spoke to Ted Holmes, who had been the manager of the Clubmoor Cinema in January, 1931. He could not remember, given the fifty-year gap, whether Miss Lloyd had been working at the cinema on the night of the murder. But he did confirm that whenever she had worked there, it had been Parry's habit to collect her after the show, just after nine o'clock and that Miss Lloyd usually arrived for work between seven-thirty and eight o'clock. From Holmes's information, Wilkes was later to conclude that Parry did not have an alibi for the night of the murder, because Miss Lloyd was working at the Clubmoor Cinema between about seven-thirty and nine o'clock, the important period for the alibi, and could not have been with Parry.

The following month, February, Wilkes made a second broadcast about the Wallace case, entitled *Conspiracy of Silence*, in which he accused the Wallace case police officers, and certain Liverpool City officials, of a cover-up, of collusion, in protecting Parry from arrest at the expense of Wallace's life.[15] Parry had friends in high places: his father, William, was Assistant City Treasurer, who employed the daughter of Superintendent Moore as a secretary and William's cousin, George Parry, was Chief Librarian of Liverpool.

What had prompted this remarkable statement from Wilkes was an interview with a retired garage worker, John Parkes, whose name had come to light in the aftermath of Wilkes's first broadcast. The story which John Parkes had to tell was the basis for the February broadcast.

In January 1931, Parkes was employed as a car cleaner at Atkinson's Taxi and Motor Engineers, of Moscow Drive, Stoneycroft, Liverpool, just around the corner from Woburn Hill where Parry lived with his parents. Parkes knew Parry, who often called at the garage, sometimes in the early hours of the morning, for a chat and a mug of tea.

According to Parkes, several hours after the murder of Julia Wallace, possibly in the early hours of the Wednesday morning, Parry gunned his car into Atkinson's garage. He was in a very agitated and frantic state, and demanded of Parkes that he clean the inside and outside of his car with a high pressure water hose.

As I was doing this, I saw a glove inside a box in the car and I pulled it out to stop it getting wringing wet. Parry snatched it off me. It was covered in blood. And Parry said to me: 'If the police found that – it would hang me.' Well, I was a bit dubious about things, and then he started rambling again about a bar which he'd hidden outside a doctor's house in Priory Road. He said he'd dropped it down a grid outside the house.[16]

Parkes had heard of Julia's death earlier from the local policeman on the beat, PC Ken Wallace. As he washed down Parry's car he was thinking:

I knew why I was washing it and I didn't dare say anything. I realised my washing the car down had washed all the evidence away, but the evidence was there on the glove – and Parry saying that would hang him, and talking about the bar where he'd hidden it.[17]

Parkes claimed that the glove in question was a leather mitten and that any bloodstains off the car would have gone straight down the grid. Parkes had been frightened of Parry and so had done what he had been ordered to do. After finishing the cleaning, he was given five shillings for his trouble by Parry, who jumped in his car and drove off into the night.

When he went off shift later in the morning, Parkes confided the incident to his employer, William Atkinson, but he did not report the matter to the police. It was only after Wallace's conviction, that he decided to contact them. He telephoned Superintendent Hubert Moore at CID Headquarters, who interviewed Parkes at the garage. Moore's reaction to the incident was, according to Parkes, to dismiss it as a figment of his imagination and there was no police follow-up.

Parkes had one more piece of significant information for Wilkes, which finally confirmed to him Richard Gordon Parry's guilt. He claimed that some time before the murder, Parry had borrowed an oilskin cape and a pair of thigh-length waders from an acquaintance in the Stoneycroft area, ostensibly for a fishing trip. But Parry had not returned the items to their owner. The absence of blood on his clothing, as noted by Parkes, and which was later confirmed by the police when they examined it, was, therefore, understandable, concluded Wilkes: Parry had worn the cape and waders when he had bludgeoned Julia Wallace to death.

In 1984, Wilkes published the record of his investigations into the death of Julia Wallace: *Wallace, The Final Verdict*. His account was so well received, that *The Daily Telegraph* announced that the Wallace case had been finally solved: Richard Gordon Parry had murdered Julia Wallace.

2

From Rowland to Goodman, and Hussey to Wilkes, there has been a supposedly steady and overwhelming accretion of evidence implicating Parry as Julia's killer. However, at no point in any of these four accounts is he measured against the evidence from the crime scenes, to see whether he fits into the frame. With the exception of Hussey, who places Parry's attack upon Julia in the kitchen, there are no attempts to place him inside the front parlour, striking Julia over the head, as she knelt in front of the gas fire. What these four writers produce is pure speculation.

The indictment raised against Parry has four basic components: he had a motive; he had a criminal record; the John Parkes story and Parry's spoilt or compromised alibi.

It is not incumbent upon the police or the prosecution to demonstrate or prove motive in the commission of a crime. It is necessary and sufficient simply to prove beyond a reasonable doubt that the accused had the opportunity to commit the crime, and that the said person was responsible for it. Motives are, therefore, irrelevant when it comes to the question of who killed Julia Wallace. However, those cited by Goodman and Wilkes fail to impress, as there is no evidence to support them.

Parry's alleged motives were that he was always short of cash and that he had a grudge against Wallace for causing him to lose his job at the Prudential. There is no evidence whatsoever for this latter assertion, and none is adduced. Parry was not dismissed from the Prudential because of financial irregularities: he left of his own accord, as Wallace himself said, several months after the incident, to improve himself, and apparently he left with a good reference, since he found employment immediately, in the same capacity, as a collection agent, with the Gresham Insurance Company. And whenever Wallace and Parry bumped into one another, their meetings were always amicable.

When Wallace made his second statement, in which he gave the names – Parry's included – of men who would have been admitted to the house by Julia, Inspector Gold asked him if he suspected any of them. Wallace replied no. During the trial, Hemmerde KC asked Wallace whether he suspected anyone, anyone at all, of murdering his wife. Again he replied no.[18]

In 1931, with over a quarter of the male population in Liverpool unemployed due to the Depression, and with many of those in work on short time and reduced wages and salaries, there were very few men in the city who were not short of cash. Both Parry and Wallace were fortunate to be in full-time employment on full salaries. Even so, Wallace bemoans his lack of finances in his diary. The entry for 25 March 1930 reads:

Our only trouble is that of millions more, shortage of pounds, shillings and pence.[19]

Goodman offers no proof that Parry was chronically short of money, except for a few, casual comments from some of his contemporaries. He came from a well-to-do family and lived in a decent residential area of Liverpool, Woburn Hill, Stoneycroft, and he had the use, if not the ownership, of a motor car. He was certainly a lot better off than many of his contemporaries; he may well have been living beyond his means, but so were many thousands of others in Liverpool at the time. But he did have access to money, considerable amounts, from his own collection rounds for the Standard Life Assurance Company. If he was so desperate for money, and if he was intelligent and devious enough to construct the Qualtrough plan, then he was sufficiently capable of stealing his own cash by staging his own mugging, in order to alleviate his financial plight, without risking the hangman's noose.

3

Parry did have a criminal record. He was convicted of car theft, embezzlement and indecent assault some years after the murder. Goodman describes Qualtrough, and hence Parry, as one of the most fastidious planners in the history of crime. Wilkes ascribes to him the status of genius, while quoting the following to illustrate Parry's criminality:

Councillor Herbert Owen found Parry sitting in his car in North John Street. When asked what he was doing, Parry said: 'Sorry, that's my car in front.' He went to the other car and produced some keys. On failing to open the door, he started to move away. Owen informed a constable, and Parry agreed to go to the detective office, but bolted. The PC followed, blowing his whistle, and Parry was tripped by a tram inspector in Dale Street and arrested. Outside the bridewell in Cheapside, he threw himself on the floor and had to be carried inside. Parry was fined five pounds with six pounds costs.[20]

This incident, more reminiscent of the Keystone Kops than a Professor Moriarty, hardly supports the contentions of Goodman or Wilkes, of Parry as the criminal par excellence. It is difficult to believe that, after several bouts of juvenile bungling, Parry suddenly assumed the mantle of the criminal mastermind, in order to plan and execute the death of Julia Wallace, only to revert to type, the inept blunderer, within a year of his great success. His criminal ventures would appear, as Professor Canter says, as if he, 'stumbled into crime'.[21]

It is more reasonable to conclude that Parry's criminal record demonstrates that he was an opportunistic criminal, who acted on the spur of the moment, without a thought for the consequences, rather than a calculating planner, who carefully weighed up his every move. In addition, he was aged twenty-two at the time of the murder, and as Professor Canter points out, violent crimes, such as premeditated murder, occur later in a 'person's developing criminal career', that is, when they are older and more experienced in their criminal activities.[22] Parry's criminal past would indicate that he was still learning his trade and that it was not until the violent assault upon the girl in Rainhill, some five years after the Wallace murder, that he had progressed from crimes against property, to crimes against the person. And this progression would indicate that in 1931, he had yet to reach the stage in his development which would have seen him attack a person, let alone resort to murder.[23]

4

The story related by John Parkes to Roger Wilkes is quite astounding, particularly in the context of Wilkes's scheme of events on the night of the murder. Parry wore oilskins when he murdered Mrs Wallace; he then drove his car containing a bloodstained mitten to the Clubmoor Cinema and waited outside for his girlfriend, Lily Lloyd, to emerge; when she did, he drove her home and sat with her in her house for a couple of hours; he then drove off to Atkinson's garage to have the interior of his car washed out by Parkes, while admitting to murder and the disposal of the murder weapon.

Was Parry wearing the waterproofs as he entered 29 Wolverton Street on the night of the murder? Or did he have them folded under his arm as he entered, and slip into them quietly in the front parlour without Julia noticing, she being too busy lighting the fire?

Waterproofs repel liquids such as blood. If Parry had been splashed and sprayed with blood, it would have run off the waterproofs, and tell-tale drops of blood would have marked his progress through the house. But no such bloodstains were found. After the murder, did he take off the oilskins and put them in a bag which he had conveniently brought so as to avoid dripping blood all over the house? Did he manage to strip off the oilskins without contaminating any of his clothing?

What does a leather mitten look like several hours after contact with blood? Depending upon the tanning and the treatment, some leathers will repel liquids such as blood, others will partially absorb it. And in the latter case, it would be very difficult, if not impossible, to identify the staining as blood, simply with the naked eye, particularly if the mitten was of a dark colour, particularly at night, particularly several hours after the first contact.

Parry supposedly wore the mitten when he killed Mrs Wallace, and so it became bloodstained. But he could not have worn it during the robbery, as he would have left behind bloody smudge marks on any objects he touched: so he must have taken it off and put it somewhere while he was inside the house. In his pocket, perhaps? But that would have left bloodstains in his pocket. Perhaps he put it in the bag together with the oilskins? But why did he take it out of the bag later and put it in the box? And what happened to the second mitten? What did Parry do with the oilskins? Put them in the boot of his car?

Parkes said he cleaned the inside of the car only, and does not mention washing down the boot. If the waterproofs were in the boot, why was the mitten not there, too? If the oilskins were in the boot, then it, too, must have been contaminated. But the boot was not washed out. What did Parry do with the bloodstained mitten after Parkes had washed the car? Put it back inside the car and re-contaminate it?

If the mitten was in a box, and since Parry had avoided contaminating his clothing with blood by wearing the oilskins, and, as the evidence of the crime scenes shows, had not trailed any blood from the house to the car, then the only contaminated part of the car was the box. Why was it necessary to wash down the inside of the car? It would have made more sense for Parry to have simply disposed of the box.

According to Parkes, Parry arrived at the garage several hours after the murder, and after the hue and cry had been raised by the police, who were searching for a man with bloodstained clothing, and stopping and questioning any suspicious-looking men. What had Parry been doing since the murder? Disposing of incriminating evidence, such as the bloody mitten?

Apparently not. According to Wilkes, Parry sat in his bloodstained car outside the Clubmoor Cinema waiting for Lily Lloyd. Did Miss Lloyd contaminate her clothing with Mrs Wallace's blood? Did she notice the box and the bloodstained mitten? Wilkes, who spoke to Lily Lloyd in 1981, did not ask her such leading questions.

Would Parry, the criminal genius, as Wilkes and Goodman regard him, having engineered his coup, leave such incriminating evidence as a bloody mitten and bloodstains inside his car for several hours while a massive police hunt was in progress, risk his girlfriend seeing, and possibly being contaminated by, the bloody mitten, then allowing the mitten to be seen and removed by John Parkes, to whom he confessed the murder?

There is no corroboration for Parkes's story whatsoever. He told Wilkes that, after his encounter with Parry, he informed his boss, William Atkinson, of what had occurred, and of what Parry had said. Atkinson was dead by the time Parkes related his story to Wilkes, so no confirmation of his story was forthcoming from him. Parkes said he finally told his story to Superintendent Moore, following the conviction of Wallace. But there is no record of any statement in the very comprehensive file of the Department of Public Prosecutions, which contains every scrap of detail and correspondence about the Wallace case, including all the police interviews. The last entry in that file is dated after Wallace's release, after Moore had interviewed Parkes.

Either Parkes was the victim of a very cruel practical joke by Parry; or he fabricated the whole story. There is not a word of truth to the story, because Parry had an alibi for the time of the murder.

5

Two years after the murder, Lily Lloyd, having been jilted by Parry, went to see Hector Munro, Wallace's solicitor, to say that she had lied in her statement to the police at the time of the murder and that she was willing to swear an affidavit to that effect. Both Goodman and Wilkes have always assumed that Lily Lloyd was playing the piano at the Clubmoor Cinema on the night of Julia's death, but that she had told the police she had spent the evening with Parry, thereby providing him with an alibi.

For Goodman and Wilkes, the spoilt or compromised alibi is the keystone to the case against Parry, as it gives him the opportunity in which to kill Julia Wallace. However, Hector Munro did not follow up Miss Lloyd's offer, and she did not swear the affidavit. Goodman and Wilkes spoke to Hector Munro about Miss Lloyd and Parry, but he was unable to help them as his memory of her visit was hazy.

Undeterred by Munro's inconvenient and inconsiderate memory lapse, Wilkes argues that:

> Although Lily Lloyd never went on record to render Parry's alibi worthless, the fact that she offered to do so is surely conclusive.[24]

That is, conclusive of Parry's guilt. And Wilkes goes on to report a conversation he had with Miss Lloyd in 1981, fifty years after the event:

> She admitted to me that she lied when she said that Parry had spent the evening of the murder with her. In her words, the statement she gave to the police a few days after the killing was only partly true, in that although she had spent part of the evening with Parry, it was the later part. She cannot remember how much later. But it is plain that it was late enough to rob Parry of the alibi he claimed for the early part of the evening, to cover the time of the killing.[25]

Wilkes does not produce Miss Lloyd's original police statement for examination and it is apparent from his arguments that he has never seen or read it. Thus the authority for the spoilt or compromised alibi is vested in the word of an old lady recalling events of her youth.

However, Miss Lloyd's memory had not failed her when she said she lied. She did lie. But not to the police. She lied to Wilkes and to Hector Munro when she offered to swear the affidavit following her parting from Parry. A woman scorned, perhaps?

Lily Lloyd, real name Lillian Josephine Moss Lloyd, had this to say to the police about herself and Parry, six days after Julia's death:

> On Tuesday the 20th inst. Parry called between 8.30pm and 9pm but I think it was nearer 9 than 8.30pm. He told me in answer to my question as to where he had been, that he had been to a Mrs Williamson, 49 Lisburn Lane. I know Mrs Williamson, she is a friend of mine. He told me that he had got an invitation for myself and him to Leslie Williamson's 21st birthday party in April. I do not remember whether or not he told me he had received the invitation that night, but I got the impression that he had. He remained until about 11pm and then

went home. He came in his car.[26]

Julia Wallace was murdered sometime between six-thirty-five and eight-forty-five on the night of Tuesday, 20 January. Miss Lloyd did not provide an alibi for Parry on the night of the murder: she first saw Parry after Julia's death. Neither does she mention that she was working at the Clubmoor Cinema that night which, in fact, she was not.

The remainder of Miss Lloyd's statement to the police is taken up with descriptions of Parry's attire on the Tuesday and Wednesday nights, a clear indication that the police were checking up on him and his possible involvement in the crime.

Josephine Ward Lloyd, Lily's mother, also made a statement to the police at the same time as her daughter:

On Monday the 19th of January 1931 Mr Parry called at my home at about 7.15pm … On Tuesday the 20th January Mr Parry called at about 9pm and remained here until about 11pm. He came in his car which he left outside.

Mrs Lloyd also gave brief descriptions of how Parry was dressed on the Tuesday and Wednesday evenings. After signing her statement, she added the following:

When Parry called at about 9pm or a little after on Tuesday the 20th, my daughter told him he was late and he said he had been to Mrs Williamson's, Lisburn Lane and to Hignetts at Tuebrook about a battery for his wireless.[27]

Mrs Lloyd does not provide Parry with an alibi for the time of the murder. However, she does provide him with an alibi for the Monday night when the Qualtrough telephone call was made. If Parry was Qualtrough then, on the Monday night, he must have been in the telephone kiosk close to Wolverton Street ringing the chess club at seven-fifteen, the time recorded for the first call. But, according to Mrs Lloyd, he was at her house, 7 Missouri Road, at that time, half a mile away from the telephone kiosk.

It is interesting to note that, in the course of researching his book, Goodman spoke to Parry's father. He claims that Mr Parry told him that his son was having problems with his car battery on the night of the murder. Perhaps Parry senior, thirty-five years after the event, confused the car battery with the accumulator battery for the radio which his son collected from Hignetts that night. And the car battery/accumulator battery conflation may be the source of Wilke's unfounded assertion that Parry claimed as an alibi that he was repairing his car in Breck Road at the time of the murder.

Wilkes asseverates that Parry claimed two additional alibis for the time of the murder, namely that he was with friends and that he was arranging a birthday celebration. From what was said in the statements by the two Lloyd ladies, it would appear that Parry did have three alibis, and that he was telling the truth.

Richard Gordon Parry made his statement to the police on Friday, 23 January at Tuebrook Bridewell:

On Tuesday the 20th inst. I finished business about 5.30pm and called upon Mrs Brine, 43 Knocklaid Road. I remained there with Mrs Brine, her daughter, Savona, 13 years, her nephew, Harold Dennison, 29 Marlborough Road, until about 8.30pm. I then went out and bought some cigarettes – Players No3, and the Evening Express from Mr Hodgson, Post Office, Maiden Lane, on the way to my young lady's house. When I was turning the corner by the Post Office I remembered that I had promised to call for my accumulator at Hignetts in West Derby Road, Tuebrook. I went there and got my accumulator and then went down West Derby Road and along Lisburn Lane to Mrs Williamson, 49 Lisburn Lane, and saw her. We had a chat about a 21st birthday party for about 10 minutes and then I went to 7 Missouri Road, and remained there till about 11 to 11.30pm when I went home.

I have heard of the murder of Mrs Wallace and have studied the newspaper reports of the case and, naturally, being acquainted with Mr and Mrs Wallace, I have taken a great interest in it. I have no objection whatever to the police verifying my statement as to my movements on Monday the 19th and Tuesday the 20th instants.[28]

Parry, Lily Lloyd and Mrs Lloyd all agree that he arrived at Lily's house at approximately nine o'clock at night, after the murder of Julia Wallace had taken place, and that he stayed there until approximately eleven o'clock. Parry really must have been a cool customer, a consummate actor, to have blithely sat with his girlfriend and her mother for two hours after just killing an elderly lady half a mile away, while her blood lay drying in his car.

What was Lily Lloyd prepared to say to Hector Munro two years after the murder that would have threatened the integrity of Parry's alibi and implicate him in Julia's murder? She could not have said anything. Probably the reason Hector Munro did not take up her offer of an affidavit was that he knew it was all a nonsense; a nonsense inspired by Parry's rejection of her. Parry's alibi was confirmed by Harold Dennison and his aunt, Olivia Alberta Brine, among others. Mrs Olivia Brine stated:

I am a married woman, my husband is away at sea. I have known RG Parry about two years. Just before last Christmas he commenced calling with my nephew William Dennison, 29 Marlborough Road. At about 5pm to 5.30pm on Tuesday the 20th inst., Parry called at my house. He came in his car. He remained until about 8.30pm when he left. Whilst he was here, a Miss Plant, Gloucester Road, called. My nephew, Harold Dennison, also called.[29]

Mrs Brine's statement has a ring of truth to it. She was a married woman and a young man was calling regularly at her home. Such behaviour more than likely would have given rise to speculation and tongue-wagging amongst her neighbours. And yet, in the interest of truth, she was prepared to come forward and speak out, not only to the police, but also to the court, and risk her reputation, perhaps her marriage. Harold English Dennison stated:

I have known RG Parry for two years. I called at 43 Knocklaid Road on Tuesday 20th inst. about 6pm. My aunt, Mrs Brine, lives there. When I called, Mr Parry was there. He remained till about 8.30pm, when he left.[30]

Richard Gordon Parry did have an alibi for the time of the murder. That alibi had nothing whatsoever to do with Miss Lily Lloyd. That alibi was thoroughly checked and verified by the police and when the tests on Parry's clothes and his car proved negative, he was rightly eliminated from their enquiries. The intervention of the mischievous Miss Lloyd, and the readiness of Goodman and Wilkes to produce specious facts and conclusions from doubtful premises, dubious research and spurious tales, has led to the maligning of an innocent man and his family. Richard Gordon Parry did not kill Julia Wallace on the night of 20 January 1931.

Part Three

Chapter 9
Profiling

The basic principle of scientific criminal investigation was formulated at the turn of the century by the French criminologist, Edmond Locard: Every contact leaves a trace.[1] One of the founding fathers of forensic science, Locard was referring to the physical, chemical and biological traces that a criminal brings to, or takes from, the scene of a crime. It is these traces, or clues – fingerprints, fibres, dust, hair, semen, for example – which investigating officers attempt to isolate and secure for forensic examination and evidentiary processing.

Crimes of violence involve contact between at least two people, and the thrust of investigations into such crimes has concentrated on the search for clues and traces, followed by inquiries aimed at connecting them to a particular perpetrator.

However, Professor David Canter, amongst others,[2] has pointed out that there is a far more subtle interpretation of Locard's tenet, one which has changed the emphasis of criminal investigations from looking for clues to match to a particular offender, to searching for a type of perpetrator to match the crime. The contact a criminal makes with a victim leaves behind a trace of the type of person he is – a psychological trace – what Canter calls a criminal shadow, at the scene of a crime.

Tell-tale patterns of behaviour that indicate the sort of person he is.[3]

That is, behaviour reflects personality.

The examination of the character of the criminal, as revealed by the behavioural traces he leaves at the crime scene, is an attempt to get beyond a mere list of clues, in order to recognise a pattern, an identifiable silhouette, a distinct shadow cast by the offender.[4]

The perspective that behaviour reflects personality was first utilised as an investigative tool in 1957 in New York, by the psychologist, Dr James A Brussel, to trace and apprehend the 'Mad Bomber', George Metesky, who had terrorised the city with a bombing campaign for sixteen years. Using

105

photographs of the bomb blast scenes, together with detailed analyses of the bomber's taunting letters to the police and newspapers, Brussel arrived at a comprehensive profile of his personality, based upon his known behaviour. Within days of receiving the profile, police arrested Metesky in his Connecticut home.[5]

However, the advance made by Dr Brussel took many years to bear fruit: it was viewed with deep suspicion and distrust, verging on hostility, by many policemen, who consigned it to the realm of the spiritualist and the psychic, seeing no place for it in their traditional world of criminal investigation. It was not until the early seventies that Brussel's technique, now known generally as criminal personality profiling, gained acceptance, not only in America, but throughout the world.

It was officers and analysts of the FBI's Behavioural Science Unit, at Quantico, Virginia, who led the way in developing Brussel's methodology, mainly in response to the rising numbers of serial murders and rapes across America. FBI Special Agents, such as Harry Teton, Bob Ressler and Jack Douglas, who had assisted in the investigations of some of the most horrific examples of these crimes, began to pool their knowledge, experience and intuition. They also began a programme of interviews with some of the most vicious killers and rapists incarcerated in prisons throughout the land, in order to try and understand what had gone on inside each criminal's mind as he committed the crime and to link those mental processes with the evidence left behind at the scene.

Over the years, often without the knowledge or support of their superiors, the FBI agents developed a corpus of knowledge, which they made available, in the form of criminal personality profiles, to inquiring, and sometimes desperate, police forces who were investigating difficult cases of murder and rape.[6] And it was the successes of this small group in solving some of the most intractable serial murders in America which led to the official acceptance of offender profiling as an investigative tool within the Behavioural Science Unit of the FBI.

Today, the FBI's profilers are gathered in the Investigative Support Unit. Police forces, not only in America, but from all over the world, utilise the FBI's experience and knowledge when confronted with intractable cases and serial and repeat crimes and they also send their experienced officers to Quantico for specialised training in the science of offender profiling.

In Britain, David Canter, Professor of Psychology at Liverpool University, has extended and developed the FBI approach to offender profiling, which still relies heavily on the instincts and intuition of the individual profilers. He places emphasis upon scientific methods, and the application of well-established psychological and objective behavioural principles to the interpretation of a criminal's behaviour.

Canter became involved in offender profiling in 1985: he was called in by

Scotland Yard to assist in the search for a serial rapist and killer who had been operating undetected for almost four years, and who had sexually assaulted more than thirty women, murdering three of them. Canter's profile of the assailant, based upon the crime scenes, their distribution and the offender's behaviour towards his victims, when placed within a behavioural framework, quickly led to the apprehension of John Duffy, the 'Railway Rapist'.[7]

Canter's approach to criminal profiling, like that of his FBI colleagues, begins with the division of the criminal's behaviour into pre and post-offence behaviour, and to such questions as: why was a particular victim chosen? what were the offender's intentions? how did he plan his crime? what took place at the scene of the crime? what did he do afterwards? and, finally, what type of person would have planned and perpetrated the offence in that particular way?

Finding the answers to these questions involves investigators who perform intricate and detailed examinations of crime scenes, working in conjunction with scene-of-the-crime colleagues, who detect, collect, and examine the traces from the scenes. From their findings, a picture is elaborated of what happened at the scene, enabling the officers to reconstruct the activities and behaviour of both offender and victim. In addition, an explication of the perpetrator's pre-offence behaviour, as well as that of the victim, may be forthcoming, from which it may be possible to deduce some further aspects of the offender's behaviour, and hence the type of person responsible.

Offender profiling has had its widest application and its greatest successes in the field of serial crime: it is obvious that the more offences of a similar nature a criminal commits, the more his behaviour will be open to inspection, interpretation and analysis. But profiling can, and does, have an application, even when the criminal act is singular and never repeated. Every contact leaves a trace, and a single contact, particularly a violent one, will leave a trace, a shadow, of the offender.

The police investigating the death of Julia Wallace did not have the technique of criminal personality profiling to hand to assist them in their search for her killer, and their examination of the crime scene left much to be desired. But the facts of her death are well documented, and are still open to examination.

The case offers for analysis and interpretation the actual murder scene itself, the front parlour of 29 Wolverton Street, the robbery scene in the kitchen, and the Qualtrough plan, which, together, cover all aspects of the killer's behaviour. Their examination and explication in the context of what happened, how and why, should give the answer to who could have committed the crimes – what type of person it was.

Chapter 10
The Killing of Julia Wallace

1

Because there were no signs of a forcible entry into 29 Wolverton Street, the police concluded that either RM Qualtrough was admitted to the house by Julia Wallace; or that her killer was already inside the house, that he was, in fact, William Herbert Wallace, masquerading as Mr Qualtrough. There are no other possibilities.[1]

During their investigation, the police decided that the robbery was so amateurish that it must have been contrived and so they prosecuted the belief that Wallace murdered his wife and staged the robbery to look as if she had died at the hands of a thief during a robbery gone disastrously wrong.

Wallace's defence was that Julia had died at the hands of Mr Qualtrough during the course of a robbery, that this theory was the true interpretation of events on the night of the murder and that Wallace was as much the victim of the illusive Mr Qualtrough as his poor wife. The defence was prepared to argue that the robbery was panic-stricken rather than amateurish.

During the trial, however, very little consideration was given to an accurate reconstruction of the murder and the robbery, and very little evidence from the two scenes was adduced in support of either side's contention, in order to ascertain which of the two theories was consistent with the facts. More time than necessary was spent by learned counsel examining the nature of the single blood clot uncovered in the lavatory pan and the spurious implications it had for the guilt, or innocence, of William Wallace.

When what little evidence was given of how Julia Wallace actually met her death, it was contradictory and inconsistent, and did not encompass all of the facts, so that a poorly defined and incomplete picture of how she was murdered emerged. In addition, vital details concerning the robbery were ignored. As a result, the question of whether she was murdered during the course of a robbery, or whether her murder was disguised as a robbery gone wrong, has never been resolved.

What actually happened at 29 Wolverton Street on the night of 20 January 1931?

The police account of events was put before the public during the trial of William Wallace by Professor MacFall on 23 April 1931, when he was examined by Edward Hemmerde KC for the prosecution, and cross-examined by Roland Oliver KC for the defence.

The murder room – the front parlour – measured thirteen feet by eleven, and was heavily furnished. Opposite the doorway was the fireplace, in front of which was a hearth rug. Mrs Wallace was found stretched across the rug, diagonally from right to left, from the fireplace towards the door, as viewed from the doorway. She was prostrate on the right side of her face, her right arm tucked beneath her, her left lying away from her body. Mr Wallace's mackintosh was found beneath the body. Flakes of burnt material from the mackintosh were scattered on the rug directly in front of the firegrate.

To the left of the fireplace, in the alcove, angled across the corner of the room, was a double-seater settee and cushion, across the arms of which rested Mr Wallace's violin case. Adjacent to the settee was the sideboard in front of which there was a chair, close to the doorway. Behind the door, two chairs, one in front of the other, were next to the piano. The seat of the second chair, which was close to Mrs Wallace's battered head, contained a stack of sheet music, the top sheet being covered in brown paper wrapping. In the recess of the bay window was a table, topped with an aspidistra plant. In front of it, to the right of the fireplace, was a chaise-longue, and adjacent to the foot of that was a small circular table, also holding a plant. Between this table and the chair with the pile of music sheets, was a music stand.

Professor MacFall inferred that Mrs Wallace had been seated forward on the edge of the settee, her head turned slightly to the left, when she was attacked. The killer struck her on the left side of the head with a heavy blunt instrument, fracturing her skull and leaving a deep fracture, one inch by three inches, in front of, and above, the left ear. The meningeal artery running beneath the fracture was ruptured and arterial blood spurted from the wound, projecting blood upwards and backwards. Mrs Wallace slumped to the floor, where her killer then administered ten more blows to the back left-hand side of her head.

The ten blows to the back of the head were, to some extent, cushioned by Mrs Wallace's hair and the pressure they induced inside the skull was relieved through the first fracture from which were squeezed slivers of bone and brain tissue. The wounds to the back of the head bled and the skull was fractured again, but no bone shards broke through the skin. The murder weapon was never found and MacFall surmised that it was a heavy metal bar.

A halo of blood, brain tissue and tiny bone fragments surrounded Mrs Wallace's head, spilling over beyond the leading edge of the hearth rug and a second pool of blood was located at the left-hand edge of the rug, just in front of the double settee. No bone or brain tissue was found beneath her head, which led MacFall to conclude that the ten blows to the back of the head were delivered while she was lying on the floor and after the killer blow to the left side of the head.

There was bloodstaining on the walls and furniture. The average height of the staining on the walls was four feet, but in some places it reached to seven. On the wall behind the door, and between the piano, there were bloodstains. Below them, on the brown paper cover of the sheet music, were further stains. Directly opposite the door, in the recess to the left of the fireplace, the bloodstains spattered the wall and two pictures hanging there. There were bloodstains on the double settee and its cushion, and upon Wallace's violin case. The surface of the sideboard, the wall above it, and above the settee, were all bloodstained.

Some of the staining on the sideboard and wall, according to MacFall, exhibited soda water bottle shaping. That is, when the leading edge of a drop of projected blood lands upon a hard surface, it adheres to that surface and causes the remaining part of the drop to skid over it, forming a shape similar to a soda water or Perrier bottle. The bottom of the bottle indicates the direction from which the blood was projected. And because of the position of these particular stains on the wall above the sideboard and settee, MacFall concluded that Mrs Wallace had been seated on the settee when first attacked, because it was the ruptured meningeal artery which had spurted and projected this blood.

Later, during the trial, William Roberts, the Analyst for the City of Liverpool, gave evidence about bloodstaining. He demonstrated that the staining covered an arc or semi-circle, centred on Mrs Wallace's head and spread from behind the door, across to the wall and sideboard, terminating in the alcove to the left of the fire. He said that the bloodstains came from several different directions. In addition, he provided detailed descriptions of the burning and staining of the mackintosh and Mrs Wallace's skirt.

The lower, right-hand side of the raincoat had been burned away, and fragments of the seared material had been scattered in front of the fire. According to Roberts, in the tests he conducted, the material of the garment was highly inflammable. It was extensively and heavily stained with blood on the left and right, inside and outside. There was also blood on the upper right sleeve and left cuff.

The front of Mrs Wallace's skirt was heavily stained with blood, and the skirt had been twisted or turned off centre from left to right. Roberts stated that in addition to the bloodstaining on the skirt, there were three, recent, horizontal burns which could have been caused by contact with the hot fire-clay of a gas fire. He located the burns at the bottom of the placquet. A placquet, or placket, on a woman's skirt is a slit or opening beneath the fastening for the skirt. In this case, it would have been an opening for the buttons that secured the skirt at the waist and she wore it on her left hip.

The evidence from Roberts concerning the burning to the mackintosh and Julia's skirt, which must have placed her closer to the gas fire rather than the settee at the time of the attack, was at odds with the version of events detailed by Professor MacFall, which completely ignored the whole question of the burnt clothing.

It was left to Roland Oliver KC to try to reconcile the evidence of MacFall and Roberts. Oliver forced the professor to concede that it was more probable that Mrs Wallace, wearing the mackintosh over her shoulders,[2] was stooped, or crouched, in front of the fire, having just lit it, when she was struck about the head by her killer, causing her to fall across the fire. Oliver had in mind that the final position of the body was inconsistent with her having been seated on the settee prior to being knocked off it and that both the mackintosh and her skirt showed signs of burning. Oliver's version placed Julia's head in front of the settee, close to the position described by MacFall, so that its placement was consistent with, and accounted for, the bloodstaining resulting from the spurting of the ruptured meningeal artery.

However, though Oliver's reconstruction of events was an improvement on MacFall's, especially the notion that Julia must have fallen across the fire in order to sustain the burning to her clothing, it still does not account for all the evidence at the scene of the crime, most notably the seared fragments of the mackintosh and the bloodstaining on the left-hand side of the hearth rug.

Indeed, Oliver's positioning of Julia in front of the fire when the fatal blow was struck is open to doubt. Had she been crouched down in front of the fire, her back must have been to her killer. For Qualtrough to have attacked the left side of her head, he must have struck his blow from left to right. Thus the projected blood from the ruptured artery would have followed the same direction as the attack; it would have fallen across the firegrate, towards the window side of the room, and away from the settee, the sideboards and the wall behind. But there was no bloodstaining in the direction of the windows. The blow, as indicated by the blood patterns, must have come from right to left.

For Oliver's version to be consistent with the bloodstaining and a blow to the left side of the head, Julia must have been stooped in front of the fire, but with her head turned into the room, a rather awkward position, when Qualtrough struck. In this case, the left side of her head would have been open to a blow delivered from right to left. However, the force of such a blow, delivered downwards and across the head, would have propelled the body away from the fire and not into it. How, then, was Julia's clothing burnt?

Both MacFall's and Oliver's accounts of Julia's death fall into inconsistency because they make the assumption that the first blow was the fatal one which caused most of the bloodstaining to the furniture and walls. And their versions are incomplete, as they fail to account for the bloodstaining on the left-hand side of the rug and the final position of body.

As reported by Roberts, the mackintosh was made of highly inflammable material. Burnt fragments of material were found in and around the hearth and beneath the body. Thus, at some point during the assault, the mackintosh caught fire, and the fire was extinguished by Qualtrough before Julia's body was placed on top of it.

At some time during Qualtrough's onslaught, Julia Wallace lay bleeding on the floor with her head close to the left-hand side of the hearth rug, thereby causing the bloodstaining in that area. From there her body must have been moved to its final resting position on top of the mackintosh, with her head close to the leading edge of the rug, where further bloodstaining occurred. The assault was not continuous, as implied by Professor MacFall and Roland Oliver. Qualtrough paused on at least two occasions during his attack, as witnessed by the charred pieces of mackintosh material, the bloodstaining, and the moving of the body to its final position.

Professor MacFall stated that there were eleven blows struck to Julia's head: the first blow, the killer one, to the left side of her head, followed by ten further blows to the back left-hand side of the head, these ten coming one on top of the other. Oliver concurred in this. But there is no evidence to show that this was the sequence of blows.

In all probability, the first blow was to the back of Julia's head as she knelt with her back to the killer in front of the fire. It was not the fatal blow, but it was the one which stunned her and caused her to collapse across the fire which, in turn, scorched her clothing. This first, non-fatal blow which, because it was cushioned by the chignon, did not fracture the skull, was later buried, or hidden, beneath a further nine blows delivered to the back of her head, leading Professor MacFall to conclude, incorrectly, that ten blows, one after another, had rained down on her head as she lay prone on her stomach.

Once the assumption that the first blow was the fatal one is discarded, a more reasonable account of what took place during the attack falls into place. Having struck the first, non-fatal blow to the back of the head, Qualtrough ceases the attack, to pull Julia away from the fire, as he can smell and see her clothes burning.[3] He places her on her back, with her head just in front of the settee, while he deals with the mackintosh which, having slipped from her shoulders, has now caught fire.

He extinguishes the burning mackintosh, scattering charred pieces of material around the hearth, and drops it in the middle of the hearth rug. He now turns his attention to Julia, who, recovering from the initial assault, is struggling into a sitting position. Her head is now in the position advocated by Oliver and MacFall, just in front of the settee. Qualtrough strikes the fatal blow to silence her. The skull is fractured, the artery ruptures, and blood spurts onto the sideboard and wall. Julia falls back, and her wounded head bleeds onto the left-hand side of the hearth rug.

But what of the final position of the body? Qualtrough, aware that Julia's clothes had been burnt, now pulls at her skirt to determine the extent of the burning and, in doing so, turns her over onto her stomach into the final position on top of the mackintosh, thereby fully inspecting the damage to the skirt, probably patting at the scorch marks to ensure they are not going to burst into flames as the mackintosh had done. This sequence of events is supported by Roberts' evidence: he stated that Julia's skirt had been twisted about her body, with the left side being brought round to the front. Qualtrough then delivers nine blows to the back of her head, covering up the initial blow, this final attack being frenzied according to MacFall.

This account fully fits the facts and is supported by the evidence in the murder room. It may not be the only interpretation possible, but any alternative version must equally account for all the evidence at the scene.

However, the most important point to be gleaned from the scenario, a point common to the accounts of MacFall and Oliver, though it would appear they did not see its relevance to their respective arguments, was that the attack was sudden, unexpected, and unprovoked.

2

Further facts and evidence from the crime scene and the post mortem support the notion of an unexpected attack. There were no signs of a struggle inside the house: in particular the furniture in the front parlour and kitchen had not been disturbed, moved or repositioned; Mrs Wallace's cardigan and blouse were not pulled or twisted, indicating that she had not struggled with her attacker and, while the palms of her hands were smeared with blood, there was no blood or skin beneath her fingernails, which were intact, to indicate that she had fought with, and defended herself against her attacker; her wrists and arms displayed no signs of bruising to indicate she had been pulled or pinioned; with the exception of a small clot of blood in the lavatory pan, all the bloodstaining was confined to the murder room.[4]

Excepting a small, recent bruise on the inside of Julia's upper left arm and the horrific injuries sustained to her head, there were no other marks of violence upon her body. In particular, there were no signs of defensive injuries. Such injuries are sustained by victims who know they are about to be attacked, or who are being attacked and throw up their arms reflexively to ward off the blows. Typically, these injuries occur to the hands and arms during a frontal assault.

From the evidence at the murder scene it is reasonable to conclude that the assault was so sudden and so unexpected, so forceful and so deadly, that Mrs Wallace had no opportunity to defend herself; that the assault took place in the front parlour, and that she was very close to the gas fire, having just lit it, when she was attacked from behind. In addition, the spread of the bloodstaining in the parlour and the placement of the furniture therein, indicate that the killer was right-handed.

3

But why was Julia in the front parlour lighting the fire? Wallace himself supplies the answer. He stated that whenever a business acquaintance called while he was out, his wife would show him into the front parlour to await his return.

Had Qualtrough called at the house on the night of 20 January asking to see Mr Wallace on a matter of business, then Julia would have let him in. But, she would have only admitted him if she knew him. Wallace was quite adamant in his testimony that she would never admit a stranger to the house.

Thus, it would be reasonable to conclude, in the light of the evidence, that Mrs Wallace, wearing the mackintosh over her shoulders against the cold, responded to a knock at the front door, and having admitted Qualtrough on that chilly January night, showed him directly into the front parlour, where she set about lighting the fire to keep him warm and that, as she knelt and lit the fire, he attacked her without warning. That is, if Julia Wallace invited RM Qualtrough into her home, then within a minute or two of entering, he brutally murdered her.

If she did admit Qualtrough to her home, then the only conclusion available from the evidence is that the killing, an assassination in fact, was an integral part of his plan. Having lured away her husband on a bogus business trip, he knew he had to deal with her: he talked his way into the house and struck her down at the first possible opportunity, before even attempting a robbery. By killing Julia Wallace, Qualtrough not only removed any possible interference to his task of robbery, but he also eliminated a possible witness.

Thus the argument propounded in defence of Wallace, that Qualtrough killed Julia Wallace during a robbery which went wrong, cannot be sustained. The evidence from the murder scene does not allow such an interpretation. Qualtrough murdered her as soon as he entered the house, before attempting the robbery.[5]

4

Julia Wallace was a frail, elderly lady: the fact that Qualtrough resorted to killing her without provocation, rather than restraining her so that he could rob the house unhindered, strongly suggests they were acquainted, and that he had to eliminate her as a witness against himself.

This perspective receives supports from the fact that Julia, according to William Wallace, would not admit a stranger to the house; it is also supported by the supposition that Qualtrough's plan was predicated upon his knowing something about William Wallace, and, by association, his wife.[6]

According to Professor Canter, entering a person's home to steal is a determined criminal act: the perpetrator must be prepared to deal with anyone encountered,[7] and to enter, with the aim of killing without provocation, rather than restraining the occupant, simply as a means to a criminal end, demonstrates a callous, cold-blooded, indifference to human life. Qualtrough sought to control the situation as soon as he entered 29 Wolverton Street, and he did so by murder. Julia Wallace trusted him, not only by inviting him into her home, at night, despite her nervous disposition, but also by turning her back on him to light the fire. But he regarded her, not as a human being, with whom to empathise and communicate, but simply as an obstacle to the smooth running culmination of his design.

Qualtrough's behaviour at the crime scene would indicate that he was an older, intelligent, organised criminal,[8] in all probability highly experienced, a careful planner, intent, to the point of murder, to reduce all risks to himself in successfully accomplishing his task and evading discovery and arrest; a man who was at the very least acquainted with the Wallaces.

<h1 style="text-align:center">5</h1>

As far as the police were able to ascertain, Julia's killer left behind no traces or clues to his identity: there were no fingerprints, no hairs, no fibres, no bloody palm prints or footsteps and no murder weapon. Qualtrough's post-offence behaviour, therefore, would strongly suggest that he was forensically aware.[9] He knew the value of such traces to the police, and sought to remove any possible links between himself and his victim.

This would again suggest that Julia's killer was an older, experienced criminal, possibly with a criminal record, and that he had learned from experience, during years of criminal activity, to avoid leaving behind forensic traces.

Professor MacFall described the attack as frenzied,[10] as if Julia's murderer was determined not only to kill her, but to obliterate her. This is at odds with the profile of Qualtrough as a hardened, forensically aware criminal: a quick, clinical dispatching of Mrs Wallace would have been expected from such a man, rather than the prolonged and bloody assault which took place; the more blood spilt, the greater the chances of Qualtrough contaminating himself and tying himself to the murder scene. Indeed, knowing Mrs Wallace to be a frail, elderly lady, some bloodless means of killing her, such as strangulation, would have been expected.

There was nothing sexual about the attack, no indications that Qualtrough sexually interfered with her or attempted to enact some form of sexual fantasy or fetish with her, or her body. But there was a great deal of anger, a great deal of savagery. Having struck the fatal blow to her head, Qualtrough had no need to hit her again; but he continued to strike her, not through necessity, but because he wanted to.

The very nature of the assault suggests an emotional aspect to the murder: that Julia Wallace and her killer were well known to one another, rather than simply being acquainted; that the rage and anger directed against her by her killer arose from a shared personal relationship; that Qualtrough was punishing her in some way.

There is a strong element of overkill, of excessive, emotional force. This was not murder as the result of a robbery gone wrong, when panic had set in and the thief resorted to excessive, deadly violence to ensure his escape. This was a carefully planned, premeditated murder, and the overkill used, the frenzied bludgeoning, and the raging, emotive force behind it, suggests a strong personal relationship between victim and killer. And, as Professor Canter has noted, the more emotional a murder, the closer to home it is, indicating some form of relationship between killer and victim.[11]

Police statistics confirm that the majority of murders happen within an established relationship rather than between strangers, and that they usually occur at home. One of the main characteristics of such murders, 'domestics' as the police call them, is that the killer attacks the victim about the face and head, seeking to depersonalise the victim.[12] The killer vents his anger, or frustration, or hatred, upon these most familiar features, attempting to destroy them, to expunge them and the victim from his memory and life. In punishing his victim he is making a statement about his feelings towards her. The parallel with Julia Wallace's murder is obvious. The frenzy and ferocity of the attack, the repeated beating on her head, would strongly indicate a very close personal relationship between Julia Wallace and her killer.[13]

Thus, the murder bears not only the marks of an experienced, careful criminal, but also the characteristics of a domestic murder, with strong emotional and personal ties between killer and victim.

6

Did Julia Wallace form a strong personal relationship with someone outside her marriage? Did that someone, desperate for money, resort to murder once he had found out from her that her husband kept large sums of money in the house?

The possibility that an affair between Julia and her killer did exist was given life by the investigations of Jonathan Goodman. Having tracked down Richard Gordon Parry to London in 1966, he reported that Parry claimed he had often called at the Wallace home in the afternoons when William was at work for 'musical interludes' with Julia, with the implication that something more salacious than music was involved. Julia, perhaps trapped in a loveless marriage, may have been flattered by the attention of a very young man, and may have been led into indiscretion.[14] Parry was the man whom Goodman believed had committed the murder.

However, Julia was almost seventy years of age and it is improbable that she was having an extra-marital relationship with Parry, or with anyone else. She was a shy and retiring woman who kept very much to herself and rarely left the confines of her home; she had few friends beyond her family and immediate neighbours and there was never a hint from either group, particularly from the neighbours, who would have been the first to know and only too willing to tell, that she was involved with another man. The structure and tempo of her whole way of life outside her marriage indicates that she was not involved in any relationship, social or otherwise, which could have put her at risk of murder.

If Julia was not involved with another man, then the only man with whom she could have had a close personal relationship was her husband. If she did not invite Qualtrough into her home, then he was already inside her home. That is, William Wallace was RM Qualtrough.

Wallace would fit the profile regarding the emotional aspect to the killing. But what of the other aspects of the profile; the careful, intelligent criminal? Could they fit William Wallace?

<h1 style="text-align:center">7</h1>

Qualtrough's withdrawal from the Wallace house, his post-offence behaviour, was orderly and organised. He ensured that he did not trail any of his victim's blood beyond the murder room, or leave behind bloody footprints or fingerprints, which, considering how cramped and confined the front parlour was and the spread of blood therein, must have required very careful attention on his part. The cash-box, which he had taken down from the top of the seven-foot high shelf, and which he had looted, was carefully returned to its original place. The gas fire and lamps in the parlour and the downstairs house lights were all turned off as he made his exit. There were no signs of panic on his part as he left the house, or any indication that he was disturbed as he went about his deadly business and fled the scene under fear of discovery. It would appear from the evidence at 29 Wolverton Street, that Qualtrough left the murder scene carrying the murder weapon, when he was ready to go, at a time of his own choosing.

Thus, between the murder, committed within minutes of entering the house, and his unhurried exit, Qualtrough perpetrated his robbery. Since his exit was cautious, careful and unhurried, it must follow that the robbery, supposedly the prime motive for his assault upon the Wallace household, was also unhurried and careful, and that he took as much time over the robbery as he did with his exit.

It is difficult to imagine a scenario in which, having killed Julia Wallace and having carefully removed all traces of himself from the parlour, Qualtrough then hurried carelessly through his main task, the robbery, only to slow to a crawl to ensure his exit from the crime scene was circumspect. Yet the evidence at the robbery scene indicates precisely this: Qualtrough did indeed hurry the robbery.

His total haul from the theft was a paltry four pounds in hard cash, scooped from the cash-box which he took down from the top of the seven-foot high shelf in the kitchen, neither the most likely place a thief would look for cash, nor the most ascertainable and accessible, and suggesting that Qualtrough knew where it lay. He did not even bother to gather up the seven shillings and few pence which fell from the box and which he left lying on the kitchen floor. Yet he did replace the cash-box in its original position.

A woman is never far from her handbag, and yet he overlooked the bag lying on one of the kitchen chairs, which suggests he did not search the kitchen, but simply made for the cash-box. No self-respecting thief would overlook such a potential source of money. Julia was wearing a brooch and her wedding ring when she was murdered: Qualtrough ignored both items.

In the front bedroom the chest of drawers held Julia's jewellery and in the wardrobe hung her fur coat: there were no indications that Qualtrough searched either for money or valuables. There were signs in the front bedroom that someone had disturbed the bedclothes and scattered some of Julia's hats. But an experienced thief would not waste time rummaging through bedclothes and hats for valuables, so it is unlikely that Qualtrough untidied the bed, or scattered the hats. In all probability he never entered that room and the disorder therein was made by Julia.

In the middle bedroom, in the jar on the mantelpiece, Wallace had placed four pounds, which Qualtrough left untouched. It would appear that he did not venture into that room in search of money or valuables, either. Nor did he venture into the back bedroom, Wallace's laboratory.

Of course, Qualtrough may have been intent only on stealing Wallace's insurance takings, and could have ignored other items of value in the house: fur coats and jewellery are traceable, money is not. But if that was indeed his intent, then he failed miserably.

Qualtrough's robbery would seem to have been of the smash and grab variety: quickly grab the cash-box, smash it open, scoop up the pound notes and ignore the loose change, without searching anywhere else in the house for the pile of cash which Wallace was supposed to have had. No experienced criminal, having murdered so that he could steal without interference, would look in only one place for the expected cash; having not found it in the first place, he would certainly look for it in other places. But the evidence suggests that Qualtrough only searched the cash-box and ignored the rest of the house.

This smash and grab robbery, hardly the work of an experienced and intelligent thief, speaks of a hurried, careless, and disorganised approach, of panic almost, which is at odds with the cautious and controlled entrance and exit from the house suggested by the evidence. It is certainly not in keeping with the notion that robbery was the main motive for the assault on the household: more time would appear to have been spent on the murder and the controlled exit, than on the actual robbery itself. Qualtrough would seem to have shown very little interest in the theft of Wallace's money.[15] He was a better murderer than he was a thief.

Further, Qualtrough, knowing the source of Wallace's cash, would have surely taken the time and trouble to observe that he was out on the streets of Clubmoor collecting the money from his customers, money he was willing to risk his neck to steal. As it was, the weekend before Qualtrough's assault, Wallace was ill and stayed at home, and so his takings were down. To have risked the rope by killing Julia Wallace as part of a robbery plan, and to have not known whether or not the money was in the house, would be very difficult to reconcile with an experienced, intelligent thief:

> *A hardened thief, intent on murder as part of the course of a burglary, would choose a victim where there was more likelihood of monetary gain.*[16]

Professor Canter points out the fact that money left at the scenes of crimes plainly indicates that robbery is not a significant motive in those crimes.[17] Not only was money left at 29 Wolverton Street, but those places where money and valuables were usually kept were ignored. The evidence at the crime scene would suggest that robbery was not a significant motive in this crime.

On his weekly collection round, Wallace gathered, in pennies and tuppences, thruppences and sixpences, premiums for life insurance and national, or work insurance and his haul would be approximately thirty to forty pounds each week, which he paid into head office every Wednesday or Thursday. However, every fourth week, there were additional premiums to collect, for endowment policies and investment bonds, and this monthly collection, as it was called, swelled the usual weekly monies to approximately one hundred pounds, which again was paid over to head office on Wednesdays or Thursdays.

Wallace had completed a monthly collection the week before, and on Tuesday 13 January he had approximately one hundred pounds garnered in his home. It is not as if the timing of the monthly collection was a secret: thousands of Prudential customers all over Liverpool knew when it was to be made.

Had Qualtrough been Richard Parry, who had worked on Wallace's collection round, and who had implied that he had formed a close relationship with Julia Wallace, then knowing he was going to kill her, it would have made more sense for him to have maximised his haul from the theft by striking a week earlier, on the 13 January, when Wallace had approximately one hundred pounds in the house.

Similarly, if Qualtrough was not Parry, but someone who had only a working knowledge of the Wallaces, then with the timing of the monthly collection round being commonly known, again it would have made more sense for this man to have struck a week earlier. That is, if robbery was the main motive for the assault upon the household.

How much simpler, how much more lucrative it would have been, for Qualtrough to have slipped a note to Wallace through his front door on Monday 12 January, asking him to call at 25 Menlove Gardens East the following night.

That Qualtrough chose Wallace's putative attendance at the chess club, rather than the night when he could maximise his gain, as the starting point for his plan, again testifies to the fact that robbery was not a significant motive in the crime.

In *Mindhunter*, Jack Douglas documents some of his investigations in which he has uncovered the artifice of staging, the doctoring of a crime scene by a perpetrator in order to deflect the blame onto someone else; or manipulating it to look like something other than what it actually was.[18] Douglas quotes instances of rapes and murders masquerading as burglaries, the perpetrators trying to make out that burglary was the main intent, and that the rape was incidental, opportunistic, an afterthought; or that the murder was an unfortunate consequence of the burglary, which had gone wrong.

The evidence at the crime scene clearly implied that Qualtrough knew Julia Wallace, that there was some emotional attachment between them. Most murders occur within an established relationship.[19]

The key to many murders of and by loved ones or family members, is staging. Anyone that close to the victim has to do something to draw suspicion away from himself, or herself.[20]

One of the most notorious and recent incidents of a staged murder was the deaths of Mr and Mrs Bamber, their adopted daughter, Sheila, and her twin sons, Nicholas and Daniel, at the hands of the Bambers' adopted son, Jeremy. He staged the crime scene to appear as if Sheila had gone berserk with a rifle and slain the entire household before turning the gun on herself. Jeremy Bamber was uncovered as the murderer and was sentenced to life imprisonment with the recommendation that he serve a minimum of twenty-five years.[21]

There can be little doubt that the robbery at 29 Wolverton Street was staged. And if the theft of Wallace's cash is removed from the equation, eliminated as the motive for the assault upon the household, then the only reason for Qualtrough's assault must have been murder. Cui bono? Who benefits from the death of Julia Wallace? Who would want to see her dead? Who would kill her and stage the murder as a bungled robbery? The answer to all these questions can only be: William Herbert Wallace.

Jonathan Goodman, in his defence of Wallace, knowing that once the robbery is recognised and accepted as staging, argues that if Wallace did stage the robbery, then why did he not make a better job of it?[22] The question he should have asked, of course, was, if Qualtrough was a thief, then why did he not make a better job of robbing the house?

But, as Douglas has pointed out, where there is staging of a crime scene following the murder of a loved one by a partner, it is usually amateurish, inept and disorganised, and easily detectable by the police: the killer has had no previous experience of staging a crime scene, and more than likely would not know, as in this case, what a successful, or partially successful, house robbery would look like.[23] Wallace, like so many killers before and after him, staged his murder to look like a bungled robbery; but his inexperience found him out. The organised killing should have been followed by an organised and systematic robbery.[24]

Wallace was an intelligent man. His job with the Prudential was not very demanding, and he exercised his mind with chess, with readings in philosophy and science and he kept abreast of the times through the radio and the newspaper. He was organised and careful and he tended to plan ahead. Like many of his contemporaries, he closely followed the more sensational murder cases of the day, both in the newspapers and in such periodicals as the *Police Gazette*. He even made a note in his diary, the entry for 27 April 1928, about the infamous PC Gutteridge case.[25]

As an intelligent, well-read man, and in particular through his work and studies in chemistry, Wallace was, in all probability, forensically aware, and knew of the basic intricacies of police and forensic investigations, such as fingerprinting and bloodstaining, and would have known what was necessary to forestall and thwart those investigations.

There are indications from people who knew the Wallaces, that there was an estrangement, a coldness, an indifference, between them from time to time, particularly as witnessed by the family practitioner, Dr Curwen, and that Wallace had a tendency to be very condescending and aloof towards his wife, treating her as the little woman whose only raison d'être was to serve him and to see him comfortable.[26] There is evidence from his diary entries that he became exasperated with her over her many illnesses, and also when she could not grasp fundamental relationships in philosophy and social theory.

It is in his coldness, condescension and intelligence, as the calculating chess player, plotting, anticipating and executing moves, that Wallace can be placed within the confines of the profile as a callous and clever killer. And, as the following chapter will show, the Qualtrough plan was littered with doubts and uncertainties, all of which can be resolved if the plan is seen as a devious ploy behind which Wallace could hide in order to murder his wife.

The police were quite correct to bring up Wallace on a charge of murder. The evidence from the front parlour clearly indicated that Qualtrough murdered Julia Wallace before he attempted to rob her, so that she did not die as a result of a robbery gone wrong and the robbery was clearly staged. Only William Wallace would stage a robbery to make it look as if his wife died during its commission.

Where the police failed and allowed him to escape scot-free, was in the presentation of their case during the trial. The evidence from the crime scene and its full implications was not fully detailed and explicated by prosecuting counsel. Nor was the Qualtrough plan critically examined. And it is in the examination of the plan that the manipulative, murderous hand of William Wallace can be detected.

Chapter 11

The Qualtrough Plan

1

Jonathan Goodman describes RM Qualtrough as one of the most fastidious planners in the history of crime, and James Agate ascribes to him the status of genius.[1] Nowhere in the Wallace literature is there an analysis of the Qualtrough plan, to see if it was, in fact, a feasible plan which should merit the accolade of being fastidiously prepared. It is assumed, particularly by defenders of William Wallace, that because the plan did work, that Qualtrough did gain access to the Wallace home to rob and kill and escape unpunished, that it must have been a good plan, the work of a genius.

All good plans are simple: the fewer the complications, the greater the chances of success. At first glance the Qualtrough plan would appear to be very simple and straightforward: to gain access to Wallace's home in his absence. However, the analysis will show that, far from being simple, it was in fact unnecessarily complex and complicated, that it was not feasible, that no intelligent criminal would have even contemplated it. The inevitable conclusion is that it was a devious ploy, behind which William Wallace hid in order to murder his wife.

Qualtrough initiated his plan with a telephone call to Wallace's chess club on the Monday night, purporting to offer him the prospect of business concerning his daughter's twenty-first birthday. The following night, he waited in the vicinity of the Wallace home to see whether he responded to his lure, and then moved in once he saw him leave home.

The underlying assumptions which inform the plan must be that Qualtrough knew that Wallace was a chess player and where he played his chess and also that he was an insurance agent. His choice of the Wallaces as victims was probably based upon the equation; insurance agent equals money and the fact that, with Wallace out of the house, only Mrs Wallace, a frail, elderly woman, stood between him and the money. Therefore, Qualtrough could have known of Wallace as a friend or acquaintance, or as business colleague; at the very least, he and Wallace may have been strangers, but he must have learnt so much secondhand about him as to be aware of his chess playing, his occupation, and his domestic situation.

The plan was never to be repeated, based on a first time success. In the event of Wallace not responding to his message, he could not keep calling him at the chess club about some business for what would have become his daughter's never-ending birthday. Nor could he repeatedly loiter outside his home, waiting for his response, without arousing some suspicion: among other things, the Richmond Park area was under police scrutiny because of the activities of the elusive Anfield Housebreaker, and its inhabitants were alert to the presence of strangers.

As noted in the previous chapter, Wallace collected in two types of premium payments; weekly and four weekly. The weekly collection garnered approximately thirty pounds, but every fourth week, that sum swelled to around one hundred pounds.

Qualtrough's plan was predicated upon Wallace's putative appearance at his chess club, rather than upon the amount of money he could realise from striking a week earlier. What is more, he chose a method of initiating his plan, a telephone call to Wallace's chess club, which was to complicate matters for him.

Wallace told the police that he decided to go to the chess club on the spur of the moment: Julia had been ill over the weekend and he was loath to leave her alone at night, particularly when she was ill. But on the Monday, Julia's condition had improved somewhat, so, in the early evening, he decided to make a long overdue visit to the club, a decision he communicated to no one except Julia.

How could Qualtrough have known that Wallace would be at the club on Monday night to receive his message if Wallace himself did not decide until the last minute that he would go? It was impossible for Qualtrough to have known in advance of his appearance at the club, and to have planned to relay his message to him there.

During the trial, defence counsel, Robert Oliver KC, calling upon hindsight, argued that Qualtrough must have known that Wallace would be at the club, simply by examining the chess club noticeboard. On the board were displayed details of the club's second class championship tournament, listing the names of those eligible to compete and the dates upon which they were to play their championship games. The list had been on display for three months prior to the murder, and anyone entering Cottle's City Café, either to eat during the day, or to play chess at night, had access to the list. Wallace's name was on the list and he was due to play against Mr FC Chandler on the night of Monday 19 January.

Thus, the argument runs, because Wallace was due to play a game on the Monday night, Qualtrough knew that he was to attend the club. During Wallace's appeal, Roland Oliver reiterated this argument to the appeal judges who, in their summing up, concurred with him that Qualtrough knew that Wallace would attend the chess club.[2] However, the best that could be said was that Wallace was expected at the club to play a game against FC Chandler. But expectation is not knowledge.

Had Qualtrough, or anyone else, then or now, perused the list, he would have discovered that Wallace had also been expected at the club on Monday 5 January to play Mr J Walsh, on Monday 8 December to play Mr T Moore and on Monday 24 November to play Mr McCartney. But, according to the list, he had failed to attend on all three occasions.[3] Had Qualtrough studied the list, he could be forgiven for concluding that the chance of Wallace attending the club on 19 January was negligible.

In addition, Oliver again argued, with hindsight, that to confirm that Wallace was going to attend the club, Qualtrough hid himself close to 29 Wolverton Street on the Monday night and when he saw him leaving home, at approximately seven fifteen, correctly assumed that he was going to the club.

Qualtrough's telephone call to the chess club was timed at seven-fifteen. Wallace said he left home at approximately seven fifteen. This would have given Qualtrough barely enough time to see him leave home before he had to make his way in the opposite direction to the telephone kiosk, a journey of four minutes at a brisk pace. He would have had no time in which to follow Wallace in order to ensure that he boarded a tramcar to the city centre and the chess club.[4]

Knowing of Wallace's poor attendance at the club from the tournament list, why would he assume that he was headed there? Why not assume he was going on a local errand, or calling on a customer, or posting a letter? As it was, Wallace did post a letter on his way to the tram stop that night.

Further, when Qualtrough made the telephone call he must have known that Wallace, if he intended going to the club, would be in transit to the club, and that he would not speak directly to him but would have to relay his message through a third person, which turned out to be the club captain, Samuel Beattie.

When he telephoned, Beattie said that he did not know whether Wallace would attend the club that night.

"Is Mr Wallace there?" asked Qualtrough. "Will he be there?"

"I can't say," replied Beattie.

"Can you give me his address?"

"I'm afraid I cannot."

"Will you be sure to see him?"

"I don't know," said Beattie.

"Can you get in touch with him, as it is a matter of importance to Wallace?"

"I'm not sure."

Qualtrough had to be satisfied with leaving his message with a third party to pass on to Wallace, *if* he attended. Can this be said to be the opening gambit of a fastidiously laid plan involving murder?

Even if Qualtrough, following the telephone call, had gone to the chess club and waited outside to see Wallace emerge just after ten o'clock, he would still not know whether he had received the message. Having received the message, Beattie, busy officiating as captain and playing chess, might have forgotten to pass it on; or he may have taken it down incorrectly and passed on a garbled version of it to Wallace. Qualtrough could not very well ask departing members of the chess club whether Beattie had passed on the message to Wallace, or what the message was, without implicating himself.

On the telephone Beattie told Qualtrough that if Wallace did not attend the club, then he might possibly be able to help.

"If I can't get Mr Wallace himself I can possibly get in touch with him through a friend," volunteered Beattie.

Beattie did not name the friend, in all likelihood James Caird, who lived near to Wallace. But it was only a possibility: Caird was a first class player and was not taking part in the second class championship with Wallace, and so he was not expected at the club that night.

What if Wallace had not attended that night and Qualtrough had observed this as he waited outside? He would assume that his message was going to be passed on by Beattie to the friend, Caird. Beattie might, or might not, have passed the message on to Caird. But how would Qualtrough know that? Even if Beattie had passed on the message to Caird, how would he know that it was the correct message? How would he ascertain that Caird, in turn, would pass it on, and pass it on correctly, to Wallace?

The point is that Qualtrough had to know, to know with certainty, that he had received his message. If he did not receive it, or if Beattie had so garbled it as to make it incomprehensible, directly or through the friend, then Qualtrough's plan was stillborn: Wallace could not respond, or respond in the way he wanted, to the message on Tuesday night.

What contingencies did Qualtrough have in place to cover Beattie forgetting to pass on the message to Wallace, or to Caird, or passing it on to Wallace, or to Caird, in a garbled form, or Caird not passing it on, or passing it on incorrectly? All these possibilities existed, and they did so because of the means which Qualtrough had employed to put his plan in motion: a telephone call. Hindsight cannot be employed here: what contingencies Qualtrough had in place must be considered from his perspective, as he saw events unfold at the time.

What was he to do? His plan was to culminate the following night: he had not left himself much time in which to employ a contingency. Did he press Beattie over the telephone for more information about Wallace and the friend, or try to recruit him for additional assistance to ensure that his message would get through to Wallace? No, he did not. Without exploring any other possibilities, without even a thought for some other avenue of approach, Qualtrough tamely resigned himself to accepting Beattie's offer of possibly passing the message on to Wallace through a friend, *if* Wallace did not attend the club. He gave Beattie his name and address and hung up. So much for fastidious planning!

There were no possible benefits to accrue to Qualtrough through his use of the telephone call to the chess club. On the contrary, his chosen method complicated matters to such an extent that he could not be sure that Wallace had, in fact, received his message. In addition, as was shown in the last chapter, choosing the week for Wallace's expected appearance at the chess club as his starting point, rather than the time of the monthly collection, he effectively reduced his take from the robbery.

Perhaps the most remarkable aspect of the telephone call was a question from Qualtrough: "Can you give me his address?" Beattie said he could not give it to him. Qualtrough obviously knew where Wallace lived: he was going to attack his home the following night. Why ask for the address?

What if Beattie had said yes, he could give it to him. Having obtained Wallace's address, what possible justification could Qualtrough have then had for asking Beattie to pass on his message? What more could Beattie do for him? Having given the address, Beattie might have simply hung up on him without further ado. What would have happened to Qualtrough's plan then?

Asking for Wallace's address was stupid: it could have compromised the plan at its inception. However, it was not a stupid question if Qualtrough knew that Beattie did not know the address. Wallace knew that Beattie did not know his address.

What better way to pass on his message to Wallace than a simple note pushed through his front door? Qualtrough could have explained himself fully in a note, besides giving him his name and address, he would have been certain that he had received the message and he could have posted the note the previous week, to coincide with the monthly collection. A note through the door would have obviated all the difficulties that developed and ensued with the telephone call.

However, if Wallace was Qualtrough, then the benefits of the telephone call are obvious: he received the message with all his friends about him. They were enjoined to participate in the debate on the location of Menlove Gardens East; they heard Qualtrough's strange name repeated several times, so that it was lodged in their memories. Thus, Wallace had many witnesses to Qualtrough's attempt to contact him, which he would not have had to a note pushed through his door. A note through the door would have been highly suspect; a telephoned message not so.[5]

By the end of his telephone conversation with Beattie, Qualtrough did not know whether or not his plan was up and running. What is more, he still had a second hurdle to jump: if Wallace did receive the message, would he respond to it the following night?

2

On Tuesday night, the only way Qualtrough could tell that his plan was moving forward was to watch the house to see if Wallace responded to his message by leaving home. There were any number of reasons why he might fail to do so: it was too short notice, he was too tired, he was ill, he did not know the area, he had a previous appointment, he had passed the information to the Prudential man in the Menlove Avenue area, he could not be bothered, Julia was ill, it was too cold, it was not worth his while, it was too far to travel.

Qualtrough would not have had to have been a man of high intelligence to realise and appreciate that any one of these potential reasons and many others, too, could prevent Wallace from responding. After all, he had not given him a great deal of time in which to consider his proposition; to rearrange a previous engagement for example. It was all very short notice.

But, getting Wallace out of the house on Tuesday night was central to the success of the plan. Therefore, to guarantee his response, it was incumbent upon Qualtrough to couch his proposal in such terms that he would find them so irresistible, so financially rewarding, that no reason on earth would prevent him from seeking out Mr RM Qualtrough. After all, Qualtrough could afford to be very generous with his offer: it was bogus.

"He wants you to call on him tomorrow evening at seven-thirty. He says it's something in the nature of your business, to do with his daughter's twenty-first."

This was how Qualtrough's message was passed on to Wallace by Beattie. The key phrases being, "nature of your business" and, "twenty-first". But neither phrase contains any great embellishment, no promises of riches to entice the grubbing insurance collector, nothing to guarantee a response.

However, the correlation of the two phrases might have meant a great deal to Wallace in terms of finance, which was not apparent to someone outside the world of insurance. But, whatever it was, he was so unimpressed by it as to tell Caird on his way home from the club that he, "might not go" to see Mr Qualtrough.

Dorothy L Sayers argues that the business proposition could have been an endowment policy which could have been worth as much as one hundred pounds per annum, with a commission of five pounds per annum to Wallace.[6] Sayers does not quote a source for her figures; equally, the business could have been worth fifty pounds per annum, or ten pounds, or even less. There was no hint in the message about the type of policy which Qualtrough was interested in, its value, or how much in commission, or bonus, its purchase would bring Wallace.

What should have been a detailed offer involving hard cash, an offer which Wallace could not have refused, an offer designed to ensure his full co-operation and the success of the plan, came across as a desultory, lackadaisical and indifferent request, which, quite reasonably, failed to impress him.

That Wallace did respond to Qualtrough's casual offer, having told his friend that he might not, and then to have sought out the elusive Mr Qualtrough the following evening with the tenacity of a bulldog, with no idea of the financial recompense, says a great deal more about William Herbert Wallace, and a lot less about the fastidious scheming of Mr RM Qualtrough.

On Tuesday evening, Qualtrough did not know with any certainty whether Wallace had received his message and he could not know whether he would take the meagre bait and leave home in search of the non-existent Menlove Gardens East. Therefore, he had to watch and wait in the immediate vicinity of the Wallace home, in order to see him leave, before he could attempt entry into the house. And this scenario, of Qualtrough watching the Wallace house on the Tuesday night, gives rise to several points of interest.

Before he could observe Wallace leaving the house, he had to ascertain that he was already at home in the first place. He might have decided, for example, to go straight to Menlove Gardens East from his afternoon collection round without going home, something which could not possibly have been foreseen, in which case Qualtrough would spend several fruitless hours, his scheme a failure, watching and waiting for Wallace to emerge from his home, when he was actually already in the Menlove Avenue area.

Therefore, Qualtrough had to be in the immediate vicinity of the house, not only to watch him leave for Menlove Gardens, but also to witness his return home from his afternoon collection round at six o'clock. Only when he had ascertained that Wallace was at home, could he then watch and wait from the shadows for him to leave. And, as matters unfolded, Qualtrough would have had to wait a minimum of forty-five minutes, from at least six o'clock when Wallace said he returned home from his round, until a quarter to seven when he claimed that he finally departed for Menlove Gardens.

During that forty-five minutes, the Richmond Park area was alive with young people skittering back and forth making milk, bread and newspaper deliveries. Men and women were walking the streets and alleyways and policemen were on patrol. And yet, on Tuesday 20 January, tucked away for at least forty-five minutes in his dark vantage point, RM Qualtrough went unobserved by this stream of humanity. Nobody – not a child, not an adult – came forward to the police during their door-to-door inquiries to report that they had noticed anyone in the vicinity of the Wallace home between six and seven o'clock on that Tuesday night. Qualtrough must have been very well hidden to have avoided detection.

The night was cold and moonless and the streets and alleyways of Richmond Park were as black as pitch, according to James Wildman.[7] The street lighting was gas, and the lamps cast a meagre umbra of light, no more than two or three feet in diameter. Only if a person was standing immediately beneath a street lamp could he be seen and pedestrians, a few feet apart, could pass unaware of one another. So it is possible that Qualtrough could have remained hidden from view while all the street activity was in progress.

However, he could not have predicted which route Wallace would choose to take: two routes were suggested to him on the Monday night by James Caird and McCartney; Wallace added a third. And there was at least one further route to the Menlove Avenue area, giving him a total of four from which to choose.[8]

In addition, Qualtrough could not have foreseen whether Wallace would leave home by the front or back door: he would have to keep both exits under observation at the same time, which was possible. But he could not keep both doors under simultaneous observation and anticipate which way Wallace would turn, upon exiting the house. Turning to the left or the right depended upon which of the four routes he had chosen to take.

Qualtrough could have positioned himself at a point where he could observe Wallace if he turned left out of the back door, or right out of the front door and that would mean that he was heading for Menlove Gardens, either on the route he did actually use, or on the Wavertree Road route. But what of the two other routes?

He could have stationed himself in such a position that he could cover Wallace turning right out of the back door, or left out of the front door, thereby anticipating his using the other two possible routes, Spellow Lane and Queen's Drive.

Positioned in Richmond Park, Qualtrough could cover three of the possible routes, but not the Queen's Drive route. But then, skulking in the open in Richmond Park itself, the main thoroughfare, would have exposed him to even more chances of being observed by the suspicious inhabitants of the area.

Qualtrough could not possibly cover all contingencies: he could not be in two places at the same time. The first two possible positions are both approximately twenty yards away from Wallace's back door, whilst the Richmond Park position is approximately sixty-five yards away. In addition, he could not afford to get in too close to the house in case he inadvertently bumped into Wallace in the dark. He would have to keep on the move, trying to cover all exits, all possible routes, whilst avoiding meeting Wallace and, at all times, trying to avoid any suspicion being attached to his movements by the locals – an impossible task.

There was no lighting in the alleyway and that in Wolverton Street was negligible. If Qualtrough did not anticipate correctly which of the four routes Wallace had chosen, which way he would turn when he exited his home, then there was a very good chance that he would miss him in the dark. And until he knew that he had left home, Qualtrough could not move in to begin his murderous assault. If he missed seeing Wallace leave, then he would wait in vain, his plan stillborn.

Qualtrough, on that dark and gloomy Tuesday night, could not have afforded to hide himself away, to be too discreet while observing the Wallace home, for fear of missing Wallace when he left. In order to cover all contingencies, all combinations of front and back doors, together with the four possible routes to Menlove Gardens East, he would have been forced to keep on the move, out in the open, risking exposure and detection and possibly being remembered by a passer-by and later being linked to the murder.

Was it possible that, for almost an hour, Qualtrough could lurk unnoticed in an area which was suffering the depredations of the 'Anfield Housebreaker', that he could go unchallenged by the suspicious and inquisitive men, women and children of the district, in addition to the police? But Qualtrough was not seen near the Wallace home on the night of the murder. That does not mean that he was not there. But it does suggest that it was highly unlikely that he was. And if he was not there, then how did he know that Wallace had left home, and that it was safe to move into the house?

4

According to Wallace, he left home at six-forty-five on Tuesday night. If Qualtrough had seen him leave, how did he know where Wallace was going? After all, he did not know for certain that he had received his message and so he could not know that when Wallace left home on Tuesday night, he was in fact was responding to it. And yet Qualtrough moved into the house after Wallace had left with assurance and determination and murdered Julia Wallace.

When Wallace left home on Tuesday night, for all Qualtrough knew, he might have been going out on a local errand, say, to post a letter, as he had done on the Monday night, or to call on a friend, or to make a telephone call. How could Qualtrough know for certain whether it was safe to move in? And, by not ascertaining that Wallace was on his way to Menlove Gardens, having begun his assault on the household, he risked him returning unexpectedly and catching him red-handed.

When Qualtrough sent his message to the chess club, he placed himself at risk of being picked up by the police investigating the activities of the 'Anfield Housebreaker'. Wallace might well have checked out the details of the message on Tuesday morning and found that the address was bogus. He could have done this with a street directory, by checking with his superintendent, Joseph Crewe, or through his head office in Dale Street. Aware that there was a successful burglar on the prowl, Wallace's suspicions might have been aroused sufficiently for him to have contacted the police. And they might well have tried to capture Qualtrough, suspecting him of being the 'Anfield Housebreaker'. When Wallace left 29 Wolverton Street to go to Menlove Gardens East, he might have left behind him a posse of policemen, waiting to arrest Qualtrough as he entered the house. There was always that possibility to impinge upon Qualtrough's scheme, because of the activities of the elusive burglar.

5

With Wallace out on a wild goose chase, Qualtrough gained entrance to 29 Wolverton Street, fully aware that he had to deal with Mrs Wallace. What did he have in mind once he was inside the house?

If he knew, or thought he knew, where the money was kept, had he planned to divert her attention, steal the money, and leave? If he and Mrs Wallace knew one another, then once the theft was uncovered, she could point the finger directly at him. Even if they did not know one another, she would still be able to identify him, and bear witness against him.

If he did not know where the money was kept, had he planned to coerce her into revealing where it was? She might have resisted, called out, fought with him. And if he had succeeded in taking the money under force, she would have been a witness against him.

Whatever the plot, unless Qualtrough killed Julia, she would be a witness against him, particularly if they knew one another. To avoid being identified as the thief, he had to kill her. And this conclusion is amply supported by the evidence from the crime scene.

6

Any intelligent criminal, as Professor Canter points out, when planning such an enterprise, and particularly when murder is an integral part of the scheme, does so on the basis of minimising the risks of detection and arrest. Criminals build into their plans what he calls 'risk-reducing strategies'.[9] But Qualtrough's plan was compromised in this respect: he had to stake out the Wallace house on the Tuesday night and placed himself in danger of being seen, and being recognised later and tied to the murder, and he was operating in an area already under police scrutiny.

The profile of Qualtrough as the intelligent, forensically-aware killer, is at odds with the picture of Qualtrough the planner, on watch outside the Wallace home, neglecting, or ignoring, risk-reducing strategies prior to entering 29 Wolverton Street. Being forensically-aware would not have been of much use to him had he been seen skulking for some time in the immediate vicinity of the Wallace house, and later identified; or if he had aroused the suspicions of the police, who might have kept him under observation, and nabbed him as he exited the house.

The Qualtrough plan was not a feasible plan: it was not simple, or fastidiously worked out; it was not the work of a criminal genius. It was complicated, it was compromised and, intrinsically, it did not possess the means to ensure success.

The criminal personality profile of the killer of Julia Wallace, derived from an analysis of the crime scene, can point the finger of suspicion at William Wallace. There can be little doubt that the evidence testifies to a contrived robbery, to the fact that Mrs Wallace was killed before any robbery commenced. Murder, not robbery, was the main motive for the attack on the Wallace home. The only person who could have contemplated and benefited from staging a robbery to hide a murder is William Wallace. When these conclusions are set alongside the analysis of the Qualtrough plan, a plan riven with unnecessary difficulties, uncertainties and potential dangers, that succeeded not through planning, but with the questionable co-operation of William Wallace, then the case against him is secure.

However, Jonathan Goodman has conclusively proved that William Wallace did not kill Julia Wallace.[10] Before continuing with the indictment against Wallace it is necessary, therefore, to critically examine Goodman's case for Wallace's innocence.

Chapter 12
Was Wallace Innocent?

1

In *The Killing of Julia Wallace* Jonathan Goodman states the case for Wallace's innocence. He produces what he considers to be one conclusive proof of his innocence and several reasonable arguments, which, taken as a whole, clearly demonstrate that he was not guilty.

Whoever killed Julia Wallace must have been at 29 Wolverton Street on the night of the murder and must have been in the telephone kiosk the night before to make the telephone call to the chess club. To successfully prosecute the charge of murder against any one person, that person has to be placed both inside the house and inside the telephone kiosk.

Jonathan Goodman has conclusively proved that Wallace was innocent by showing that he could not have been inside the telephone box on the Monday night. If Goodman's proof stands up to critical examination, then the case against Wallace must fail.

As the investigation progressed, the police became convinced that Wallace was her killer and they assumed that he must have made the Monday night call. It is this assumption that Goodman challenges and arrives at the conclusive proof that William Wallace was innocent.

Wallace stated that on the Monday night, after leaving home, he eventually boarded a tram at the junction of Breck Road and Belmont Road. This tram took him to North John Street, where he alighted and walked the short distance to the chess club, finally arriving just before seven-forty-five.

Both the police and the prosecution argued that Wallace's route was different, that in truth he walked in the opposite direction, not towards the junction of Breck Road and Belmont Road, but towards the junction of Breck Road and Rochester Road, where the telephone kiosk was situated. From there, it was alleged, he made the call before boarding a tramcar at the stop adjacent to the telephone box, arriving at the chess club at seven-forty-five.

Goodman quite rightly points out that:

So much emphasis was placed upon the importance of the time-factor on the night of the murder that it seems to have been forgotten that there was a time-factor on the Monday night as well. Clearly, the police did not attach any importance to it; there were no tram tests to establish how much time was needed to get from the telephone box to the City Café. At the trial it received only two brief mentions ... Yet the time-factor on the Monday evening was of paramount importance ... if Wallace had made that call he would not have been able to get to the City Café at the time he did.[1]

Therefore Wallace must be innocent: he cannot be placed in the telephone box on the Monday night.

Goodman says that there are two main times to be taken into consideration:

The time the Qualtrough telephone call ended and the time of Wallace's arrival at the City Café ... We know that it was 7.15 when the caller first tried ... to get through to the café; we know, too, that it was 7.20 before he succeeded. This time is definite ... Having got through, the caller had a short conversation with Gladys Harley, and asked if Mr Wallace was there ... After telling the caller (who will be referred to as Qualtrough from now on) to hold the line, the waitress put down the phone, walked through to the section of the café reserved for the chess-players, and spoke to Samuel Beattie, who listened to what she said, looked round the room, told her that Wallace was not there, and then agreed to speak to Qualtrough ... Beattie got up from the chess table and crossed to the phone ... His conversation with Qualtrough consisted of about two hundred words; then he told Qualtrough to wait a moment while he poked around in his pockets for a used envelope and a pencil; having found them, he wrote the name as it was spelt out for him, the address as it was dictated to him ... End of call.

Goodman then poses the question of how long the call took.

Even if everything was done in jig-time, which it was not, the call must have lasted at least four minutes. Say four. So the receiver was put down at 7.24 – and if the caller was Wallace, he then went rushing across to the tram-stop in Townsend Lane.

According to Goodman, there was a tram service of eight to nine minutes on the route connecting Townsend Lane with North John Street.

Therefore, if Wallace had left the call-box at 7.24 and been unlucky enough just to miss a tram, he would have had to wait until well after 7.30 before the next tram came along. But suppose fortune smiled upon him – that he crossed from the call-box to the tram-stop in a quarter of a minute and that he waited only three-quarters of a minute for a tram to take him to the City Café. A minute altogether. So he left Townsend Lane at 7.25.

Next Goodman turns his attention to Wallace's arrival at the City Café in

North John Street: he was first seen by James Caird at approximately seven-forty-five.

Caird's estimate may be accepted. But the fact that he saw Wallace at about quarter to eight must not be taken to mean that he saw him as soon as he arrived.

Caird may have only noticed Wallace minutes after his actual arrival at the club. Goodman then goes on to beg the question by describing Wallace's fixation with punctuality, and the club rule that tournament matches had to commence by seven-forty-five. He concludes:

Almost certainly, then, Wallace was at the City Café before 7.45. The important question is: How much before? Surely no one – not even the most ardent anti-Wallaceites – can complain that two minutes is extravagant?

Goodman's estimated time for Wallace's arrival at the City Café is seven-forty-three.

Then Goodman adds up the various times: Wallace finished the Qualtrough call at seven-twenty-four; he boarded the tram at seven-twenty-five and he arrived at the chess club at seven-forty-three. Therefore, the journey from the tram stop nearest the telephone kiosk to the chess club …

… occupied eighteen minutes. But the minimum time for the journey (indeed, one could go so far as to call it the all-time record for the journey, which even the Anfield Harriers could not have bettered) was twenty-one minutes … In other words, Wallace could not have got from the telephone-box to the City Café in the time available.

As it reads, this is a very simple, yet powerful, argument based upon facts and evidence which were available to the Wallace defence at the time of his trial and at his appeal, but which were overlooked and not deployed in Wallace's favour. Goodman, to his own satisfaction, and that of many other Wallace scholars, has demonstrated clearly and succinctly that it was impossible for Wallace to have made the Qualtrough telephone call and to have arrived at the City Café at the time he did. Therefore Wallace truly was an innocent man.

However, leaving aside the questionable time of Wallace's arrival at the chess club, a few minutes before seven-forty-five,[2] Goodman's argument is seriously and unredeemingly flawed: one of the basic premises of his thesis is false.

Goodman writes, in a footnote to Chapter 13 of his book, wherein he produces his proof:

There is no doubt that Wallace travelled by tram. The only other means of transport – taxi-cab or private car – are ruled out for reasons so obvious that there is no need to state them.[3]

The reasons so obvious being that the police would have, and indeed did, check taxi-cab companies and private hire car firms to see whether Wallace had used one or the other of them, either on the Monday night, or the

Tuesday. Wallace had not used either a taxi, or a hire car, for the journey to the chess club. And so Goodman bases his whole argument on the fact that he had to use a tram for the journey, a journey which would take a minimum of twenty-one minutes.

But there *is* a doubt, a very big one indeed. Wallace made his first statement to the police at Anfield Bridewell, just before midnight on the night of the murder. Goodman reproduces this statement as a single appendix in his book. After the preamble of the first paragraph, Wallace goes on to describe the events of Tuesday 20 January, beginning at ten-thirty in the morning, collecting throughout the day, and finishing up work in the evening.

My last caller being either 19 or 21 Eastman Road. I boarded a bus at Queens Drive and Townsend Avenue, alighted at Cabbage Hall and walked up to my house at about 6.05pm.[4]

The most important word in that brief extract, which Goodman has overlooked, is 'bus'. And that bus would have been either the number ten or the number eleven.[5]

On Monday night, Wallace had the choice of two trams, the numbers 13 and 14, for the journey to the chess club in North John Street. They both originated in Carr Lane, Clubmoor, and ran along Townsend Avenue, Townsend Lane and Breck Road, past the junction with Belmont Road, where Wallace said he boarded the tram, then round the houses, before entering the city centre. Their routings through the centre of town to the terminus at the Pier Head differed, but both trams passed North John Street, the nearest stop to the chess club and either tram would have suited Wallace.

Two buses shared part of these two tram routes, the numbers ten and eleven. The number 10 originated in Fazackerly, a newly-developing Liverpool suburb which had no tram service. This bus ran along Lower Lane and Lower House Lane to the tram terminus at Carr Lane. And here the number 11 bus originated. The two buses then followed the tram route down Townsend Lane, into Breck Road and past the junction with Belmont Road. But, just beyond the junction, instead of following the tram routes round the houses, the two buses took a shorter, more direct route to the city centre, where they both terminated in Castle Street, having passed North John Street. Either bus would have carried Wallace to the chess club.

Wallace claimed that on the Monday night he caught a tram from the junction of Breck Road and Belmont Road. The two buses also picked up passengers from a stop adjacent to this tram stop. Both of the trams also stopped at the tram stop next to the telephone box in which Qualtrough made his call. There was also a bus stop next to the tram stop, from where the two buses also collected passengers.

Could Wallace have made the Qualtrough telephone call, boarded a bus by the telephone box rather than a tram, and arrived just before seven-forty-five at the chess club? The answer is, yes.

The timetables for the two buses overlapped, and they ran along Breck Road at four to five minutes intervals. The journey by bus into the city centre was shorter by a quarter of a mile, and while trams averaged six miles an hour on their routes, buses averaged ten miles an hour. If, as Goodman says, the journey by tram from the telephone kiosk to North John Street took twenty-one minutes, then the same journey by bus would take fifteen minutes.

If the telephone call ended at twenty-four minutes past seven, as Goodman has argued, and even if the caller then had to wait four or five minutes for a bus, he could still arrive at the chess club just before seven-forty-five. And if the caller was Wallace, then he can be placed in the telephone kiosk making the Qualtrough call; he can still arrive at the chess club by seven-forty-five.

This does not prove that Wallace did in fact make the Qualtrough telephone call. It simply demonstrates that he could have, that he did have the time, and that Goodman's conclusive proof of Wallace's innocence is untenable. Wallace, in the guise of RM Qualtrough, could have made the telephone call and still have arrived in time at the chess club.

2

In support of his conclusive proof, Goodman adduces an argument concerning the actual telephone conversation which Qualtrough had with the chess club captain, Samuel Beattie. Goodman asks the question: could Wallace have spoken to Beattie, a man he had known for eight years, in the guise of Qualtrough, without giving away his true identity? Goodman concludes that he could not have done so. Therefore he was innocent.

During the trial, the prosecution alleged that Wallace made the call using an assumed voice. Samuel Beattie, who had the longest conversation with Qualtrough, when questioned by the defence, categorically stated that his voice sounded nothing like Wallace's. Beattie was very firm and unshakeable on this point.

How easy is it to disguise one's own voice? Almost impossible, claims Goodman and he cites the judgement of an unnamed member of the BBC Drama Repertory Company:

An experienced radio actress, whose whole working life is occupied with the task of imitating other voices, so as to disguise her own.

In the opinion of this actress:

It is almost impossible successfully to disguise one's voice, without 'putting on' a foreign accent, a strange dialect, or some form of speech defect. Even with such 'vocal moustaches' added, it is extremely difficult to change the rhythm of one's mode of speech – and, although not generally realised, it is as much by the rhythm, as by the sound, that one's voice is recognised by others. This becomes increasingly true as a person grows older and, as the vocal pattern solidifies, as it were. It would also be true to say that the older the person is, the more difficult it is for him (or her) to alter the tone of voice over a wide register.[6]

An unnamed radio actress claims that it is almost impossible to disguise one's voice; Goodman agrees, and without considering any further evidence, he concludes that Wallace could not have disguised his voice over the telephone and deceived his friend, Samuel Beattie. Beattie was very categorical in court that the voice he heard did not belong to Wallace. Therefore, Wallace and Qualtrough are two separate individuals, and Wallace is innocent.

The three telephone operators, Alfreds, Kelly and Robertson, who spoke with Qualtrough prior to both Gladys Harley and Samuel Beattie doing so, all said that he spoke with an ordinary voice. And an ordinary voice to three Liverpool ladies is a voice with a Liverpool accent. For Wallace to have spoken with a Liverpool accent, says John Brophy, would have been difficult, if not impossible, because his accent was immutably Cumbrian.[7] And, like Goodman, Brophy concludes that Wallace must be innocent on that basis.

This argument of Goodman's is not, in fact, a proof of Wallace's innocence. He does not prove that Wallace did not, could not, disguise his voice. What he offers is informed opinion to the effect that disguising one's voice to fool a friend is difficult. Difficult it may well be, but not impossible.

Goodman's argument assumes a friendship between Wallace and Beattie, which did not exist, while it ignores Wallace's own background, which is highly relevant to the discussion.

Goodman places too much stress on the fact that Beattie and Wallace had known one another for some years: he assumes they were friends. They were, in fact, simply acquaintances, whose only point of contact was the chess club. Even though Samuel Beattie had known Wallace for eight years, he did not know, as he admitted in his statement, what he did for a living, or where he lived, facts which hardly speak of friendship. And Wallace, despite what has been written in the literature surrounding the case, was not a regular attendee at the club.[8]

Socially, they were miles apart. Wallace was a collection clerk, belonging to the lower echelon of the middle classes, living a life of genteel poverty in a poor, cramped, working class district. In contrast, Beattie lived in a large house in the select suburb of Mossley Hill, on the outskirts of the city, within easy reach of the countryside. He was the manager of a firm of cotton brokers, a high-flying businessman, well known in Liverpool social and financial circles and he employed clerks such as Wallace in the hundreds, to perform the menial tasks about his brokerage firm. He was also captain of the chess club, a first class player, whereas Wallace only qualified for the second class team. They would not have met socially, or at any other time, but for their mutual love of the game.

A huge social gulf, not as deep today as it would have been then, lay between the two men. Each would have been aware of it and their attitudes to one another would have clearly shown it: Wallace would have deferred to Beattie. Their conversations together in the club would not have ranged beyond their common interest. Nor would these conversations have been prolonged, not when the meetings at the club were mostly given over to playing chess rather than talking about it.

During these conversations, Wallace would have been aware that he was talking to a social superior, a man on the same high level as the manager at the Prudential, who had clerks and superintendents by the dozen at his beck and call. Wallace's voice, his manner of speaking, the form of his language, his intonation, his body language, would have reflected the social gulf. How Wallace spoke to Beattie, both in form and content, would have been very different from how he spoke to his friend and equal, James Caird, which in turn would have differed from the way he spoke to his wife, which again would have been different from how he addressed his customers in Clubmoor.

Whereas the three telephone operators described Qualtrough's voice as ordinary, in contrast, Gladys Harley described it as deep and strong, while Samuel Beattie said it was gruffish. And while these descriptions are subjective, it is, nevertheless, of interest, that Beattie and Harley did not hear an ordinary voice, a voice with a Liverpool accent, but would appear to have heard a different voice, one that had altered from being ordinary to being deep, strong and gruffish. Beattie and Harley did not hear a voice with a Liverpool accent.

Of the five people who spoke to Qualtrough on the telephone only two, Harley and, in particular, Beattie, would have been a position to recognise the Qualtrough voice as that of Wallace and it is strange that the voice becomes strong and gruffish rather than remaining ordinary, when Harley and Beattie listen to it. It was as if the voice had been changed to accommodate them.

But Beattie was unequivocal in his belief that the voice he heard was not that of Wallace. However, psychologists have known for many years that the conviction and confidence with which a witness holds a belief, the certainty with which he gives evidence in court, bears no relationship whatsoever to the actual veracity or validity of that belief or evidence.[9] There are many instances of witnesses who have presented statements and evidence in courts of law with confidence, assurance and certainty, and who, in doing so, have convinced juries, when later, those same witnesses have been shown to be mistaken. Some have been shown to have been outright liars.

Because Beattie was so certain that he did not recognise the voice as that of Wallace, it does not mean that it was not Wallace speaking to him in a disguised voice. Three factors in particular mitigate against Beattie's certainty. Firstly, the last person Beattie expected to hear when he was called to the telephone was Wallace, and so he did not hear Wallace. Expectation plays a major role in what we hear, as it does in all forms of sensory perception, and it is the habituation of expectation which, at times, leads to the senses being deceived. Beattie expected to speak to a stranger, and so he heard a stranger.

Secondly, Beattie was not listening to the voice in order to ascertain who was speaking: he was listening to, and concentrating upon, the message which the voice was conveying to him, the content rather than the form; he was not listening to the voice with the inner ear, as it were, of his auditory memory, the faculty which would have enabled him to have recognised the voice as that of Wallace.

Thirdly, Beattie was accustomed to speaking to Wallace face to face at the chess club, usually about chess matters, and in this context he knew his voice. But, on the telephone, he was listening to a disembodied voice, concentrating on what was being said about a business meeting, and writing it all down. A situation, a context, in which he and Wallace had never before participated. And context is just as much a factor in voice recognition as are tone and rhythm.

It can be argued that the Liverpool, Cumbrian, and Yorkshire dialects are all strange to people from other areas and that any one of them would qualify as a vocal moustache behind which a voice could be disguised, as suggested by Goodman's radio actress.

Brophy contradicts himself when he argues that accents are immutable, only to add that Wallace's immutable Cumbrian accent may have been possibly refined by his own literary tastes and the example of his wife. Immutable means unchangeable, not subject to variation; while refined means purified, that is, changed from the original state.

Accents are not immutable. An accent is simply a particular, or idiosyncratic, way of pronouncing the words of a language and a person speaking with an accent can be taught by elocution, or by long term exposure to another accent, to pronounce the language with a different accent, or perhaps without any strong accent at all. People can, and do, assimilate and adopt other accents, by exposure to them or with formal training.

A dialect is a form of speech or language of non-standard pronunciation, vocabulary, phrasing, or grammar, peculiar to a particular region or locality of a country. The dialects of Britain have been mapped and studied and there is a wide and colourful variety. A person speaking English only in dialect form can be taught to speak, or can assimilate by immersion, another English dialect or Standard English.

Speech is energy and movement and among the prosodic features that endow speech with life and power are the dynamic characteristics of stress and pitch. No word is possible without stress and pitch, and no utterance without rhythm and intonation. The rise and fall of the musical pitch of the voice confer intonation or harmony upon an utterance. All ethnic languages, dialects included, possess their own peculiar intonations or harmonies, what may be called rhythms, melodies or main tunes. Thus a Scouser speaks quite differently from a Geordie.

Within these main tunes or rhythms of a language or dialect, there are infinite variations, secondary tunes, which are determined, among other things, by the speaker's subjective attitude to what he is saying: the emotions of anger, sorrow, joy, and fear, will all sing different tunes. These variations are also determined by the situation or context in which the speaker finds himself: conversations of man-to-man, man-to-women, woman-to-woman, adult-to-child, employee-to-boss, colleague-to-colleague, will all produce varying, secondary tunes.

In a strongly stressed language such as English, it is the tune at the end of sentence which has the greatest significance. And it is this final tune, or cadence, that changes the least. It is at this point that a speaker's main tune minimises interference by secondary influences, emotionally or contextually based, so that the speaker's voice is recognisable to the listener, regardless of the variations and changes that may have occurred before the cadence.

No one today knows how Wallace spoke, neither his accent nor his dialect, but he is described as being soft-spoken and reserved. Wallace was born in Millom, in Cumbria, and spent his formative years there. Millom has its own distinctive accent and dialect and there can be no doubt that in his early years, this dialect and its particular accent was his native tongue, and would have stayed with him throughout his life. But this does not mean that it was not modified as he grew older and travelled the world.

Wallace left Millom to live in Blackpool at the age of ten, and two years later the family moved to Dalton-in-Furness. From Dalton he went to live and work in Barrow-in-Furness. He was thus exposed, while still young, to the dialects and accents of Blackpool and the Furness area, which are quite distinctive and different from that of Millom. The young are quick to recognise change; they are malleable and eager to experiment and readily adapt to change.

Later, Wallace lived in Manchester, and had to contend with the accent and dialect of that metropolis. In 1902, aged twenty-four, he sailed for India, where he lived for two years. In Calcutta, he would have met with a variety of accents and dialects from the British inhabitants of the city, together with the various forms of pidgin English spoken by the native Indians.

From India he travelled to Shanghai, where a similar pot-pourri of the English language assailed his ears. Then he returned to Manchester for some time, before he went to live in Harrogate, Yorkshire, where, as agent for the local Liberal party, he met a variety of Yorkshiremen and women of diverse backgrounds, including his future wife, all with their own peculiar dialects and accents. Finally, he settled down in Liverpool, where, for sixteen years, he was immersed in the Liverpool dialect and accent.

It would be naive to believe that in 1931, after such a peripatetic existence, after such exposure to so many British dialects and accents, Wallace would still speak purely in his native Millom dialect and accent, having left forty-one years earlier. It would also be naive to believe that his speech would not have been modified by his long-term immersion in the Liverpool dialect and accent, which he heard day in, day out, as he walked the streets of Clubmoor collecting insurance premiums.

Besides describing Qualtrough's voice as gruffish, Beattie also said it was the voice of a man who was sure of himself, that Qualtrough was a strong-voiced man. How easy would it have been for Wallace to have cast aside his usual, deferential manner of speaking to Beattie and to have adopted the strong voice of a man sure of himself, a voice with a Liverpool or a Millom or a Barrovian accent perhaps, with a gruffish tone, which would have disguised that final, rhythmic cadence with which Beattie was familiar?

William Wallace had heard, had been immersed in, very many different English dialects and accents in the course of his life: consciously and subconsciously his speech pattern, his phrasing, his vocabulary, his accent and pronunciation, the rhythms of his speech, would have been modified and changed. And in all probability he could change those characteristics of his speech at will, moving from say, a Cumbrian accent and dialect, to a Liverpool one, or from a Yorkshire to a Mancunian dialect. Of all the protagonists in the Wallace case, it is William Wallace above all who stands out as the one person capable of changing and disguising his voice.

Wallace's innocence cannot be proved on the basis that he could not have disguised his voice to fool Samuel Beattie: the possibility existed that he could. Nor can his innocence be proven by arguing that he could not have made the Qualtrough telephone call and still have arrived at the chess club in time. Wallace can be placed in the call box on the Monday night, and he could have made the call. The case against Wallace can be sustained.

3

Goodman produces two further arguments about the crucial telephone call, which are again not proofs of Wallace's innocence, but which, he argues, lend credible support to his claims of innocence. Firstly, he asks, why did Wallace, if he was Qualtrough, choose to make the telephone call to the chess club from a kiosk so close to his own home? And, secondly, why, when making the call, did he act so indiscreetly and cause so much confusion, that the telephone call was recorded at the exchange, thereby allowing it to be traced by the police?

There were several public telephones in close proximity to the Wallace's home, besides the one in Rochester Road from where the call was made.

There were pay telephones in the library, which stood next to Holy Trinity Church, in the post office opposite, and in a confectioner's shop nearby, according to the evidence of Leslie Heaton, the post office telephone engineer, given during the trial. But they were not enclosed, and they were all on well-lit premises, which were still open to the public at the time the Qualtrough call was made. Anyone using any of those telephones would have been seen and, more than likely, overheard. Naturally, being overheard was what Wallace wanted to avoid.

In and around Lord Street, where Wallace alighted from the tram for the chess club, there were several telephone boxes. But these boxes were electrically illuminated, on well-lit streets and they were close to the club. If Wallace had used one of them for the call, he risked being seen and remembered by fellow chess players on their way to club; or by a member of the public. What is more, the police would have been highly suspicious of a call arriving for Wallace, just minutes before his own arrival at the club.

So what other option did Wallace have besides the kiosk in Rochester Road? The kiosk in Rochester Road was isolated, enclosed, and in a poorly-lit area, the nearest light being twenty-four feet away. And there was no light inside the kiosk, the bulb having blown. Using the darkness as a cover, Wallace made his way to the box, slipped in and made the call in the dark.

There was little chance of him being interrupted; the telephone was then a luxury beyond the means of most of the working-class inhabitants of the area: those who had telephones had no need for a public telephone and those without one generally had no need for a call-box, for their friends and relatives, living in similar circumstances, had no telephones either.

From Wallace's point of view, the kiosk in Rochester Road was not only convenient, but was also his only option if he wanted to make the call in private, without being disturbed or overheard, without being seen and recognised.

When discussions arise about Qualtrough's behaviour during his telephone call to the club, it is always forgotten that there were two stages to the tracing of the call to the Rochester Road kiosk, four hundred yards from Wallace's home. First, Gladys Harley remembered that it had been the Anfield Exchange connecting the call, and, second, that Annie Robertson at that exchange had made a note of the call.

The call was put through at seven-fifteen by Louisa Alfreds. A few minutes later, Lillian Kelly engaged Qualtrough, who complained that, "I have pressed button A but have not had my correspondent yet". Kelly then told him to press button B to return his money and she saw the red light on her console light up, indicating that he had done so, and that the money had been refunded. Kelly spoke briefly with Louisa Alfreds, who confirmed that this was the same caller whom she had connected earlier to the chess club, before summoning her supervisor, Annie Robertson.

Robertson noted that the money had been returned and spoke to Qualtrough, who asked to be reconnected.[10] Robertson made the connection, passed it on to Kelly, and he was put through to Gladys Harley at the club.

Annie Robertson had put the call through gratis. She made a note on a slip of paper of the timing: it was twenty minutes past seven when the final, successful connection was made. And on her note she had written 'NR' , meaning no reply, as the reason for giving Qualtrough a free telephone call.

Gladys Harley, at the chess club, was certain that the telephone only rang once and she answered it immediately to hear the voice of RM Qualtrough. She passed him on to Samuel Beattie.

There was a fault in the Rochester Road box, Anfield 1627, which needed repair, according to Leslie Heaton, and he repaired it the following day. It is probable that the problems making the call were due to this fault: if Qualtrough pressed button A but did not get through when first connected, then his money should have remained in the box, and should not have been refunded when he later pressed button B. That he had his money returned indicates that he was not put through, and that there was a fault in the box.

The call was logged not because of problems in making the connection, but because the second call was put through gratis. It was Robertson, and not Qualtrough, who was responsible for the call being logged. It was not something Qualtrough did, but something Robertson did: she gave him a free telephone call. Had he paid for the call when connected by Robertson, she would have had no reason to log it.

When Superintendent Moore telephoned the Liverpool Telephone Exchange on the Wednesday following the murder to inquire whether the call could be traced, he was told it would be impossible. However, when Gladys Harley stated that the operator had said, "Anfield calling", when she answered the telephone, Moore then contacted Anfield Exchange and asked to speak to all the operators who had been working on Monday night. Once police interest was shown at the exchange, Alfreds, Kelly and Robertson stepped forward with Robertson's brief note of the proceedings.

If Harley had not remembered that the call came from the Anfield Exchange, had the call not been put through gratis by Robertson, then it would never have been traced.

Goodman's contention, that if Wallace had made the call, he would not have been so indiscreet as to cause it to be logged, cannot be sustained. Wallace was not being reckless: he wanted to make a telephone call to set his plan in motion. His first attempt failed and so he would try again to be connected. It was that simple. He was put through free of charge: if he had known that a free telephone call would be logged at the exchange, then, no doubt, he would have insisted on paying.

Goodman continues his argument and claims that the devious, criminal mastermind, RM Qualtrough, sought to implicate Wallace in his crime: he deliberately created such an ado on the telephone, in order to get the call logged, so that it would be traced eventually to the Rochester Road kiosk, thereby bringing Wallace under suspicion.

This presupposes that Qualtrough knew that such behaviour over a telephone call would result in it being logged; it presupposes a knowledge of the workings of the exchange, a knowledge of the complaints procedure, a knowledge of the level at which supervisors were called in, or had to intervene. Such knowledge would not have been common currency with the general public in 1931.

Again, if Gladys Harley had not remembered it was the Anfield Exchange, and if Robertson had not put through the call gratis, then it could not have been traced. According to Goodman, Qualtrough's plan to implicate Wallace was therefore based upon Harley's memory and Robertson's altruism and clerical correctness, an improbable basis for such a scheme.

But in what was Qualtrough attempting to implicate Wallace? Goodman believes that he was a thief intent only on stealing Wallace's cash, and that he killed Mrs Wallace only when she caught him stealing. That is, when Qualtrough made his call he was setting in motion a robbery only.

Therefore, by purposefully having his telephone call logged, Qualtrough could only have been attempting to implicate Wallace in the theft of his own money, which makes no sense at all.

Goodman's argument can only make sense if he, like Roger Wilkes, argues that Qualtrough, or as Wilkes would have it, Richard Gordon Parry, set out intentionally to murder Mrs Wallace and then to frame William Wallace for the crime. Wilkes believes Parry did just that to avenge himself against Wallace for having him sacked from his post at the Prudential. Thus, Parry would have arranged to have the telephone call logged.

Again this presupposes that the caller knew what it took to get a call logged. Why would an insurance agent know the working procedures of a telephone exchange? But why go to all the bother of scheming Mrs Wallace's death with a logged telephone call, a bogus trip, and a staged robbery, in order to frame Wallace, when there was always the possibility that the police, or the court, would believe him innocent, as the Court of Criminal Appeal finally did? If the motive was revenge against Wallace, rather than to kill Mrs Wallace, why not lure him to Menlove Gardens East, a very dark and quiet location, and kill him there?

It is difficult enough to plan a murder, to execute it, then to escape retribution, without adding the burden of trying to frame someone else for that murder. But this notion that Qualtrough tried to frame Wallace, pervades the arguments of all Wallace's defenders. A gigantic conspiracy, which encompassed the police, was aligned against Wallace, and the telephone call was part of that conspiracy. What is ignored is the fact that Wallace did not have Parry removed from his job at the Prudential.

From the evidence of Harley at the chess club, and Robertson and her operators at the Anfield Exchange, it would appear that there was some difficulty and confusion with the Qualtrough telephone call and its connection to the club, but that it arose unintentionally rather than purposefully. Wallace or Qualtrough, or whoever made the call, was setting in motion a criminal enterprise; when he could not get through at the first attempt, he certainly was not going to be put off. He was going to try again and again and again, if necessary, regardless of the problems, because the call was essential to his scheme. That the call was put through gratis ensured that it was logged, rather than Qualtrough's behaviour over the call.

<h1 style="text-align:center">4</h1>

One further argument needs to be examined. This concerns the murder weapon, or rather the absence of one at the murder scene and Goodman, among others, has advanced its absence in defence of Wallace.

Sarah Draper, Mrs Wallace's charwoman, following her inspection of 29 Wolverton Street under police supervision, identified two items that were missing from the house: a steel poker, nine inches long, with a knob on one end, from the kitchen, and an iron bar, "about one foot long and about as thick as an ordinary candle", from the front parlour.[11] The last time she saw it was on 31 December 1930, according to her statement.

Wallace stated that he had not known he ever possessed an iron bar which had been kept in the parlour; the missing poker, he suggested, had probably been thrown out with the fire ashes. He reported that a heavy dog leash was missing from the house, but said it had no metal parts to it.

The police concluded that the murder weapon was the missing iron bar from the front parlour. The house was searched thoroughly, but it did not come to light. An alert was put out and the neighbourhoods of Richmond Park and Menlove Avenue were scoured for the bar. However, it was never recovered.

At the trial, Professor MacFall asserted that whatever weapon had been used, it must have been heavy, and delivered with terrific force and that an iron bar, of the dimensions suggested by Draper, could have answered the description. However, in his original police statement, MacFall said that the weapon …

… *must have had a large heavy head covering a big area, as seen in the penetrating wound above the left forehead.*[12]

This latter description would appear to indicate something other than an iron bar. In addition, in the post mortem protocol, MacFall described the murder weapon as a 'hard instrument', which would suggest something such as a hammer, rather than a simple iron bar.

Laura Gomez, who, as a young girl, served behind the counter in a general grocery store in the area, says that an ordinary candle was about six inches long and approximately half an inch in diameter.

> We sold them half a dozen at a time. Rather than light the gas lamps when going upstairs to bed, or when rising in the dark in the morning, people used candles instead and these candles gave a quick, bright light when lit. They were thin, with a thin wick.[13]

Sarah Draper is the only one who knew of the existence of the iron bar. Wallace claimed that he had never had one in his front parlour. MacFall's evidence in court that an iron bar, similar to the one described by Draper, was possibly the murder weapon, contradicts his own statements on the matter. Could an iron bar, twelve inches long and half an inch thick, inflict such horrific injuries? Could it be reasonably described as heavy, as having a heavy large head, as being a hard instrument?

An iron bar one foot long with a diameter of half an inch would weigh just over half a pound; with a diameter of one inch, it would weigh just over two and a half pounds. But a candle with a diameter of one inch would be a large candle, certainly not ordinary. Neither bar would have been capable of inflicting the injuries sustained by Julia Wallace. It is only when the diameter of the bar reaches two inches, which would give it a weight of ten and a half pounds, could it be considered as the murder weapon. But in 1931, how many people of Sarah Draper's background would have referred to a candle with a diameter of two inches as being ordinary?[14]

It is highly doubtful that the missing iron bar from the front parlour, if it existed, was the murder weapon. However, if it was the murder weapon, what happened to it? That it was never found is used as an argument in favour of Wallace's innocence.

Dorothy L Sayers says that whoever committed the murder, it was to his advantage to leave the weapon in the house.

> In this case the weapon was identified only with the house itself, and if the murderer came from outside, the use of a weapon identified with the house would assist him in throwing the blame on Wallace, whereas, if Wallace himself was the murderer, by far the readiest way of fixing suspicion upon himself was to use a weapon belonging to the house and remove it, since its removal created a strong presumption that no weapon had been brought from outside. Whichever way one looks at it, the carrying away of the weapon was an idiotic and entirely unnecessary error, involving the risk of discovery.[15]

However, Sayers' argument is valid only if it can be proved that the missing iron bar was the murder weapon.

Had the killer come from outside, then, as the evidence at the crime scene suggests, he had come to murder Mrs Wallace. He may well have brought his own weapon with him, in which case he would have taken it with him: being forensically aware, he would not want to leave behind a weapon which might have held traces of himself, most notably fingerprints; nor would he want to leave behind a weapon which one day the police might be able to prove belonged to, or was associated with, him. Even if the killer had arrived unarmed, and had used something from the house as a weapon, he might still have taken it away with him, just in case it held a trace which the police might have been able to link with him.

Suppose that the iron bar was the murder weapon, and that Wallace had used it to kill Julia, then he might well have thought that with his wife dead, no one else would know about it, that its removal from the house would go unnoticed and would give the police the impression that the killer had come from outside, had brought the weapon with him, and had taken it away with him. Wallace's claim that he had no knowledge of an iron bar in the parlour would support this notion. Sarah Draper's intervention might have spoilt his ploy. However, without trying to lay a false scent for the police, he might still have removed the iron bar, simply as a precaution, just in case there was any trace of himself on it.

Jonathan Goodman reports that, several years after the murder, the Sunbeam gas fire in the front parlour was removed by the new occupants of 29 Wolverton Street and that, in the space behind the fire, a workman found an iron bar. The workman apparently examined the bar, but found no traces to indicate that it had been used as a murder weapon. He duly handed it over to the police, but it disappeared.

This bar was, according to Goodman, without doubt, the missing iron bar and he argued that it must have rolled under the fire and had been lying there, 'since the beginning of January 1931'.[16] And since the workman had found no evidence that it had been used as a murder weapon, then it could not have been the murder weapon.

Goodman goes on to conclude that this find is an indicator of Wallace's innocence: the real murder weapon was brought to the house and taken away again by the real killer, who later disposed of it in his own time, in a place of his own choosing.

However, the Sunbeam gas fire was removed from the front parlour by the police, along with many other fixtures and fittings over a period of three days following the murder. The reason Wallace spent the time up to his arrest at his sister-in-law's flat in Ullet Road, was because 29 Wolverton Street was made uninhabitable by the removal of so many fixtures. In fact, several weeks after the trial, the landlord, Samuel Evans, had to write to the police asking when the fixtures were going to be returned, as he wanted to make the house habitable again.[17]

The police had been alert to the possibility that the bar might have rolled underneath the fire. Having removed the fire, they examined the vacated space but did not find it and when it was not found elsewhere in the house, the conclusion was that it was indeed the murder weapon, and that the killer had taken it with him.

The bar found by the Goodman's workman could not have had anything to do with the iron bar which Sarah Draper claimed was missing from the front parlour and any conclusions which can be drawn from its presence behind the fire are invalid.

If the iron bar was not the murder weapon, what was used to kill Julia? How did the killer dispose of the weapon? These questions will be examined in the final chapter.

None of the arguments propounded in support of Wallace can conclusively prove his innocence: he can be placed inside the telephone kiosk on the Monday night; he could have disguised his voice when speaking to Beattie; his best option was the Rochester Road telephone box; his behaviour when making the call had nothing to do with it being logged and eventually traced; the absence of the murder weapon indicates neither guilt nor innocence.

Chapter 13
Menlove Gardens East

1

If it cannot be conclusively proved that Wallace was innocent, can it be conclusively proved that he was guilty? Broadly speaking, there are three types of evidence: direct, expert, and circumstantial. Any evidence adduced in support of a verdict of guilty will be, as it was the case in 1931, purely circumstantial: there was no trace evidence linking Wallace to the murder, no expert evidence and no witnesses to the evil deed, no direct evidence.

The real test of the value of circumstantial evidence is: does it exclude every reasonable probability? I can even put it higher: does it exclude other theories or possibilities?[1]

Exploration of the circumstances surrounding the death of Julia Wallace has shown that the robbery, supposedly the prime motive for the assault upon the household, was staged. This begs the question of who would want to stage a robbery to cover a murder? The answer is: William Herbert Wallace.

But there are other circumstances to be examined, circumstances beyond the confines of the front parlour wherein Mrs Wallace died, circumstances which involved only William Wallace. When Wallace left home on the Tuesday night, if he left behind him the body of his dead wife, then his behaviour from that point on, until the arrival of the police at his home, was part of his post-offence behaviour, behaviour purposely designed to demonstrate his innocence.

Thus it can be argued that the tram journeys to Menlove Gardens and the ensuing fruitless search for Mr Qualtrough were nothing more than cynical ploys to establish his presence four miles from home at a time when he hoped the police would conclude that his wife was being murdered: if the police failed to reach such a conclusion, Wallace hoped that sufficient uncertainty would have been generated by his movements as to leave reasonable doubt about him having had the time in which to kill her.

While travelling to Menlove Avenue and creating the circumstances in which he would be remembered, and then wandering about the Menlove Avenue area inquiring about Mr Qualtrough, Wallace was not trying to establish an alibi. An alibi, as Goodman says, is:

A plea which avers that the accused was in another place at the time of the commission of the offence, and therefore cannot be guilty.[2]

Had Julia's murder been witnessed or overheard at a time when Wallace was known to be in transit to Menlove Avenue, then Wallace could be said to have had an alibi.

But, there were no witnesses to Julia's death, and the timing of it could not be established with any precision. If Wallace killed his wife, then he could not have an alibi. The best he could do was create the circumstances in which it could be said there was reasonable doubt about whether he could have killed her in the time available.

If Wallace's behaviour on the journeys to Menlove Gardens and his search for Mr Qualtrough can be shown to be purposefully designed to create those circumstances, then that behaviour can be rightly designated as post-offence behaviour. And if he was engaged in post-offence behaviour, then he must have committed the offence, he must have murdered his wife.

2

It has been assumed by many writers investigating the case that Wallace travelled to the Menlove Avenue area from Smithdown Lane on a number 4 tramcar to Penny Lane, and then on from there on the 5A tram. It is true he used the 5A tram, but he did not use the number 4 route.[3] The error arose from the fact that Tram Conductor Phillips had started his working day on the number 4 route, but had changed to the number 5 route by the time he picked up Wallace at Smithdown Lane.

Because this error has gone uncorrected since the time of the murder, a detailed and critical examination of the routings of Wallace's journeys from Smithdown Lane, along Smithdown Road to Penny Lane and beyond to Menlove Gardens, has not been forthcoming. And it is precisely this area wherein lies the circumstantial evidence which clearly demonstrates that Wallace's behaviour throughout these journeys was bogus, and that his only intention was to have himself noticed and remembered: he was engaged in post-offence behaviour, hoping to demonstrate his innocence.

On the Monday night after he had received the Qualtrough address, he claimed that he did not know the area where Qualtrough lived. The consensus of opinion among the men at the chess club was that Menlove

Gardens East was somewhere off Menlove Avenue and there were three suggestions made as to the best route he should take to get there: McCartney, Wallace's chess opponent, suggested a tramcar from Spellow Lane to Smithdown Road and onwards; James Caird, walking home with Wallace later that night, advised taking a tram from Clubmoor along Queen's Drive to its junction with Menlove Avenue, and Wallace himself told Caird that he would, "Get a tram to town and another out again from town, as I know the way".[4]

Three important points emerge from the impromptu discussions among the chess club members. First, that Menlove Gardens East was in the vicinity of Menlove Avenue; second, that Caird's and McCartney's suggested tramcar routes were bound in the direction of Menlove Avenue; third, that Wallace said he did not know the area, that is, the Menlove Avenue area, but that he knew how to get there.

Wallace did not look up Menlove Gardens East in a street directory before he set out on the Tuesday night. The suggestion by his fellow chess players that it was in the vicinity of Menlove Avenue was, thus, firmly fixed in his mind and the search for Menlove Gardens East would commence after he had reached the Menlove Avenue area.

Leaving home, Wallace claimed that he walked through the back streets to Belmont Road, turned left, walked down to St Margaret's Church on the corner of Belmont Road and Rocky Lane, where he boarded a number 26 tramcar which carried him to the junction of Tunnel Road and Smithdown Road, which he then crossed to join the queue at the tramcar stop in Smithdown Lane.

It should be noted that Wallace's route was not the one he himself had suggested to Caird; nor was it either of the routes suggested by Caird and McCartney. The route he was taking must have been a route he knew, for he would hardly have discarded his own route in favour of one he did not know. However, apparently this is what he did do.

Five trams stopped at the Smithdown Lane tram stop. Originating at, or close to, the Pier Head in the city centre, they were the number 5, destined for the Penny Lane terminus; the 5A, for Calderstones Park; the 5W, to Calderstones Park and Woolton; the number 7, bound for Calderstones Park and the number 8, going to Mather Avenue. All five trams travelled along Smithdown Road; all went as far as Penny Lane, the interim destination suggested by Beattie.[5]

Before it was immortalised in song by the Beatles, Penny Lane was a major terminus, transfer point and depot on the Liverpool City tram and bus networks: it was a latter-day Spaghetti Junction of tramcar tracks, which looped and turned to accommodate four different tramcar routes and the trams from the Smithdown Road tramcar sheds. Once seen, it would have been difficult to forget.

Penny Lane was named in all transport timetables, including those displayed at tram and bus stops, along with other major depots and transfer points such as the Pier Head, the Old Swan, Spellow Lane, and Litherland. From Penny Lane, a passenger could travel anywhere within Liverpool and its suburbs.

Wallace's sister-in-law, Amy Wallace, lived at 83 Ullet Road, a major road off Smithdown Road and the Wallaces used to visit her at her home just as she, in turn, visited them in theirs. They had last called on 16 November 1930. To get to Ullet Road, they would travel on the number 26 tram to the junction of Tunnel Road and Smithdown Lane, cross to the stop in Smithdown Lane, and board any one of the five trams that stopped there. Three-quarters of the way along Smithdown Road, just before Penny Lane, they would alight at Ullet Road.

They also used to visit Calderstones Park for nature walks, two or three times a year, a fact recorded in Wallace's diaries. To get there, they would again take the number 26 tram from Belmont Road to the stop in Smithdown Lane. Of the five trams which stopped there, only three, the 5A, the 5W and the number 7, went directly to the park via Smithdown Road and Penny Lane. But they could also take one of the other two trams, the 5, or the 8, provided they changed trams at Penny Lane and from there took the 5A, or the 5W or the number 7.

From Penny Lane, the 5A, 5W and number 7 ran into Allerton Road and then crossed Queen's Drive. Allerton Road then veered sharply to the right where it met Menlove Avenue, but the trams veered off to the left and into Menlove Avenue.

Two hundred yards up Menlove Avenue, on the left, was the entrance to Menlove Gardens West, where the tram stopped. This was the point at which Wallace alighted from the number 5A tram on Tuesday 20 January. But to get to Calderstones Park, the Wallaces would stay on the tram and as it moved on from that stop and along Menlove Avenue, it would cross Green Lane before reaching the stop nearest to the main entrance of Calderstones Park, where they would get off.

In 1929, Wallace took up the violin and was given lessons by his Prudential supervisor, Joseph Crewe, who lived at 34 Green Lane. Crewe advised him how to get to his home. Wallace took the number 26 tram from Belmont Road down to the junction of Tunnel Road and Smithdown Road, and caught a tramcar from Smithdown Lane.

Green Lane runs between Menlove Avenue and Allerton Road, and I live about midway between the two, so that a number 8 tram up to Mather Avenue, or a number 5A or 7 along Menlove Avenue, would be equally convenient.[6]

This was Crewe's advice to Wallace on how to reach his home.

The number 8 tram ran along Smithdown Road, passed Ullet Road and Penny Lane and entered Allerton Road, then crossed over Queen's Drive and, turning away from Menlove Avenue, continued along Allerton Road to Mather Avenue. Green Lane is at the junction of Allerton Road and Mather Avenue. Wallace would alight there and walk two hundred and fifty yards up Green Lane to Crewe's house. Alternatively, Wallace could have caught a 5A, 5W or 7, as if going to Calderstones Park, and alighted at the top of Green Lane, where it crosses Menlove Avenue, and walked down Green Lane to Crewe's house.

Thus, Wallace was very familiar with the tramcar route along Smithdown Road to Ullet Road, Penny Lane, Menlove Avenue, Allerton Road and Green Lane. And it would not be too wild an assumption to conclude that he had travelled at least once on each of the five trams which ran those routes.[7]

But what is most important is that, with his knowledge of the Smithdown Road route, it is inconceivable that he did not know where Penny Lane, the major transport terminus in the area, stood, in relation to Ullet Road and Menlove Avenue. With his experience of the route, he could not have failed to appreciate that Penny Lane came after Ullet Road, that it came before Menlove Avenue and therefore before the assumed location of Menlove Gardens East and that any tramcar destined for Penny Lane, such as the number 5, while it would take him to Ullet Road and Penny Lane, would not take him to the Menlove Avenue area.

He was also familiar with the Menlove Avenue area, despite his protestations of being a stranger there: he may not have known all the street names in the area, nor all the side streets, but he knew some. For a man who made a living on the streets, collecting insurance premiums, noticing and noting streets and their names, and how to get to them, must have been second nature.

Given what was to occur after he boarded the number 5 tram on Tuesday night, the behaviour of Wallace throughout the journey to Menlove Gardens can only be viewed with the gravest suspicion.

3

All Liverpool tramcars had a permanent number embossed on the front and rear. Trams were designated a route number and a destination, which were both displayed, front and rear, within a glass-fronted panel, which was lit up at night.

As the number 5 tram, bound for Penny Lane, approached the Smithdown Lane stop at approximately six minutes past seven on the Tuesday night, both its number and destination would have been clearly visible in the lighted panel on the front of the vehicle. Before embarking, Wallace asked the conductor, Phillips, "Does this tram go anywhere near Menlove Gardens?"

Since Wallace was working on the assumption that Menlove Gardens was in the Menlove Avenue area, and as the number and destination on the tramcar were both clearly visible, the only reason for his question was that he wished to attract the conductor's attention: he knew Penny Lane came before Menlove Avenue and thus the assumed location of Menlove Gardens, and that a tram bound for Penny Lane would not take him to the Menlove Avenue area.

The only other possible reason for Wallace's question was that somehow he had failed to see the illuminated panel on the front of the vehicle, which clearly highlighted the destination – Penny Lane – and the route number – five.

Phillips told him that, no, his tramcar did not go to Menlove Gardens, and advised him to take the 5A, or the 5W or the number 7. Then, after a moment's consideration, he told Wallace to board and to purchase either a penny ticket, or a transfer ticket for Penny Lane, where he would have to change trams to one of the three he had mentioned. Wallace boarded the tramcar.

With the information supplied by Phillips, together with his own knowledge of the route, particularly the fact that Penny Lane came before the Menlove Avenue area and after Ullet Road, Wallace should have been fully equipped with everything he needed to know to get to his destination. He should have been assured and confident that he was heading in the right direction, where to change trams and which trams to take thereafter.

But, from the moment he boarded the tram and throughout the journey to Penny Lane, at every possible opportunity, he harassed both Phillips and Angus with questions and demands. The answers to his persistent questions were redundant in the light of his experience. He behaved as if he was travelling a route he did not know.

As Wallace boarded the tramcar he told Phillips: "I'm a stranger in the district, and I have an important business call. I want Menlove Gardens East." Phillips had not only told him that his tramcar did not go there, but also which trams he needed to take from Penny Lane.

Less than two minutes later, as Phillips took his fare, Wallace again spoke: "You won't forget, guard? I want to go to Menlove Gardens East." Phillips told him again to change at Penny Lane.

Within a minute or two of this exchange, Ticket Inspector Angus approached Wallace.

"I want Menlove Gardens East," Wallace told him.

"Change at Penny Lane. Then you want the 5A, 5W or 7."

Descending from the upper deck a few minutes later, Phillips was again accosted by Wallace.

"How far is it now? Where do I change?" he demanded.

"Penny Lane," replied Phillips.

By now, Wallace had been told several times to transfer at Penny Lane. What was the point then, of his repeated demands of Phillips and Angus about his transfer point? Had he forgotten the sprawl of the Penny Lane terminus? Had he forgotten that Penny Lane came before the Menlove Avenue area? Had he forgotten all his previous journeys along Smithdown Road? Why was he behaving as if he did not know the route? If he did not know the route, why had he decided to take it instead of the route he said he knew?

What is more, when Wallace asked Phillips how far it was before he reached the transfer point at Penny Lane, the tramcar had not yet travelled halfway along Smithdown Road; it had yet to reach Ullet Road, where he had often visited his sister-in-law. Nevertheless, he asked Phillips how far it was. Why? He knew Ullet Road came before Penny Lane and that if the tram had yet to reach Ullet Road, then it had yet to reach his transfer point at Penny Lane. Even if Wallace is given the benefit of the doubt, and it is granted that he did not know how far it was between Ullet Road and Penny Lane, his question should have been asked after the tramcar had passed Ullet Road, and not before. His question suggested that he did not know the whereabouts of Ullet Road, how far along Smithdown Road it was.

However, on the Thursday night following the murder, Wallace left Dale Street police station, and met with Samuel Beattie and James Caird as they left the chess club. They spoke, and then Wallace boarded a number 8 tramcar to take him to Ullet Road: he was then living at his sister-in-law's flat. He did not ask the conductor if the tram would take him to Ullet Road before he boarded; he simply got on.

He was followed by a detective, who later reported nothing untoward occurring on the tram journey. That is, the tram travelled through the city centre and up to Smithdown Lane, then along Smithdown Road to Ullet Road. And Wallace was not at all concerned or worried: as the tramcar travelled along Smithdown Road, not once did he ask the conductor how far it was to Ullet Road; he knew exactly where he was, where along Smithdown Road Ullet Road was, and where to get off. And yet two nights previously it would appear that he did not know.

What had happened to Wallace on the Tuesday night? He was an intelligent man, reserved and taciturn; the phlegmatic, reticent Stoic, who kept to himself. He was a man who was later to sit impassively through his own trial, and who, under examination, never once showed any signs of excitement or distress; he was a man who, without a care, had travelled throughout England in search of a livelihood, who had moved from one town to another without concern; a man who had bravely shipped out to the mysterious Orient without a second's thought, in search of better prospects in the strange and overcrowded cities of Calcutta and Shanghai.

However, here he was on a number 5 tramcar, totally out of character, reduced to a state of concern and dithering anxiety, demanding constant reassurance about travelling a simple route he knew so well, through a familiar part of the city where he had lived for sixteen years. Can his behaviour be seen as anything other than suspicious? Can it be seen as anything other than an attempt to impress upon Phillips and Angus the time of the journey and its destination? Can it be seen as anything other than post-offence behaviour?

What was the reason for Wallace's journey? He told Phillips it was for a, "very important business transaction". Again out of character, Wallace was suddenly very talkative, and proffered information unbidden, that he had important business to deal with, that he was a stranger to the area, which was untrue. On the Monday night Wallace had told Caird that he might not pursue the Qualtrough prospect and Qualtrough had not been very specific about his proposition. In the space of twenty-four hours, Qualtrough's lackadaisical and unappealing proposition had grown into an important business transaction, which the once reluctant Wallace was now pursuing with a determination and vigour so out of character, as to render him unrecognisable.

When interviewed by the police, both Phillips and Angus remembered Wallace without a moment's hesitation because of his persistent questioning; one passenger among the thousands they had served that day, easily and clearly remembered. They both recalled precisely what he had asked of them, what he had said to them and they both had the impression that he was apprehensive and anxious, and that he did not know the route.

Wallace's behaviour on board the number 5 tram can only be construed as highly suspicious. It was a pretence and a sham for him to have acted the way he did about a route and a destination he knew so well. And his behaviour, so out of character, clearly demonstrated that he wanted to attract attention to himself, that he wanted to be remembered by Phillips and Angus, that he wanted the time he boarded the tram to be noted. Phillips and Angus could not help but comply with his wishes. Wallace was already preparing his defence with this post-offence behaviour.

5

At Penny Lane, Wallace boarded the number 5A tram and asked the conductor, Arthur Thompson, to put him off at Menlove Gardens East, which Thompson agreed to do. Thompson told him to get off at Menlove Gardens West, informing him that Menlove Gardens East was probably a continuation of the former. Having alighted at Menlove Gardens West, Wallace left Thompson with a parting shot: "I am a complete stranger around here". He had also said as much to Phillips, as he had done to his fellow chess players on the Monday night, claiming that he did not know – that he was a stranger to – the Menlove Avenue area.

This was an obvious lie: as he alighted at Menlove Gardens West, ahead was Green Lane, where his superintendent, Crewe, lived and further on, the entrance to Calderstones Park, where he had taken Julia many times. Wallace was not a stranger to that area of Liverpool. Conductor Thompson, like Phillips, would remember that he had been on his tram and that he had been set down at Menlove Gardens.

Under examination at his trial, Wallace said that whenever he went to Calderstones Park with Julia, they travelled to the Smithdown Lane stop and then would ask the conductors which tram to take to get there. Further, when asked about his visits to see Joseph Crewe, he maintained that he had only been advised by Crewe to take the number 8 tramcar. This latter assertion, given what Crewe said in his statement, was untrue; but it was not pursued by the prosecution.

Unfortunately, Wallace was not required to say whether he asked the conductors which tram he should take whenever he visited his sister-in-law in Ullet Avenue. For a man who had used the Smithdown Road route as much as a dozen times a year, for at least ten years, to claim that he did not know which of the five trams from the Smithdown Lane stop he needed to take, is beyond belief.

The contention is that Wallace murdered Julia before setting out in search of Qualtrough. Therefore, he could not provide himself with an alibi. The best he could do was to create doubt among the investigators through his post-offence behaviour: could he have killed Julia and made it to Smithdown Lane by six minutes past seven? Perhaps, yes, perhaps, no. And that is exactly what he did: he established his presence miles from home by his persistent and mendacious avowals to Phillips, Angus and Thompson, about the tramcar route he knew, about being a stranger in a familiar area and he created thereby the necessary doubt and confusion which ultimately led to his release.

6

If Wallace's behaviour on the tramcar was a cynical attempt to establish himself as far as possible from home in the shortest time, then his search for Qualtrough in Menlove Gardens was both a continuation and an extension of the same process. Having made a fuss and bother over getting to Menlove Gardens, as if it had been a matter of life and death, to be consistent, he had then to show he was determined, however long it took, to find and contact Mr Qualtrough.

Having alighted at Menlove Gardens West, Wallace went in search of Mr Qualtrough. He questioned eight people about Menlove Gardens East, seven of whom informed him that no such address existed in the area. Yet, despite these negative replies to his inquiries, he persisted for an hour in his quest. The police and the prosecution argued that Wallace's continued search, in the face of so many denials, was, like his attention-seeking on the tramcars, nothing more than a sham to establish his presence four miles from home at a time which he hoped the police would conclude that Julia was murdered.

James Agate, the critic, diarist and bon-vivant of the inter-war years, was obsessed with the Wallace case,[8] and though he concluded that it was insoluble, he tended to favour Wallace's innocence. In part six of his autobiography-cum-diary, *Ego*, Agate makes reference to the case on three occasions. He comments on Wallace's dogged determination to find Qualtrough at Menlove Gardens East and argues that nothing suspicious or untoward should be read into it.

Agate cites a personal experience which, he argues, provides a parallel: while trying to locate the home of Lady Juliet Duff at 3 Belgrave Place, where he was due to dine, Agate was misinformed and misdirected by two policemen and four passers-by, before eventually finding the place, having wandered for an hour around the Belgrave Square area, where he had assumed, incorrectly, that Belgrave Place was located.[9]

Jonathan Goodman also quotes a similar, personal example in his book on the case, supporting both Wallace and Agate. This time the location is Belgrave Mews North, and Goodman, and later a friend, wander around Belgrave Square in search of the Mews, persistently asking for directions, until they find it.[10]

That Wallace's persistence in trying to locate Menlove Gardens East was no more than the determination of an innocent man to complete a task which he had started, is given additional support by Dorothy L Sayers. At the trial, Wallace said that the Qualtrough business, with his daughter coming of age, "might result in a policy of something like a one hundred pound endowment, or something of that nature".[11] Sayers then argues:

> To a man in Wallace's position, that would have been business worth getting ... All through this case one has to remember that Wallace lived in a small way and worked for very small profits. Nobody is more pertinacious than your small insurance agent. He will go miles to secure a few shillings ... It was nearly as certain as death and taxation that Wallace would never rest content till he had investigated the whole matter personally and on the spot.[12]

The very similar experiences related by Agate and Goodman are the only arguments that have ever been cited to counter the charge that Wallace should have given up the hunt for Qualtrough much earlier than he did and that the fact that he did not was highly suspicious and incriminating. Goodman's and Agate's accounts do not, in fact, parallel Wallace's search for Qualtrough. Whereas they were both in search of real addresses which people knew, and they were, on some occasions, misdirected by the people they inquired of, Wallace's search was for a non-existent address and he was repeatedly told that the address did not exist. What would have been Agate's and Goodman's reactions to the information that the addresses they were searching for did not exist? Would they have continued their searches?

There is a lot of truth in what Sayers has to say. But Wallace's persistence in the face of so many denials and his own belief, very early on in his search, that the address was bogus, stretch the imagination to the point of incredulity. And it must be remembered that on the Monday night Wallace had told Caird that he might not go to Menlove Gardens East. By the Tuesday night, he not only had made the trip, but was as tenacious as a bulldog in trying to track down the elusive Mr Qualtrough at the non-existent address. From indifference to zeal in less than twenty-four hours is not the attitude usually associated with the staid, plodding William Herbert Wallace.

The first person whom Wallace spoke to in his hunt for Mr Qualtrough was Sidney Green, who told him, without a great deal of preamble, that there was no such place as Menlove Gardens East. Wallace himself had noted that there was a Menlove Gardens North, West and South, but not East. When Wallace spoke to Kate Mather of 25 Menlove Gardens West, she told him that Mr Qualtrough did not live at her house and he then said to her: "It's strange, there is no East." That is, no Menlove Gardens East. At this point, Wallace himself believed there was no Menlove Gardens East in the immediate vicinity of Menlove Gardens North, South and West and he could have been forgiven for believing that Samuel Beattie had taken down Qualtrough's particulars incorrectly. But why did he persist? Where was the gain in him in wandering around deserted streets in the dark, having been told, and believing it himself, that the address he was looking for did not exist?

Wallace then returned to Menlove Avenue, where he accosted the only person he could find, a stranger to the area, who could offer no help to him. He then turned off Menlove Avenue and walked for half a mile down the length of Green Lane, which was deserted. At his trial, he claimed that he did not know where he was, or where he was going. So why did he walk down Green Lane? What was he hoping to accomplish by wandering down a dark, deserted road with which he was unfamiliar? The better option would have been to have walked back down Menlove Avenue to Allerton Road and Queen's Drive, where there were shops and people; where he might have obtained help. Instead he chose a route he did not know, or said he did not know, one that could have led him anywhere.

At his trial, Wallace told the court that he was halfway down Green Lane before he suddenly realised that it was the same Green Lane in which his superintendent, Joseph Crewe, lived. This was quite an astonishing statement and one that should have been forcefully taken up and attacked by the prosecution. The fact that it was allowed to pass, is an indication of how poorly prepared the prosecution were in this area.

Wallace had admitted visiting Crewe several times at his home; the trees in Calderstones Park could be seen from the back of Crewe's house. When Wallace crossed Menlove Avenue and entered Green Lane, the entrance to Calderstones Park, the very same park he had passed through with Julia, was to his left. Did he really expect people to believe that he thought this Green Lane, and this Calderstones Park, and the Green Lane wherein Crewe lived, behind which stood Calderstones Park, were two different Green Lanes, two different Calderstones Parks?

What is more, in his statement, Crewe related how he had told Wallace the route to his home on the 5A and number 7 tramcars, which involved alighting from the tramcar in Menlove Avenue, and walking down Green Lane. Yet when he did walk down Green Lane from Menlove Avenue on the night of the murder, he did not recognise it as such. Or so he told the court.

Wallace then told the court that he had knocked at Crewe's house, hoping that he would be able to tell him the location of Menlove Gardens East, but no one answered, there being no one at home.

Wallace was interviewed several times by the police and he made four statements. In the first two he gave details of his search for Qualtrough in the Menlove Avenue area. He failed to mention, during the interviews, or in his statements, that he had called at Crewe's house. He only mentioned the call under examination by Hemmerde KC, after hearing Crewe give in evidence the information that he was out on the Tuesday night, enjoying a visit to the cinema.

After failing to contact Crewe, Wallace claimed that he walked down Green Lane to the junction with Allerton Road, because he knew where he was by then and that there were shops and people in the area. So, he admitted that he was looking for shops and people to help him in his search. If this was the case, why had he not walked back to Queen's Drive earlier to the shops there, along a route he knew, instead of wandering along an allegedly unfamiliar road, where there might not have been shops and people?

At the junction, Wallace spoke to Police Constable 220F James Serjeant, who was later to state that he was nervous and stammered as he spoke. Wallace, more than usually talkative, supplied Serjeant with all the details of his quest and again he was told there was no Menlove Gardens East. Serjeant advised him to try 25 Menlove Avenue, a suggestion which he ignored and, as Wallace set off for the post office, he took out his pocket watch and asked Serjeant for a time check. The ever punctilious Wallace claimed that he checked the time to see whether he was too late for the post office. But why did he need to check the time with the policeman, when simply looking at his own watch, one he always kept correct, would have sufficed?

Wallace went to the post office in order to use, rather belatedly, a street directory. The post office assistant dispatched him across the road to a newsagent's. There, Nancy Collins allowed him to browse through a street directory at the counter, where he was interrupted by Lily Pinches, the manageress, who again told him that the address did not exist, and that she knew no one by the name of Qualtrough in the area. It was at this point, after almost an hour of fruitless searching, that Wallace gave up his search and decided to head for home.

Pinches would later state that he appeared cheerful, while Wallace later claimed that he was growing apprehensive and was anxious to get home.

It would have been reasonable for Wallace to have concluded, a great deal earlier than he did, in the face of so many denials of the existence of Menlove Gardens East, that Beattie had taken down the address incorrectly and that there was no benefit to be gained from pursuing the matter further. His dogged persistence, in the face of so many denials, verges on the ridiculous, if not the criminal.

From outside the Plaza Cinema in Allerton Road, Wallace boarded the number 8 tramcar, the only one serving the Allerton Road route, which took him back to Smithdown Lane, from where he took the number 27 to Belmont Road, and then home on foot.

During their investigation, when the police canvassed the Liverpool tram conductors for help, Phillips and Thompson immediately came forward, as did Ticket Inspector Angus. But the conductor of the number 8 tram, and those on the 26 and 27 trams, going to, and coming from, Smithdown Lane, did not come forward, probably because Wallace did, or said, nothing memorable.

Wallace had not used that route, Allerton Road to Smithdown Lane on the number 8, since the winter of 1929, when he ceased visiting Joseph Crewe. And yet he hopped on board that tram on Tuesday night, suspicious about the events of the night, anxious to get home as he later testified, but without a repeat of his behaviour from his earlier journey into the area. Since the tram conductor from the number 8 did not remember Wallace, then it can be assumed that he had not said anything to be remembered by, despite his apparent anxieties. That is, he did not pester and harass the conductor about whether this was the tram to take him part of the way home. Why not? Because he remembered the route.

Yet he had used the route along Smithdown Road to Calderstones Park throughout 1930; he had used it many times before he had started visiting Mr Crewe. But, strangely enough, it was the Smithdown Road/Menlove Avenue route, the more familiar of the two, which caused Wallace the anxiety, which resulted in all the questions; the less familiar route he took in his stride, without a question. It seems that Wallace's memory was highly selective when it came to the subject of tramcar routes.

7

The telephone message relayed to Wallace contained a false name and a bogus address. Was there an error in the transmission of Qualtrough's message to Wallace via Beattie? Or did Qualtrough make a mistake? Or was he too elaborate in his scheming?

It is understandable that the person who made the Qualtrough telephone call would give a false name. But a false address also? Experienced criminals know that the fewer lies told, the less chances there are of being caught out in a lie. A false name and a false address is an elaboration, an unnecessary complication.

If Wallace was innocent, he could have looked up the address in a street directory. The name is unimportant in this context, as the person could have been living in a flat at the address, or could have just moved into the area, in which case the name would not have appeared in the directory. The address is all important. The street directory would have established conclusively that 25 Menlove Gardens East did not exist. What does Wallace do now? Contact Beattie at work to check the details again? Telephone the Prudential and ask someone to look up the address in the latest directory? Call the police, suspecting some criminal intent behind the call? Decide not to go? Forget all about it? Decide to go on the off chance that the address might be locatable?

Qualtrough had jeopardised the success of his own plan from the start by being too elaborate with a false name and a bogus address. It would have been far better, far simpler, to have used a real address: Wallace may well have given up immediately when he did not find Qualtrough at the address, but that still would have given a murderer an hour's time in which to strike.

However, if Wallace was guilty, then the question of over-elaboration with the false name and the bogus address could also speak of inexperience, the same inexperience he demonstrated in staging the robbery.

Alternatively, since Wallace knew from his journeys with Julia to Calderstones Park that there was a Menlove Gardens West, he might have assumed, mistakenly, that there would be an East too and decided to use Menlove Gardens East in his plan. Then again, the false address could have been an error by Wallace.

On the Monday night at the chess club, when Beattie dictated the address to him, Wallace wrote it down and repeated it as 25 Menlove Gardens West. Beattie then interrupted him to stress East and not West and Wallace wrote down East in his book in block capitals. Why should he, having heard Beattie say East, repeat it as West? It was almost as if he was trying to anticipate what Beattie was going to say. Could there have been an error when the message was relayed to Beattie?

Wallace may have decided to use Menlove Gardens West as the address, but, when speaking on the telephone to Beattie in a disguised voice, the word West may have been heard as East by Beattie. And when Beattie started dictating the address to him, Wallace was expecting to hear the word West. If Wallace, as he claimed, did not know the Menlove Gardens area, he should not have known that the phrase Menlove Gardens could be followed by affixes North, South and West. So why should he have said West when Beattie clearly said East?

8

When Wallace returned home after his fruitless search, he tried to enter by the front door with his key, and found it locked against him. He went round to the back of the house, found the yard door unlocked and tried the scullery door, which would not yield. Returning to the front door, he tried again, unsuccessfully, with his key, and then knocked, but could not gain entrance. Mrs Johnston, next door, heard Wallace knocking. And it was on his second trip to the back of the house that he encountered the Johnstons on their way out.

The prosecution alleged that Wallace held back from entering his home until the Johnstons had put in an appearance and that he used them to witness his entry and the discovery of his wife's body. Hemmerde KC did not even bother to ask, as Goodman rightly points out, how Wallace could have known that the Johnstons were going out that night, at that time.

Goodman assumes that Wallace's meeting with his neighbours was purely fortuitous: he did not know that they were going out that night, and therefore could not have timed his arrival home to coincide with their exit. Bumping into the Johnstons in the entry was not planned, and no suspicion, therefore, can be attached to the fact that he had two witnesses on hand when he entered his house.[13]

But the houses in Wolverton Street were very thin-walled. Mrs Johnston in number 31 reported hearing Wallace knocking at the door on his return, while at six thirty in the evening, Mrs Holmes in number 27 had heard a knock on the front door of number 29. In other words, there was very little that could be done in and around a house in Wolverton Street without the neighbours overhearing.

If Wallace wanted witnesses standing by when he entered his home, then it could reasonably be said that he was creating a commotion at the front and rear doors of his home in order to attract the attention of his neighbours and that if they had not come out to him, he would have gone in search of them, either the Johnstons, or Mr and Mrs Holmes, and brought them outside to his back door so that they could witness his entry.

The first thing that he asked of the Johnstons as they stood in the entry by his back door, was whether they had heard anything unusual. Then Wallace told them he could not get in, but was sure that Julia was in, as she had such a bad cold.

On Tuesday afternoon, Julia had spoken to Arthur Bliss, the window cleaner, to her sister-in-law, Amy Wallace, who spent almost an hour with her, and the bread boy, Neil Norbury. In the evening, she had spoken to Allan Close when he delivered the milk. None of these people, in particular Amy Wallace, mentioned that she had a bad cold.

She had eaten dinner and tea with her husband, which would indicate that she was not ill. Wallace himself told the police that while she had been ill over the weekend, she had gone to the doctor's on Monday morning and that by the evening she had been sufficiently recovered for him to go to the chess club. He did not like leaving her alone at night when she was ill.

If he went out on the Tuesday night in search of Qualtrough, a task he was reluctant to take on, then Julia must have been well. However, upon his return home, when he could not get in, he told the Johnstons that she had a heavy cold and so would not have gone out. The problems he was having were therefore mysterious and perplexing. Had the Johnstons heard anything unusual?

Then Wallace told them that the scullery door was locked against him. Under normal conditions, had the Johnstons met Wallace in the entry, they would have passed on after exchanging greetings. Wallace had not only awakened their curiosity, but had also instilled in them the feeling that something was amiss. He did not directly ask them to witness his entry into the house; but he inveigled them to stay.

Under their watchful eyes, the scullery door opened readily. Hemmerde said that this was an indication that Wallace had been feigning, pretending that he could not get in, until he had witnesses around.

Sarah Draper, Julia's char lady, testified that sometimes the scullery door lock jammed and had to be manipulated in a particular way to force it to yield. This could be the explanation for Wallace claiming that the door was locked against him and he could not gain entrance to his home that way.

However, he should have been aware of this peculiarity of the scullery door lock, and of how to deal with it, even more so than Sarah Draper: she was only in the house once a week and thus had a limited knowledge of the door's peculiarity, whereas Wallace lived there and, mornings and afternoons, week in, week out, he left and entered the house through that door on his way to and from work.

Superintendent Moore tested the front door lock in Wallace's presence on the night of the murder. He said he could open the door but that the lock was defective. Wallace commented that, "it was not like that this morning". This was a curious reply since he had not used his key to open the front door that morning: he had left and returned to work through the back door. And he told detectives that he only used the front door when he was returning home late at night.

There was a great deal of debate among the detectives as to whether the front door was actually bolted from the inside to prevent Wallace from gaining entrance had his key worked. The locksmith, James Sargison, testified that both the front and back door locks were worn and would be likely to cause problems.

Yet Wallace made no mention of the tendency of the front door lock to jam. By way of explanation, what he did say to the police early on in their investigation was that he had the feeling that there was someone in the house, besides Julia, when he first tried to enter. Later, at the trial, he withdrew his statement, maintaining that he had been mistaken, that there was no one inside the house upon his return.

Perhaps he intended the police to believe that Qualtrough was still inside the house when he returned and had locked the front and back doors against him and, upon hearing Wallace at the front door a second time, had quickly unlocked the scullery door and made his escape. That the door then opened without a problem when Wallace tried it in the presence of the Johnstons was, therefore, understandable.

This type of incident, with Wallace making a statement and then withdrawing it later, is a notable characteristic of his behaviour throughout the investigation. When questioned by the police about his interrogation of Beattie outside the chess club on the Thursday following the murder, he intimated that he had some ideas of his own as to where the investigation should be directed. When pressed by Superintendent Munro for these ideas, he replied that they were not important and dismissed them.

After Wallace made his second statement to the police, the one in which, by anyone's interpretation, he directed them towards Richard Gordon Parry, he was asked by Inspector Gold whether he suspected any of the men he had named. Wallace said he did not. At his trial, Hemmerde asked him the same question: Wallace answered no. It is worth pointing out here that when Wallace named Parry in his second statement, he could not at first remember where he was working. But, not only did he know the name of Parry's girlfriend, Lily Lloyd, but also her address. Had he researched Parry's background in anticipation of setting him up for Julia's murder?

However, within days of his release from prison, Wallace committed to his diaries the fact that he knew the identity of his wife's killer. He did not actually name him, but he was undoubtedly referring to Parry. The case was still open at this time and Wallace wrote in his diary of taking his suspicions to the police and of steeling himself for a confrontation with the killer. He also wrote of trying to uncover the evidence which would lead the police to arrest Parry.

These three incidents, of Wallace stating something and then withdrawing it later, are reminiscent of a phenomenon well known to the police, that of a perpetrator attempting to insinuate himself into the investigation of his own crime. It is not a common phenomenon, but one which has occurred with sufficient frequency world-wide, that the police are always wary of too much help coming from the same person during an investigation, particularly one involving murder, and especially when that person points the police in a certain direction, claiming to know the identity of the killer.[14]

But when Wallace said he thought someone was in his home upon his return, he was implying that he had disturbed Qualtrough, that the thief was still in the process of robbing the house.

However, Qualtrough's exit from the house was orderly, and not effected under the pressure of being disturbed: the lights were all turned out throughout the house and a thief caught in the act is not going to stop to turn off the lights as he hurriedly makes his exit. Perhaps this contradiction became obvious to Wallace later on, and he knew that the police would see it. So, he withdrew the observation, claiming he had been mistaken, that there had been no one in the house when he had returned.

From the moment that Wallace left home on the Tuesday evening, until his return and the discovery of his wife's body, his behaviour can only be described as suspicious, if not criminal. He killed his wife and staged the robbery, then left home in order to establish that he could not have done either. There can be no doubt that his behaviour on the journey to Menlove Gardens, the search for Mr Qualtrough, and the presence of the Johnstons on his return, were all part of his post-offence behaviour.

Chapter 14
The Murder

1

The crux of the case against Wallace is a matter of time. On the Monday night the question was: Did Wallace have sufficient time in which to make the Qualtrough telephone call and arrive in time at the chess club? For Tuesday night, the night of the murder, the question is: Did he have sufficient time in which to murder his wife?

Wallace prided himself on his time-keeping, almost to the point, according to Goodman, of being fanatical.[1] It is not surprising, therefore, that time factors play an important part in the case. Because he could not provide himself with an alibi for his wife's murder, he used time as an ally, and manipulated time frames and sequences to produce what he hoped would be reasonable doubts about his involvement in his wife's death.

Wallace never went anywhere without his pocket watch, and he ensured that it was correct by regularly adjusting it to the signals given out by BBC Radio. Not everyone had, or could afford, a pocket watch and whilst wristwatches are a standard article of dress today, in 1931 they were very expensive and very few inhabitants of the areas where Wallace lived and worked would have possessed one. Most people in the streets gleaned the time from public clocks, such as the Holy Trinity Church clock, or by asking someone for the time, or by listening out for factory hooters and whistles. Today, most people have a keen awareness of time; in 1931 few people had.

On Tuesday evening Wallace said he returned home just after six o'clock from his afternoon collection round, and sat down with Julia to a meal of buttered scones and tea. After eating he described how he entered the front room to sort out some papers which he thought he might need for the transaction with Mr Qualtrough. Then he went up to the bathroom, washed his hands and face, changed his collar and combed his hair in the middle bedroom, and left the house at a quarter to seven. Twenty-one minutes later, he boarded the number 5 tramcar.

In his statement to the police of Wednesday 21 January, Allan Croxton Close stated that he had spoken to Julia Wallace as he had delivered her milk between six-thirty and six-forty-five. Later, with the assistance of the police, he changed his mind and agreed the time was approximately six-thirty.

The average time for the tram tests performed by the Anfield Harriers was eighteen minutes, that is, for Wallace's journey by foot from Wolverton Street down to the tram stop at St Margaret's Church, and then by tramcar to the Smithdown Lane stop. As six minutes past seven is a fixed point in the time frame, the time when Conductor Phillips first spoke to Wallace at the Smithdown Lane stop, the police concluded that Wallace left home at twelve minutes to seven and that, between six-thirty, when Julia spoke to Allan Close, and twelve minutes to seven, a period of eighteen minutes, Wallace murdered his wife, cleaned up, staged the robbery and disposed of the murder weapon.

James Allison Wildman made his statement to the police on 2 March:

I was halfway in the entry from Twyford Street to Richmond Park delivering papers, and I looked at Holy Trinity Church and it was then six-thirty-five.

After making two deliveries in Richmond Park, Wildman made his way to 28 Wolverton Street and then crossed over to number 27 to deliver the newspaper.

I saw a boy standing on the doorstep of number twenty-nine. He had two or three milk cans in his hand. The door of twenty-nine was wide open. I did not see anyone come to the door … I delivered the paper at twenty-seven and then went away, it would then be about twenty-two, or twenty-three minutes to seven … The next morning I heard of the murder, and I told my mother I was in Wolverton Street about six-thirty-five the previous night … I always look at the church clock as I am going through the entry to see how I am going on with my deliveries, sometimes I am early and sometimes late and I regulate my speed accordingly.[2]

The milk boy on the doorstep of number 29 was undoubtedly Allan Close, wearing his Collegiate College cap, which Wildman noticed. Even today, Wildman, the last surviving participant in the Wallace case, is still adamant that his timings are correct, that it was twenty-two or twenty-three minutes to seven when he saw Close on the doorstep.

I can still see the face of the church clock showing twenty-five to seven, and that was before I got to Wolverton Street.[3]

During the trial, Close was a poor witness under cross-examination by Roland Oliver KC: he sulked and at times refused to answer when pressed about his recollection of the time, particularly his certainty that it was definitely six-thirty when he spoke to Mrs Wallace, rather than between six-thirty and a quarter to seven, the timing from his original police statement.

Wildman, on the other hand, supported by his friends, Elsie Wright, Kenneth Caird and Douglas Metcalfe, was the better witness, and there can be no doubt that the jury believed him, rather than Close. His testimony formed part of the deliberations set before the Appeal Court, which led to the conviction against Wallace being quashed.

If Wildman's testimony is correct, that Close spoke to Mrs Wallace at twenty-three minutes to seven, and if, as the police maintained, Wallace in fact left home at twelve minutes to seven, then he had only eleven rather than eighteen minutes in which to murder his wife. And if, as the defence maintained, Wallace actually left at seven-forty-five, then he had only eight minutes in which to kill.

Florence Johnston, living next door to the Wallaces, was the most competent and consistent of the witnesses who gave evidence at the trial. Her story, in statement form, verbally at the police court, and even later at the trial, never varied. She had no axe to grind and simply told her story as she saw it happen. This is what she said in her second statement:

My milk was delivered from Mr Close of Sedley Street at about six-thirty that night. I have my jug in the lobby and the front door open. The boy shuts the door after he has put the milk in the jug. I heard the door shut that night and I fetched my milk at once.[4]

If Mrs Johnston's milk was delivered at six-thirty on the night of the murder, then so was Mrs Wallace's.

At number 27 Wolverton Street on the Tuesday evening, Bertha Holme was serving tea to her husband, Walter. She heard a noise at the front of the house.

"Is that a knock at our front door?" she asked of her husband, who replied, "No, it's at the Wallaces'."[5]

In their statements given to the police the day after the murder, both Mr and Mrs Holme said it was six-thirty when they heard the knock on the door at the Wallace house. Was this Allan Close knocking on the door to make his milk delivery?

James Wildman said he noted the time of twenty-five to seven on the church clock as he was halfway along the alley which ran between Twyford Street and Richmond Park. Midway along the alley is the best place from which to see the clock: at other points along the way the clock face is partially obscured by the alley walls and the angle of the clock tower itself.

However, when viewing the clock from Wildman's position, it is necessary to look up at an angle of twenty-five degrees, displaced a further ten degrees to the right from the vertical. In addition, the fingers of the clock are wide and black and it is configured in black Roman numerals and what

Wildman would have seen was an inverted Roman numeral number seven (VII) on an unlit clock face on a moonless, winter's night. Under these conditions, Wildman's claim that it was exactly twenty-five to seven when he saw the clock is improbable. At what point on the inverted seven on a dark night is it exactly twenty-five to, particularly when viewed from an angle?

The day after the murder, Wildman told his mother that he had been in Wolverton Street at, "about six-thirty-five". Mrs Johnston said her milk was delivered at approximately six-thirty; Bertha Holmes heard what would have appeared to have been a knock at the front door of number 29 at six-thirty. Allan Close wore a wristwatch, James Wildman did not.[6] In all probability, therefore, it was three or four minutes after six-thirty that Mrs Wallace closed the door on the milk boy.

2

Wallace was the chief suspect. Everything he said to the police, therefore, had to be treated with caution, and had to be checked out thoroughly. What is surprising about that part of the investigation which was called the tram tests is that the police uncritically accepted Wallace's word about the route he took on foot from home to the tram stop at St Margaret's Church.

On the Tuesday night, Wallace stated that he left home at six-forty-five, turned left out of his back door, and right again along the alley running between 79 and 81 Richmond Park. He crossed over Richmond Park, entered the alleyway at the side of the parish hall behind Letchworth Street, from where he emerged into the top of Sedley Street. From there he walked into Pendennis Street and then Castlewood Road, along which he walked to the junction with Belmont Road. There he turned left and walked down Belmont Road to St Margaret's Church, from where he caught the number 26 tramcar to the Smithdown Lane stop.

At Smithdown Lane, it was six minutes past seven when he boarded the number 5 tram and, having left home at six-forty-five, Wallace claimed the total journey time was twenty-one minutes. On the tram tests, which followed Wallace's route, the police had an average of eighteen minutes for the same journey.

However, Sergeants Bailey and Fothergill did not follow Wallace's route on their first tram test. At the top of Castlewood Road they turned right into Belmont Road instead of left, and walked a few yards to the tram stop where they boarded a number 26 tramcar. Thus they saved several minutes, avoiding the walk down to the church, by allowing the tram to take them there. Their total journey time from Wolverton Street to Smithdown Lane was fifteen minutes.

Roger Wilkes claims that Wallace was a sick man, and that he probably walked a lot more slowly than the police did from Wolverton Street to the church, because of his various ailments.

But he walked an average of one and a half miles a day on his collection round. He may have been victim to periodic bouts of illness, particularly with his kidney complaint, but he was certainly used to walking and, despite his illnesses, must have been reasonably fit. If walking was such a problem to him, as Wilkes alleges, why did he walk down to the church? Why did he not turn right into Belmont Road, as Bailey and Fothergill did, and catch his tram from the nearer stop? Had he done so, he would have saved himself the walk. Bailey and Fothergill clearly demonstrated that Wallace could have used their route and saved himself time, that it could have taken him much less than twenty-one minutes to make the journey down to Smithdown Lane…

If, as it is alleged, Wallace killed his wife and then set out to establish himself several miles from home in the shortest possible time, thereby casting doubts on his having had time in which to kill her and make the journey to the stop, then, by using a shorter route than the one he claimed to have used, it would help him in his scheme.

If Wallace did take the shorter route, timed at fifteen minutes by Bailey and Fothergill, then from the fixed point at six minutes past seven, he could have left home as late as six-fifty-one and if Mrs Wallace had closed the door on her milk boy at six-thirty-four, then Wallace would have had seventeen minutes in which to kill his wife, clean up, stage the robbery and leave the house.

3

The time of Mrs Wallace's death has never been fixed with any precision. Professor MacFall, accompanied by Dr Hugh Pierce, gave a time of death at approximately six o'clock. This estimate was based upon the progress of rigor mortis through the body which they observed in the front parlour. Dr Pierce was prepared to qualify his time with a two-hour correction on either side of six o'clock. But Professor MacFall insisted that the correction should be no more than an hour either way and that it was more likely only half hour.

Determining the time of death from the progress of rigor mortis is notoriously fallible and there are many factors, including age, health, stature, ambient temperature, clothing, all of which, either singly or in combination, can effect the onset and progress of rigor. The initial onset of rigor mortis occurs in the smaller muscles of the body, in the eyes in particular; but MacFall and Pierce relied upon the larger muscles of the legs and neck to measure its progress. The method they should have used, in situ, was rectal temperature measurement, which, though fallible in its own way, would have been an improvement over the rigor mortis technique. Nowadays, pathologists rely on chemical testing of bodily fluids and the contents of the eyeballs, liver temperature and electrical testing of the musculature, among other techniques, for estimating the time of death. But, as Professor Simpson has said:

Armed with all this data, the pathologist can still only give a time of death as a 'peak probability' and no more.[7]

The analysis of the stomach contents of a dead person can also assist in estimating the time of death. Professor MacFall, during the post mortem, did make a record of Julia's stomach contents.

The stomach contained about four ounces of semi-fluid food consisting of currants, raisins and unmasticated lumps of carbohydrate.

That is, the partially digested remains of her last meal, tea and scones, taken just after six o'clock on the Tuesday evening, were present in her stomach.

One has to be extremely prudent, on the finding of partially digested food in the stomach, what time lapse occurred between the last meal and death. Although it is usually stated in textbooks of physiology that a light meal leaves the stomach about two hours after being ingested, and that a heavy meal takes about four to six hours, there are various factors which can prolong gastric emptying, or even cause the stomach to cease emptying, and which can also slow down, or even stop the digestive process altogether. Not only head injury, but factors such as fear, stress, excitement, also, can significantly retard gastric motility and digestion.

Despite the forgoing caveats, one can, with justification, state without fear of refutation, that the contents of Mrs Wallace's stomach were fully consistent with her having drunk a cup of tea and eaten a couple of scones at about six o'clock, and being killed during the next two hours. Unfortunately, it is not possible to be more exact.[8]

Perhaps the best indicator that Julia Wallace was killed earlier rather than later, that is, at least an hour before Wallace's return home, is that no one who entered the front parlour immediately after the body was discovered, including Wallace himself, Mr and Mrs Johnston and PC Williams, reported the smell of burnt material.

The mackintosh was extensively burnt down the right side, so burnt, in fact, that charred pieces of material were scattered in the hearth and on the rug. Yet the smelly fumes from the burning material had dissipated by the time the body was discovered. Had the raincoat been burnt less than an hour before the body was discovered, there can be no doubt that some residual smell of burning would have remained inside the front parlour.

What is known is that, just after six-thirty, Julia Wallace was alive, and that she was dead by eight forty-five when discovered by her husband. She could have been killed any time within that period of just over two hours. And any medical evidence adduced cannot make it any more precise than that.

4

Whoever killed Julia Wallace must have turned off the light in the front parlour before making his exit from the room. He would not only have had to manoeuvre around the furniture and the prone body, but also around the bloodstaining. Unless he was equipped with a torch, the killer probably accomplished this with the aid of a lighted match and he managed to leave the room without knocking over any furniture or, more importantly, trailing any blood into the rest of the house.

Even with the aid of a torch, that would have been quite an accomplishment. But if the killer knew the exact layout of the furniture in the crowded room, he would only have to concentrate on the body and the bloodstaining. One step, two step, and he was by the door, having avoided all obstacles, especially the blood.

Wallace claimed that he struck a match to see into the front parlour and that that was when he discovered Julia lying prone on the floor. He said he thought she had had a fit. Thus, by his own admission, he should not have been expecting the large quantity of blood dispersed in the room, and he should not have taken any diversionary steps to avoid it. He stepped into the room, lit the right-hand gas lamp, and only then did he see the murderous devastation before him, at which point he rushed out to alert the Johnstons.

Wallace had entered a dark room, over-filled with furniture, unaware of the bloodstaining, which the flaring match could not have fully illuminated: just two steps from the doorway would have taken him to the leading edge of the hearth rug and his wife's battered head. And yet he managed to avoid the bloodstains.

Having seen his wife's dead body, and verging on panic, he rushed from the room, again avoiding the bloodstaining. He made two subsequent visits to the room to kneel close to his Julia's body and hold her hand, one with both the Johnstons and the other with Mrs Johnston. Yet through all this he did not pick up a single trace of his wife's blood, not on his hands, not on his clothing, not even on his shoes.

If Wallace had killed his wife, he could have left the murder room with the gas lamp still burning, cleaned up, and left the house. On his return, with the Johnstons waiting in the backyard, he need not have entered the front parlour to 'discover' his wife's body. He could claim that he had done so, that he had entered and lit the gas lamp, but in truth he had not, the lamp had been burning since the murder. In that way he could have avoided contaminating himself and his clothing.

5

If Wallace did kill his wife before he left home, he did not have a great deal of time, seventeen minutes at most, in which to do it, clean up, stage the robbery and escape. So, if he did it, how did he do it?

At the trial, prosecuting counsel, Edward Hemmerde KC, created a sensation when he averred that when Wallace killed his wife, he was naked except for the mackintosh, which he wore to prevent contaminating himself with blood and which he later tried to burn, so as not to incriminate himself.

Originally, Professor MacFall had said that the killer would have been splashed with blood during the murder. Then, as the police investigation progressed and Wallace fell under suspicion, to account for the lack of bloodstains on his clothing, under suggestion from Superintendent Moore, both MacFall and Dr Pierce reassessed the situation, concluding that the killer could have escaped contaminating himself had he struck Mrs Wallace about the head from a particular angle.

However, commonsense prevailed: with the amount of blood shed in such a confined space, the police and the prosecution really could not envisage the killer exiting the front parlour without having some blood traces on his clothing and shoes. Even had Wallace worn the raincoat over his clothes, there was still the chance of contamination, since the coat would not have covered the lower part of his trousers. Hence Hemmerde's suggestion that all Wallace wore when he murdered his wife was his mackintosh.

The suggestion of a naked, or near-naked killer, was not as far-fetched as it seemed at the time. On 15 September 1741, James Hall was hanged at the Strand for the murder of his employer, Peter Penney. Having knocked Penney unconscious with a cudgel, Hall stripped naked before cutting his throat.

One of the more sensational murders of the nineteenth century was that of Lord William Russel in 1840. His manservant, François Courvoisier, who resented being disciplined by the seventy-three-year-old lord, cut his throat while he slept. Tried and convicted for the murder, it was only hours before his execution at Newgate on 6 July, that Courvoisier confessed that he had been naked when he had cut his Lordship's throat, thereby ending the mystery of why his clothing had been free of bloodstains.

Neville George Heath, on the run for the murder of Margery Gardner in a London hotel, booked into the Tollard Royal Hotel in Bournemouth at the beginning of July 1946, under the name of Group Captain Rupert Brooke. He met a young lady, Doreen Marshall, staying at the nearby Norfolk Hotel, and they dined together at the Tollard on 3 July. Five days later, her naked mutilated body was found in Branksome Dene Chine, a gorge leading down to the sea, about two miles from the Norfolk Hotel.

Heath was eventually arrested and charged with both murders. He confessed that after dinner with Miss Marshall they had gone for a walk down to the Chine. There, Heath punched her into unconsciousness, dragged her into some bushes, and bound and gagged her. Then, stripping naked, he cut her throat, tore off her clothes, and savagely and sadistically mutilated the body. Having satisfied his blood lust, Heath then walked naked down to the sea, washed away all incriminating traces of his crime, returned to the scene, dressed, and wandered back to his hotel as if nothing had happened. He was hanged at Pentonville Prison on 26 October for the double murder.[9]

However, the suggestion of Wallace being naked beneath his raincoat as he killed his wife, was as far as the prosecution ever went in attempting to reconstruct how he had committed the murder. But this scenario did not answer the question of how the mackintosh was burnt – that Wallace tried to burn it after the murder makes no sense at all. Julia, wearing the raincoat on her shoulders when she was killed, does not fit into Hemmerde's scenario, either. However, Hemmerde's hypothesis of a naked, or near-naked killer certainly has its merits.

William Roberts, the City Analyst, said in evidence that some of the bloodstaining on the hearth rug was not spilt blood from Julia's wounds, but had been, in his opinion, pressed into the rug, as if the killer had wiped blood from himself, possibly from his feet, onto the rug.

The following reconstruction of the murder of Julia Wallace might appear far-fetched.[10] But, in the light of what has been said, and with further evidence in support, it is a distinct possibility that the murder was accomplished as follows.

Soon after finishing his meal on Tuesday night, William Wallace tells Julia he is not going to keep his appointment with Mr Qualtrough. He will have a bath, and then they will have an evening of music together in the front parlour to make up for having missed their practice the previous Sunday.

Wallace goes upstairs, runs a bath, undresses and waits at the top of the stairs. There is a knock at the front door. Wallace sees Julia go to the door to retrieve the newspaper. It is six-thirty. The bath is now as full as he wants it and he turns off the water. Minutes later there is a second knock at the door. Julia answers it to find that the milk boy has left a jug of milk on the doorstep.

Julia carries the jug to the scullery, pours the milk into her own jug, and returns to the front door to be greeted by Allan Close. She hands over the jug, bids the boy goodnight and closes the door. As she turns away, Wallace, knowing there will be no more interruptions, tells her to go into the front parlour to light the fire. She slips his raincoat over her shoulders before entering the frosty room. Naked, and armed with an iron bar, Wallace creeps down the stairs.

Julia has lit the right-hand gas jet above the mantelpiece. Wallace stands in the doorway of the parlour watching her stoop to light the fire, then moves in and strikes her on the head with the bar. She collapses across the fire. Perhaps momentarily stunned by the enormity of his deed, he stands back aghast, thereby allowing the mackintosh to catch fire and Julia's skirt to scorch.

He pulls her away from the fire, and tamps down the flames on the mackintosh, throwing it in the middle of the rug; and, as Julia begins to recover from the first blow and tries to sit up, he strikes the killer blow to her head, rupturing the meningeal artery. She falls once more to the floor on her back and dies. Noticing the scorch marks on her skirt, he rolls the body over to check there is no danger of further fire, and then delivers nine blows in a frenzy to the back of her head.

Any blood splashes on his body he smears over his skin to prevent them from dripping, wipes his feet and hands on the rugs, leaves on the gas light, and runs upstairs to the bathroom carrying the murder weapon. He could accomplish all this within four or five minutes.

As he climbs into the bath, he may well have deposited a small clot of blood on the inside rim of the toilet.[11] He bathes quickly, scrubbing his body, particularly his hands and fingernails, with the nail brush, to ensure that all traces of blood have been washed away, pulls the plug and dries himself on the towel as he stands in the bath.

In the middle bedroom he dresses, before returning to the bathroom. Turning on one of the bath taps, he uses his damp towel to sluice the bath clean, perhaps even adding some bleach or caustic soda from his laboratory to ensure that all traces of blood are removed. With a second towel, he dries the bath, the floor and the murder weapon, which he then wraps up in the first towel. In the rush, he leaves the wet brush on the edge of the bath. A further seven or eight minutes have passed.

Downstairs he dons his overcoat, wraps the towel containing the iron bar in an old newspaper, puts that in his pocket, hangs the second towel on the rail in front of the range in the kitchen, loots his cash-box, breaks off the cabinet door, and leaves the house by the back door, having turned off all the lights in the kitchen. With no more than four minutes having passed by on this phase of the plan, he could have accomplished the whole task in approximately fifteen minutes, if not less.

If Wallace then took fifteen minutes to reach the tram stop at Smithdown Lane, he would arrive there just before six minutes past seven, just in time to catch the number 5 tram to Penny Lane. Had he missed that tram and had to wait several minutes for another, no doubt he would have struck up a conversation with someone at the stop; a memorable conversation, probably with a reference to time, which would have involved checking his watch, just as he did with PC Serjeant at the bottom of Green Lane.

The timings given here are not absolute. It is possible to kill by beating a person eleven times about the head within two minutes; it is possible to wash and dress in under seven minutes and it is possible to stage a robbery, as poorly staged as it was, within three minutes. The important point to note is that when Wallace set out on this venture, he had no time limits; he created them as he went along. All he wanted to do was to accomplish everything as quickly as possible in order to create confusion and cause doubts to be raised about the time and his culpability. In this he succeeded.

Back home once more, after his fruitless search for Qualtrough, with the Johnstons looking on, he enters the house, collects the towel, now dry, and replaces it in the bathroom, then goes downstairs to the front parlour to 'discover' his wife.

Is there any evidence to support this scenario?

Wallace may well have been naked; that is a reasonable assumption. To have managed to avoid contamination with his wife's blood during the murder, after its discovery, and on his visits to the parlour later, suggests that he planned to ensure that no traces of blood, even if they were picked up innocently, were to be found on him. Going naked into the attack would have ensured that his clothing was uncontaminated; bathing afterwards would have ensured that all traces were washed away; knowing where the blood was when he entered the parlour on his return, enabled him to avoid contact.

Evidence that he bathed immediately following the murder is suggested by what Sherlock Holmes might have called the 'unusual circumstances' of the dry towel and the wet nail brush.

Before leaving home on Tuesday night, Wallace claimed that he washed his hands and face in the sink in the bathroom. Detectives at the scene of the crime found that the right-hand side of the sink overlapped the bath by ten inches; the bathroom towel was dry; the bristles of the nail brush on the edge of the bath were damp; the bath and the linoleum-covered floor were dry, too.

There was no face cloth or sponge in the bathroom, so if Wallace was telling the truth, with one or both taps running, he must have washed his face with his hands, rinsing off the soap by scooping up handfuls of water to his face. He then dried his face and hands on the towel, which was made of very thin cotton.

Yet, as he washed and rinsed and the taps splashed, not one drop of water fell, or was spilt, into the bath, or onto the floor. And as Wallace turned away from the sink to reach for the towel on the edge of the bath, with his hands and face dripping with water, not a drop fell to the floor, or into the bath.

According to Inspector Gold and Professor MacFall, the thin cotton towel was dirty but dry. The towel should have been damp, perhaps only slightly damp, but certainly not dry. There was no heating in the bathroom, and it was a cold winter's night. The towel was draped over the bath, and it would have been difficult for drying air to circulate around it. If the bristles of the nail brush showed signs of recent use, then the bathroom towel should have, too. It was made of thin cotton, the type that soaked up and held water.

But why was the nail brush damp? Wallace did not mention scrubbing his hands while washing. And how was a damp brush placed on the side of the bath without a drop of water falling into the bath, without any water being beneath it? Why was the brush placed on the side of the bath and not on the sink, where, if Wallace had used it while washing in the sink, it would have been a more natural place to put it after use? That the brush was on the side of the bath would suggest that it had last been used in the bath.

The arrangement of the bathroom does not lend itself to Wallace's story of washing his hands and face. The bathroom, in particular the bath, was too dry. There should have been more signs of recent use, a damp towel, water splashed in the bath, on the floor. And yet the one sign of recent use, the wet nail brush, placed on the side of the bath, cannot be accounted for by Wallace's story.

Did Wallace, after scrubbing away all traces of blood as he sat in the bath, place the wet nail brush on the side of the bath when he had finished? Did he, as he hurriedly dried up afterwards, lift up the damp brush to dry beneath it, then, inadvertently return it to the same place? Did he dry the very damp towel above the kitchen range and return it dry, too dry, to the bathroom before 'discovering' his wife's body?

If Wallace was the originator of the Qualtrough plan, as the evidence suggests, then he was capable of planning to kill his wife when naked, and of cleaning up afterwards in the bathroom. However, he was too fussy as he tidied up the bathroom, and gave himself away with the dry towel and the damp nail brush on the side of the bath.

6

What was the murder weapon, and what did Wallace do with it?

Possibly the murder weapon was some type of iron bar, probably with a knob or protrusion at the striking end, which would agree with Professor MacFall's first assessment of the type of weapon used: something hard, with a heavy head. It may even have been a hammer, or the blunt end of a chopping axe.

An axe was found beneath the stairs among some old clothes when Wallace searched his own house accompanied by Gold and Bailey. There were no blood or hair traces on the axe. But it had been used to chop wood for the kitchen fire, and Wallace told the detectives that it had been missing for twelve months. However, despite losing the axe, Wallace had not replaced it and it is not known what he had used to chop up his firewood after it disappeared.

Possibly the axe was the murder weapon and Wallace hid it beneath the stairs after the murder. But when he discovered that Sarah Draper was reporting on missing items from the house, and that she might claim the axe was missing, he decided to own up to its presence. But, having washed it after the murder, it is more than likely that Wallace felt confident enough to bring it out into the open. It was a strange place in which to lose an axe, in a basket of old clothes beneath the stairs.

If the murder weapon was a heavy iron bar with a knob, then Wallace could have obtained it without a great deal of trouble, and without anyone knowing he had it. In 1931 there was no set refuse collection from bins. Whatever household refuse could not be burnt on the fire, was dumped at a midden or rubbish heap. Every two or three streets there would be such a dump and householders deposited their waste there, later to be collected by the trucks of the Liverpool Corporation Sanitation Department which, in turn, carried the rubbish to a central dump area.

Anything, an old iron bar included, could turn up at a midden and Wallace walked a big area of Clubmoor on his collection round, and passed many a midden on the way. It could have been from a midden that he secured the murder weapon.

Following the murder, when Wallace reached Menlove Gardens West, he walked up towards the top of that road and, at its junction with Dudlow Lane, he met Sydney Green, who told him there was no Menlove Gardens East. Then Green continued on his way down Menlove Gardens West towards Menlove Avenue, leaving Wallace behind at the junction.

Sixty-five yards from that junction, further up Menlove Gardens West, was a walled enclosure, one hundred yards long by fifty yards wide, belonging to Liverpool Water Works. Within the enclosure, in the top right-hand corner, stood a small water pumping station. The remainder of the enclosure, with the exception of a short tarmac driveway inside the main gate, was given over to grass, bramble and shrub, which were all wildly overgrown. The wall was six feet high and lined with closely planted trees. Having seen Green on his way, Wallace had time to walk up to the pumping station enclosure and throw the murder weapon over the wall and into the undergrowth.

While the police did make great efforts to find the murder weapon, searching the grids, middens and alleyways around Richmond Park and Menlove Avenue, the fact that they did not find it does not mean that it was not there. It could have been overlooked, or disregarded, particularly if the police were looking for an iron bar from the house, a foot long and a quarter of an inch in diameter, which, in all probability, was not the murder weapon.

There is no record in the police file of a search of the grounds of the pumping station. Had they searched the grounds and found nothing, again that does not mean that the murder weapon was not there: they may have overlooked or disregarded it. And if they did not search the grounds, then no one will ever know whether or not the murder weapon, probably wrapped in an old newspaper and towel, was there: the enclosure has been redeveloped as luxury apartments.

Conclusion

On 28 November 1958, in Thanksgiving week, Lowell Lee Andrews shot to death his mother, father and elder sister at their home in Wolcott, Kansas. Then he opened a window, prized loose the protecting screen, and rifled through every drawer in the house, scattering their contents on the floor to give the impression that his family had been shot to death in the course of a house robbery. He dismantled the murder weapons and dropped the parts into the Kansas River.

He drove forty miles to the town of Lawrence, home of the University of Kansas, where he was a first-year student, and stopped at the campus house where he lodged. Usually a solitary, shy and uncommunicative young man, he engaged the landlady of the campus house in a long conversation, explaining to her that it had taken him nearly two hours to drive to Lawrence because of the bad weather, and that the reason for his journey was that he had come to pick up his typewriter.

Collecting the machine, he then drove to the cinema where, again uncharacteristically, he chatted with one of the ushers and a popcorn vendor before going in to view the feature film. Upon returning home, he telephoned the sheriff's office to report a robbery.

When the sheriff's men arrived, Lowell was sitting on the front porch stroking the family dog. He casually told them to look inside and when they did so they were stunned by the carnage framed by the signs of a robbery. What impressed the law officers during their initial investigation at the house was Lowell's callous nonchalance and indifference to the fate of his family: he seemed more concerned about the dog and when asked by the coroner what funeral arrangements were to be made, he replied that he did not care.

The robbery at the house was obviously staged, according to the police and when they found out that Lowell's conversations with the landlady, the usher, and the popcorn vendor, were definitely out of character, they obtained a confession from him with the assistance of the family pastor.[1]

The similarities between the Lowell murders and the Wallace case are striking: take away the Qualtrough telephone call and the method of murder, and the two cases are identical, Lowell copying Wallace. Neither man had an alibi; both were usually reticent but relied upon attracting attention to themselves at a distance from the murder scene, unbidden; both proffered information about the necessity for their journeys; robberies were staged at the murder scenes; both men became focal points for police attention by their callous and indifferent attitudes to the deaths of loved ones.[2]

Lowell Lee Andrews, Andy to his very few friends, was diagnosed as a simple schizophrenic. That is, he suffered no delusions, hallucinations, or false perceptions; he understood what he was doing, knew right from wrong and that the act of murder merited severe punishment. His illness was the total disassociation, or separation, of thought and feeling: he had no emotions.[3]

There is evidence, not only from Wallace's own Stoicism, a philosophy which eschewed emotional attachments in favour of indifference, that Wallace was a cold fish. "Cool, calculating and despondent," was how a colleague, Alfred Mather, described him. And while it may not be possible to show that he, like Andy, was a simple schizophrenic, sufficient detail is known about him to say that, at the very least, he was psychologically stressed.

His kidney ailment brought him great pain and he also suffered from constant headaches and lumbago, each of which disrupted his ordered day to day life. He had lost his left kidney in 1907 and he knew his life depended upon the healthy functioning of the other. When that organ began to deteriorate, it must have caused him great mental anguish, as did his other illnesses, not to mention the recurrent ailments of his wife.[4]

The malfunctioning kidney and the treatments he received to alleviate the problem, might not of themselves have caused any mental illness or imbalance in Wallace.[5] But the psychological effects of knowing that his life was on a knife's edge must have been acutely stressful. His diary is littered with brief mentions of the kidney ailment, and the depressions and headaches he suffered as a consequence. As his condition worsened, the stress would have increased.

Wallace's entire adult life might have been different, successful, brilliant, even, but for the illness. But for the kidney complaint he might well have remained in Shanghai and, through the auspices of his brother, have made a success of himself. He would never have met Julia Dennis if he had not had to return home. And in Julia he found a woman who was both a companion and a burden, a woman who was constantly ill and ailing.

Andy admitted that he had a motive for his murders: he wanted to inherit the family farm and sell it in order to move to Chicago to become a hired killer, a man of respect, the centre of attraction. This is a far cry from the lonely, taciturn, overweight, bookish student that he was. This was his dream, his fantasy, which, on that cold November night, he sought to turn into a reality by slaughtering his family. But given his character, it is doubtful, had he escaped retribution, that he would have attempted the move to Chicago. It was the dream which sustained him, rather than its realisation: it would always have been something he was going to do. But something must have triggered his violence and pushed him to attempt the realisation of his fantasy.

It is known that Andy had had a violent argument with his parents some days before the murders and it is probable that he resented them as a result and suddenly viewed them as obstacles to the culmination of his dreams. As

Douglas points out:

> *You generally see a precipitating stressor in the hours, days, or weeks before the crime. The two most common … to do with jobs and relationships – losing one or the other – but any type of hardship, particularly an economic one, can trigger the violent outburst.*[6]

Wallace, as he himself pointed out in his statement at the end of the committal proceedings, had not been credited with a motive for his wife's murder.[7] Because it would appear that he had no motive for killing his wife, it is argued that, therefore, he did not kill her. The traditional motives of financial gain, another woman, a flaring of domestic violence, were all ruled out.

All through his early life, Wallace strove to improve himself and his situation, but his ambition was thwarted by his kidney complaint. And when he appeared to be on the path towards bettering his position, when lecturing at the college in Liverpool, he gave it up without giving a reason. More than likely it was the stress of simultaneously holding down both the teaching post and the Prudential work, coupled with the strain of his own illnesses and the additional burden of Julia's.

If that was the case, then not only would he have resented the illnesses visited upon himself, perhaps demanding, why me? but he would have also resented Julia's contribution to his failure. Additionally, his own rancour would have been displaced to Julia, who would have been blamed totally for his failure; she would have been seen as the main obstacle to his breaking free from the common herd. He was, as Mrs Wilson said, a man who had suffered a keen disappointment in life, one which stayed with him to the end. He was bitter, resentful and highly stressed.[8]

Yet, despite his age and his illness, he was able to write in his diary, two weeks before the murder, that he had one more chance to put in some hard work, in order to pull himself free of the boring and repetitive Prudential collection rounds; he was still hoping for success, to better himself, to attain the rightful position and status which he thought his intelligence merited. Like Andy, he was fantasising about what he hoped to become. And, also like Andy, he blamed someone else – his wife – for his failure to produce a practical reality from his fantasy. Was the removal of Julia Wallace his one last chance?

Had he realised, following his month's stay in hospital in the summer of 1930, that he did not have long to live, not long in which to make something of himself? Was this the breaking point for Wallace, his precipitating stressor, which led to a well-planned outburst of violence? Did the diary entry signify that he was going to rid himself of Julia, whom he felt had been holding him back? Did it signal the removal of all the resentment which had festered deep inside him? Did it indicate that he was breaking free of his clinging wife to actualise his dreams and realise his true potential?

In terms of traditional motives, Wallace did not have a reason for killing his wife. But her murder was probably fuelled by resentment.[9]

Judson Ray was a colleague of John Douglas in the FBI. In 1982, Judson's wife hired a contract killer to murder him. Ray survived the attack and his wife and the assassin received long prison sentences.[10] One of the consequences of Ray's experience was that he took a great deal of interest in spouse murders, particularly those which were planned and premeditated. What he discovered was that the domestic atmosphere, very often fraught and belligerent, mellowed and calmed in the weeks immediately prior to the murder: the murderous partner called a truce.

When Ray analysed his own experience, it showed that this was indeed the case: there had been a rapprochement between himself and his wife, which she had engineered, in the weeks before the attempted murder. He had relaxed and let down his guard, anticipating a reconciliation in response to his wife's change in behaviour. It was his policeman's instincts which saved him from the assassin's bullets.

A radical, or even subtle but significant change in a partner's behaviour can mean that he or she has already begun to plan for a change in the status quo … has already come to regard that change as inevitable or imminent.[11]

There is evidence in his diaries that Wallace had adopted a more caring and considerate attitude towards Julia in the last two years of her life. He does continue to mention her various illnesses and ailments but the style of reporting has changed: he appears more concerned and details all aspects of her illnesses from onset to recovery, describing Julia as an …

… invalid for years a great worry and care.[12]

On 15 December 1930, Julia, on a visit to friends, was late returning home at night and Wallace, rather than waiting patiently at home, reported her as missing to the police at Anfield Bridewell, making a great fuss about his concern for her well being. The entry for 7 January 1931 stands out because he attempted to involve Julia as an equal in his observations, where usually he used her as a sounding board, and was critical of her when she could not grasp what was being said:

A night of keen frost … After dinner persuaded Julia to go to Stanley Park and she was equally charmed.[13]

In addition, there are several diary entries about Richard Gordon Parry:

Bamber points out how Parry wants watching in insurance work.[14]

It was as if Wallace was preparing the ground, both for the murder, and for Parry's indictment as Julia's killer.

Jack Douglas, as part of the initial FBI programme of interviewing serial killers in order to understand their behaviour, interviewed David Berkowitz, 'Son of Sam', at Attica State Prison, New York State in 1979. Berkowitz was, according to Douglas:

More of an assassin personality than a typical serial killer. Berkowitz is not what I would call a charismatic guy, and he was always searching for some bit of recognition or personal achievement ... He's pretty emotionally undemonstrative ... a loner who indulges in obsessive journal writing ... one way he resembles an assassin personality.[15]

The death of Julia Wallace was an assassination.

There are similarities between Andy and Wallace, Wallace and Berkowitz, in their profiles, in their personalities, in their attitudes towards life, towards other people, and towards the ways in which they compensated for their problems. Wallace was, like Andy and Berkowitz, a loner, neither charismatic nor emotionally demonstrative: each was looking for some form of recognition. Andy and Berkowitz both harboured a deep distrust of women, and if Wallace knew of Julia's age when he married her, then that would tend to suggest that he, too, distrusted women and that he married a woman much older than himself who would pose no threat to him.

For the sixteen years in which he lived in Liverpool prior to the murder of his wife, Wallace led a very ordinary, if not boring existence, having few friends either at work or in his immediate neighbourhood. And yet he took the time, on a daily basis, to record, sometimes in great detail, the tedious minutiae of his mediocre existence, just as Berkowitz did.

Obviously Wallace's diary writings meant a great deal to him, to the point of obsession. But why he should have bothered to record such ordinary fare, on such a very regular basis, is a question that has never been asked. He was a reasonably intelligent man and he did think he was a cut above the average. Did he imagine that he was a man of such high intelligence that his life story, his thoughts and opinions, as recorded in his diary, would be of interest to others?

And as a very occasional diarist, I also feel that the moment a man sets his thoughts down on paper, however secretly, he is in a sense writing for publication.[16]

Was Wallace, like Berkowitz, writing for posterity? He and Berkowitz were loners and a characteristic of such men is that they use, amongst other things, a diary as one of the primary means of communication. The Wallace case has remained unsolved and has been written about for many years, continually discussed and argued over. Was this how Wallace sought recognition, through the crime of murder, through his diary entries?

The murder of Julia Wallace was an assassination. Berkowitz assassinated his victims as did Andy. Berkowitz committed his thoughts to a diary, though he never detailed any of his murders. But he sought justification for them in the pages of his diaries, and apportioned blame to others for the deaths he was forced to bring about.

Similarly Wallace, after his release, used his diary not only to promote his innocence, but also to try and incriminate Richard Parry. He wrote that he knew who was his wife's killer, and of going to the police with his suspicions, of pointing Superintendent Moore in the right direction: he wanted the case re-opened and he was going to lead the way in catching the real killer. Again he was hoping to insinuate himself into the investigation. And he used the articles in the *John Bull* magazine to the same effect: proclaiming his innocence while pointing the finger at Parry.

Despite his carping over his neighbours for their alleged mistreatment of him following his release, nevertheless, like Berkowitz, Wallace enjoyed being in the spotlight, and relished the attention given to him by the press, both locally and nationally. He enjoyed being a focal point and took great pleasure in disseminating his own views on his own intelligence, his grief, and most importantly for him, the chance to start anew. He had and enjoyed his fifteen minutes of notoriety.[17]

If William Wallace was tried for the murder of his wife in a court of law today, there can be no doubt that the circumstantial evidence arraigned against him, supported by a behavioural profile, would be sufficient to secure a conviction; one that would not be overturned by the Appeal Court.[18]

William Herbert Wallace committed the perfect murder. He escaped scot-free.

Appendix

William Herbert Wallace – Statements to the police.
Note: The following statements are set out in their original form.

Anfield Detective Office
Tuesday 20/01/31
William Herbert Wallace says:

I am 52 years and by occupation an insurance agent for the Prudential Insurance Company, Dale Street. I have resided at 29 Wolverton Street with my wife Julia (deceased) age believed 52 years, for the past 16 years. There is no children of the marriage. My wife and I have been on the best of terms all our married life. At 10.30am today I left the house, leaving my wife indoors, doing her household duties. I went on my insurance round in Clubmoor district, my last call being 177 Lisburn Lane shortly before 2.0pm. I then took a tramcar to Trinity Church, Breck Road arriving at my house at 2.10pm. My wife was then well and I had dinner and left the house at about 3.15pm. I then returned to Clubmoor and continued my collections and finished about 5.55pm. My last call being either 19 or 21 Eastman Road. I boarded a bus at Queens Drive and Townsend Avenue, alighted at Cabbage Hall and walked up to my house at about 6.05pm. I entered my house by the back door, which is my usual practice, and then had tea with my wife, who was quite well and then I left the house at 6.45pm leaving by the back door. I caught a car from Belmont Road and West Derby Road and got off at Lodge Lane and Smithdown Road and boarded a Smithdown Road car to Penny Lane. I then boarded another car up Menlove Avenue West, looking for 25 Menlove Avenue East where I had an appointment with Mr RM Qualtrough for 7.30pm in connection with my insurance business. I was unable to find the address and I enquired at 25 Menlove Avenue West and I also asked at the bottom of Green lane, Allerton, a constable about the address. He told me there was no such address. I then called at a Post Office near the Plaza Cinema to look at the directory, but there was none there, and I was unable to find the address. I also visited a newsagent where there was a directory but I was unable to find the address. It was then 8.pm and I caught a tramcar to Lodge Lane, and then a car to West Derby Road and Belmont Road and walked home from there.

I arrived at Wolverton Street about 8.45pm and I pulled out my key and went to open the front door and found it secure and could not open it with my key. I knocked gentle but got no answer. I could not see any light in the house. I then went around to the back, the door leading from the entry to the backyard was closed, but not bolted. I went into the back door of the house, and I was unable to get in, I do not know if the door was bolted or not, it sticks sometimes, but I think the door was bolted but I am not sure. There was a small light in the back kitchen, but no light in the kitchen. I then went back to the front, I was suspicious because I expected my wife to be in, and the light in the kitchen. I tried my key in the front door again, and found the lock did not work properly. The key would turn in it, but seemed to unturn without unlocking the door. I rushed around to the back, and saw my neighbours Mr and Mrs Johnston, coming out of 31 Wolverton Street. I said to them, "Have you heard any suspicious noises in my house during the past hours or so?" Mrs Johnston said they hadn't. I said then I couldn't get in and asked them if they would wait awhile, while I tried again. I then found the back kitchen door opened quite easily. I walked in by the back kitchen door. I found kitchen light out, I lit it and found signs of disturbance in the kitchen. A wooden case in which I keep photographic stuff in had been broken open and the lid was on the floor. I then went upstairs and entered the middle bedroom, but saw nothing unusual. I then entered the bathroom, but it was correct. I then entered the back room and found no disturbance there. I then entered the front room, struck a match, and found the bed upset, the clothes being off. I don't think my wife left it like that, I then came down and looked into the front room, after striking a match and saw my wife lying on the floor I felt her hand and concluded she was dead. I then rushed out and told Mr and Mrs Johnston what had happened, saying something but I cannot remember what I did say. After my neighbours had been in, Mr Johnston went for the police and a doctor, I asked him to go. I afterwards found that about £4 had been taken from a cash-box in the kitchen but I am not sure of the amount. When I discovered my wife lying on the floor I noticed my macintosh lying on the floor at the back of her. I wore the macintosh up to noon today but left it off owing to the fine weather. My wife has never worn a macintosh to my knowledge. You drew my attention to it being burnt, but it was not like that when I last saw it and I [can't] explain it, I have no suspicion of anyone.

(Signed) William Herbert Wallace

There was a dog whip with a lash in the house which I have not seen for 12 months but I have not found it up to now. It usually hung in the hall stand. The handle was of wood 12" long and 1" thick, I don't think there was any metal about it.

Dale Street Detective Office
22/11/31
William Herbert Wallace further states:

Mr Gordon R Parry, of Derwent Road Stoneycroft, is a friend of my late wife and myself. He is now an agent for the Gresham Insurance Company. But I'm not sure of the company. He was employed by the Prudential up to about 12 or 15 months ago, and he then resigned to improve his position. Although nothing was known officially to the company detrimental to his financial affairs, it was known that he had collected premiums which he did not pay in and his superintendant, Mr Crewe, of Green Lane, Allerton, told me that he went to Parry's parents who paid about £30 to cover the deficiency. Mr Crewe's office is at 2, Great Nelson Street. Parry is a single man about 22 years of age. I have known him about three years and he was with my company about two years. I was ill with bronchitis in December in 1928 and Parry did part of [my] collecting for about two or three days a week for about three weeks. I discovered slight discrepancies and I spoke to him about it. He was short of small amounts when paying in and he had entered all the amounts collected in the book. When I spoke to him he said it was an oversight and that he was sorry and he [would] put the matter right. Previous to Parry doing my work he had called at my house once on business and left a letter for me which he wrote in my front room. I was not in at the time but my wife let him in. While he was doing my work in December 1928 he called very frequently to see me about business, and he was well acquainted with our domestic arrangements. He had been in the parlour and kitchen frequently and had been upstairs in the middle bedroom a number of times to see me while I was in bed. I do not think he called to see me after I resumed work in January 1929 but if he had have called, my wife would have had no hesitation in admitting him. I have often seen him since he has been working for his new company and have spoken to him. About last November I was in the City Café one evening, I think it was on a Thursday, playing chess, and I saw Parry there. He was not playing chess. He was by himself walking across the room. I said, "Good evening" and he returned my greeting. I think that was the last time I saw him. He is a member of an amateur dramatic society which holds its meetings at the City Café on Thursday evenings. I do not think he drinks. He is engaged to a Miss Lloyd, 7 Missouri Road Clubmoor. He would be on a weekly salary from his company plus commission on business and his earnings would be about £4 per week.

There was another man named Marsden who also did part of the work for me while I was ill in December 1928. I do not know his address. He was an agent for the Prudential Company for two or three years and had left before he did my work. I gave him the job because he was out of work. Parry recommended him. I have heard that Marsden left the Prudential on account of financial irregularities. While he was working for me he often came to my house to see me on business. He also knew the interior arrangements of my house. I have seen Marsden several times since he worked for me. I do not know if he is working now and I do not know anything about his private affairs. If he had called at my house my wife would have asked him in. Both Parry and Marsden knew the arrangements of my business with regard to the system of paying in money collected to the Head Office, Dale Street. There is a definite order of the company's that money must be paid in on Wednesday's but this is not strictly enforced and I paid in on Thursday usually. I have had the cash-box from which the money was stolen for about 16 years. I always put the company's money in that box and it was always kept on the top of the bookcase in the kitchen during the daytime. At night I always took it upstairs to my bedroom. Parry and Marsden knew I kept the money in the box because while they worked for me. I always put the money into it when they called to pay over to me their collections. They had both seen me take it down and put it back to the top of the bookcase in the kitchen often. Marsden is about 28 years of age, about 5foot 6/7inches, brown hair, and fairly well dressed. Parry is about 5foot 10inches, slimmish build, dark hair, rather foppish appearance, well dressed and wears spats, very plausible.

Superintendant Crewe, his assistant, Mr Wood, 26 Ellersley Road, Mr J Bamber, Assistant Superintendant, 43 Kingfield Road, Orrel Park, employees of the company, would be admitted by my wife without hesitation if they called. There are personal friends of ours who would also be admitted if they called. They are Mr FW Jenkinson, his son Frederick, 20 years? his daughter 16 and his wife. They live at 112 Moscow Drive. Mr James Caird, 3 Letchworth Street Anfield, his wife and family. He has two grown up sons. Mr Davis, the music teacher of Queens Drive, Walton, who is teaching me the violin. Mr Hayes my tailor of Breck Road.

I forgot to mention that I believe Mr Parry owns a motor car or has the use of one, because I was talking to him about Xmas time in Missouri Road and he had a car then which he was driving. He gave me one of his company's calendars.

When I left the house at 6.45pm on Tuesday night last, my wife came down the backyard with me as far as the yard door, she closed the yard door. I do not remember hearing her bolt it. On Monday night, the 19th inst. I left home about 7.15pm to go to the chess club. I got there about 7.45pm and started to play a game of chess with a man whose name I think is McCarthy, but I am not sure of him and I do not know his business. He is a member of the club. We had been playing for about ten minutes when Captain Beattie came to me and told me there had been a telephone message for me from a Mr Qualtrough asking me to go and see him at 25 Menlove Gardens East at

7.30pm on Tuesday the 21st, on a matter of business. Captain Beattie had the name Qualtrough and the address 25 Menlove Gardens East, and the time and date of the appointment written on an envelope and I copied it into my diary. Mr Caird was present and we all discussed the best way to get to Menlove Gardens. When I left home on Monday night to go to the chess club I think I walked along Richmond Park to Breck Road and then up Belmont Road, where I boarded a tramcar and got off at the corner of Lord Street and North John Street.

When I was at Allerton looking for the address 25 Menlove Gardens East, in addition to the people I have already mentioned, I enquired from a woman in Menlove Gardens North. She came out of a house near the end by Menlove Gardens West. She told me it might be further up in continuation of Menlove Gardens West. I went along as suggested by her and came to a crossroad, I think it was Dudley Road, and I met a young man about 25 years, tall and fair and I enquired from him but he could not inform me. I walked back down the West Gardens to the South Gardens and found all even numbers. I did not knock and came out on to Menlove Avenue itself, when I saw a man waiting for a tram by a stop where there was a shelter. I went up to him and asked him if he could tell me where Menlove Gardens East was, and he said he was a stranger and did not know. I think these are all the people I spoke to that night at Allerton.

When I got back home, and after getting into the house and making the discovery of my wife's death, Mr Johnston went for the doctor and police. Mrs Johnston and I stayed in, and some time after a knock came to the front door. I answered it and it was thus I found that the front door was bolted. The safety catch was not on the latch lock. I opened the door and admitted the constable. That was the first time I went to the front door after getting into the house.

When I left my house at 6.45pm, my wife was sitting in the kitchen, that is when I had got my hat and coat on ready to go, and as I have already said, she came down the yard with me. The tea things were still on the table. When I got back, the table had been cleared of the tea things.

There is a Mr Thomas, a member of the chess club and a Mr Stan Young who used to be an employee of our Company, who would be admitted by my wife if they called. I do not know their addresses. My wife had no friends unknown to me as far as I know. I have now found by the calendar that Mr Parry's employers are The Standard Life Assurance Company, whose head office is at 3, George Street, Edinburgh.

(Signed) WH Wallace

Dale Street
23/1/31
William Herbert Wallace further states:

Before I got on the tram at Smithdown Road on Tuesday night, I asked the conductor whether it went anywhere near Menlove Gardens. The conductor said I had better go to Penny Lane and have a transfer. I then boarded the car and sat inside on the first seat on the right. A few seconds later a ticket inspector entered the car and he told me to get off at Penny Lane and then take a 5a and he told me the numbers of other cars which I cannot remember and that either of those cars would get me to Menlove Gardens. I took a penny ticket and got off at Penny lane. The conductor pointed to a tram, a 5a, which was standing there and told me that would take me to Menlove Gardens. I boarded it and took a penny ticket and asked the conductor to put me off at Menlove Gardens and he did so. I remember looking at my watch and noticing that I had about 10 minutes to spare before the appointment was due at 7.30pm, So it must have been about 7.20pm when I got off the tram.

(Signed) WH Wallace

83 Ullet Road
29/1/31
William Herbert Wallace further states:

On Monday night the 19th inst. When I left home to go to the chess club I think I went out by the back door and up the passage to Richmond Park and then up to Breck Road and got the tram at Belmont Road. I do not remember seeing anyone I know. I am not sure but I have an idea that I posted a letter in the pillar box opposite the library in Breck Road. I have a lot of correspondence and I have no special reason for remembering about whether or not I did post a letter that night because I post so many.

When I returned home at 8.40pm on Tuesday the 20th inst. I went to the front door because it was my usual practice if I was out late at night. It was my usual practice to use the back door in daylight and if I went out by the back way after dark my wife usually came down the yard and bolted the yard door after me when I went out.

As far as I can recollect I do not know anyone named Hall living in the neighbourhood of Wolverton Street, or Richmond Park, or any of the streets adjacent, but I have an idea that I have heard my late wife mention someone of that name in connection with Holy Trinity Church, but my recollection of that is very hazy. In the summer of 1929 I remember my wife and I had been out for a walk. I had forgotten to take my key and we had to borrow a key from Mr Gosling who lives on the opposite side of Wolverton Street and his key opens our front door. Some years ago a man named Cadwallader, who lives at 33 Wolverton Street, had a key that opened our door, because he used to drink and on several occasions he made a mistake and came into our house instead of his own. He has been dead several years and his widow and son still live at 33 Wolverton Street.

(Signed) WH Wallace

Notes

Introduction

[1] The Liverpool City Police title of the case file. This force was amalgamated with Bootle Police in 1967; in 1974, this unit formed the central core of a much larger police force, covering a much wider area on both sides of the River Mersey, the Merseyside Police.

[2] Raymond Chandler, creator of the eponymous private eye, Philip Marlowe, in a letter to his literary agent, Carl Brandt, 14 December 1951. Chandler had been approached by *American Weekly* to write a series of articles on disputed murder convictions. Among the cases suggested was the Wallace case, which Chandler told Brandt, would be difficult: 'I call it the impossible murder because Wallace couldn't have done it, and neither could anyone else'.

[3] At least thirty-five non-fictional and approximately nine fictional accounts of the Wallace case have been published. Roger Wilkes of Radio City, Merseyside has made two radio broadcasts: *Who killed Julia Wallace?* aired on 20 January 1981, the fiftieth anniversary of the murder and *Conspiracy of Silence*, broadcast on 26 February 1981. Martin Fido, in his *Murders After Midnight* series for London Broadcasting Company Radio, aired the Wallace Case in 1988. BBC television broadcast a reconstruction of Wallace's trial in the *Jury Room* series in 1965, and in January 1990 they screened a television play, in the Screen Two series, *The Man from the Pru*.

Members of Parliament from Liverpool, Glasgow and Greenwich questioned both the Home Secretary and the Attorney General about the Wallace case in the House of Commons in May 1931. In March 1981, Robert Parry, Labour MP for Liverpool, Riverside, tabled a question for the then Home Secretary, William Whitelaw, asking why Merseyside Police had not released certain information about the Wallace case to the public.

In 1977, Robert Montgomery, a Liverpool barrister, prosecuted Wallace in a mock trial held by the Merseyside Medico-Legal Society.

Even today, in Liverpool, the case is still avidly discussed and argued over and articles and monographs are regularly published locally. See for example, *The Insurance Man* by the Reverend Richard Waterhouse, a limited private edition published in 1994, and *Wallace or Parry?* by Ian Kidd, first published in *Merseybeat* (1991) and later in *Outlook* (1993). Ian Kidd, a Liverpool policeman, regularly lectures on the case to groups and societies in the Liverpool area.

[4] *The Liverpool Classic*, in *The Meaning of Murder,* by John Brophy: Whiting and Wheaton, 1966, page 227. Referred to as Brophy in the notes.

[5] *The Killing of Julia Wallace* by Jonathan Goodman: Harrap and Company, 1969. Referred to as Goodman in the notes. The preceding quote is from the foreword by Edgar Lustgarten, eminent jurist and writer.

[6] *Murderer Scot-Free* by Robert F Hussey: David and Charles, 1972. Referred to as Hussey in the notes.

[7] *Wallace: The Final Verdict* by Roger Wilkes: Triad/Panther, 1985. Referred to as Wilkes in the notes.

[8] *The Murder of Julia Wallace*, by Dorothy L Sayers in *The Anatomy of Murder*: The Bodley Head, 1936. Referred to as Sayers in the notes. Sayers also wrote an abridged version of *The Murder of Julia Wallace* for the *Yorkshire Post*, 6 November 1934.

Two Studies in Crime, by Yseult Bridges: Hutchinson, 1959. Referred to as Bridges in the notes.

Raymond Chandler Speaking, by Raymond Chandler: Hamish Hamilton, 1962.

The Wallace Case, by John Rowland: Carroll and Nicholson, 1949. Referred to as Rowland in the notes.

Murder Casebook, The Perfect Murder, volume 25: David Jessel, media and planning consultant; Colin Wilson, adviser on the psychology of the criminal mind: Marshall Cavendish, 1990. Referred to as Jessel in the notes.

William Herbert Wallace, by Colin Wilson in *Unsolved Murders and Mysteries*, edited by John Canning: Futura Publications, 1988. Referred to as Wilson in the notes.

Colin Wilson has co-written at least three additional accounts of the Wallace case. He is consulting advisor on the psychology of the criminal mind in *Murder Casebook* (see above); with Pat Pitman he compiled *William Herbert Wallace* in the *Encyclopaedia of Murder,* and with Damon Wilson he wrote *The Wallace Case* in *World Famous Unsolved Crimes*. All four accounts are at variance with one another; the most accurate account of the case is in the *Encyclopaedia of Murder*.

Part One

In this reconstruction, all dialogues are from, and all events are based upon, the statements of witnesses, the evidence given at the committal proceedings, and the trial testimony (TT), all of which can be found in the Wallace files at the Merseyside Police Headquarters (MPH) and the Department of Public Prosecutions (DPP).

Chapter 1
Prelude to Death

¹ The church of St Mary's was still under construction when William Wallace married Julia Dennis, and the wedding was celebrated in the temporary church, the Tin Tabernacle, constructed of corrugated sheet iron and wood.

² The 'overhead', sometimes known as the 'Dockers' Umbrella', was the Overhead Railway Line, an elevated railway system which carried passengers through the Liverpool docks from Seaforth to Garston. Sadly it was closed and dismantled in the late fifties.

The dockers congregated in stands or pens to await work assignments. If there was no work, they still had to report to the stands twice a day in order to qualify for dole.

In 1931, because of the Depression, shipping was very scarce in Liverpool, so scarce in fact that when the SS *Baltic* of the White Star line berthed at Gladstone Dock on 10 March, over two thousand dockers rushed to the dock and a riot ensued as men fought for assignment to the ship, according to the *Daily Post and Mercury* of 11 March 1931.

The *Daily Post and Mercury* was Liverpool's morning newspaper, and *The Liverpool Echo* was the main evening paper.

³ The workhouse was an institution to provide accommodation and employment for paupers and the destitute, and sustenance for the infirm. Provision for the poor and needy went through many forms through the ages, but the Poor Law Amendment of 1834 stated that all who wanted relief had to live in the workhouse. Conditions were deliberately harsh to discourage the poor from relying on the parish and unions for relief. At the turn of this century, conditions did improve somewhat, but it was for many a shameful and degrading course to have to enter the workhouse in order to survive.

The social welfare services and social security system supplanted workhouses after the Second World War.

Some of the older hospitals in the major cities in Britain were once workhouses. Belmont Road Workhouse became Newsham General Hospital which, in turn, has been converted into a retirement home complex. Walton Hospital, the largest in Liverpool, was once West Derby Union Workhouse.

⁴ Most homes in the working class areas were yet to be supplied with electricity and major advertising campaigns were launched to encourage householders to convert to the 'wonders of electricity'. The 1931 Liverpool Corporation Tramways Timetable carried such advertisements.

In order to listen to the radio in a home without an electrical supply, an accumulator battery was needed as a power source for the radio. Most households kept two such batteries, one in use, and one being recharged at the local radio shop.

[5] Equivalent to one hundred and fifty pounds a week today.

[6] In 1931 in Britain, fourteen percent of all houses were owner-occupied, nine percent were rented from local authorities, and seventy-seven per cent were rented from private landlords, according to the Halifax Building Society.

Wallace was paying a weekly rent equivalent to £22 today.

[7] In his statement to the police on 21 January 1931, Beattie stated that he did not know Wallace's business: "I told him the message, said it was something about business although at the time I did not know what Wallace's business was". It is difficult, therefore, to understand the following: "Beattie ... made a mental note to pass on Qualtrough's message. Wallace was an insurance agent with the Prudential ... Qualtrough was contemplating an endowment policy for his daughter ... Wallace could stand to earn quite a substantial sum by way of commission". Wilkes, page 28; and, "Beattie knew that Wallace was a Prudential Assurance agent, and he guessed before he picked up the receiver that this telephone call might have something to do with his work". Goodman, page 20.

Chapter 2
Murder

[1] A bridewell was a small prison in the seventeenth century, and later a police lock-up; what nowadays would be called a police station. The original bridewell was the City Bridewell, Blackfriars, London, formerly a royal palace built over the holy well of St Bridget, commonly known as St Bride. After the Reformation, Edward VI turned it into a reformatory and penitentiary for unruly apprentices and vagrants and the name bridewell was then applied to all lock-ups in London, and later to those in the major cities of Britain.

[2] Collegiate College, a Grammar School for boys, was in Shaw Street, Liverpool. It was destroyed in an arson attack in 1986.

[3] In the Wallace literature, this tram stop is sometimes referred to as being situated at the junction of Tunnel Road and Smithdown Road, sometimes at the junction of Smithdown Road and Lodge Lane. Travelling south down Tunnel Road towards the docks, the tram reaches a junction: to the left is Smithdown Road, to the right is Smithdown Lane and straight ahead is Lodge Lane. The tram stop for journeys along Smithdown Road to Penny Lane and the Menlove Avenue area was in Smithdown Lane, just around the corner from Tunnel Road. The stop will be referred to throughout as being the Smithdown Lane stop.

[4] Goodman, page 33; Wilkes, page 39; Jessel, page 870 - are but three whose geography of Liverpool is wrong, and who incorrectly state that Wallace boarded a number 4 tram destined for Penny Lane. The number 4 tram did not go to Penny Lane or travel along Smithdown Road: it ran from the Pier

Head in the city centre to Wavertree via Wavertree Road and Picton Road, terminating at the Picton Clock.

The Smithdown Lane stop was in Edge Hill not Wavertree. Wilkes, page 39.

Goodman reproduces an accurate map of the area of the tram journeys but shows the number 4 tram travelling along Smithdown Road. Goodman, page 89.

When Phillips, the conductor, started work on Tuesday afternoon, he did work the number 4 route. But his route was changed later that evening to the number 5 route and it was on his second run on the number 5 route, from the Pier Head to Penny Lane, that he encountered Wallace. TT, page 43.

[5] It was the number 26, Outer Circular Route North and the return in the opposite direction was the number 27, Outer Circular Route South.

[6] Sergeant Bailey, who took the notes into evidence, only found four pound notes, one of which was stained with blood. Whether this was a new bloodstain that possibly Wallace left on the note, or whether it was an old one, was never determined during the course of the investigation.

Chapter 3
Julia Wallace

[1] Wilson, page 31. Colin Wilson and Pat Pitman say that Julia died aged fifty: Julia married in 1914, gave her age as thirty-seven, and died in 1931. Her age should have been fifty-three or fifty-four. *Encyclopaedia of Murder*, by Colin Wilson and Pat Pitman: Pan Books Ltd, 1964, page 631. Referred to as *Encyclopaedia* in the notes.

Jessel, pages 871, 875. Goodman, page 83. Sayers, page 159. Hussey, page 17.

[2] From the Wallaces's wedding certificate, wherein Julia gave her age as thirty-seven in 1914.

[3] George Smith Dennis, one of Julia's brothers, wrote to the police from his home in Redcar on 26 April 1931. MPH file.

[4] All data on the Dennis family is from census records, birth, death and marriage certificates, supplemented by information from Douglas Birch, a great nephew of Julia Wallace.

[5] So-named after a Mr Katton, a Scottish drover, who herded cattle from Scotland to the markets in North Yorkshire. East Harlsey was a stopping over point for the drovers and Mr Katton, whose forte was the bagpipes, would entertain the congregation of itinerant drovers and locals with his renditions. 'Katton's bagpipes' was corrupted into Cat and Bagpipes.

[6] A burgess was an inhabitant of a borough, male or female, entitled to vote in borough elections, providing he or she met certain qualifying criteria. Hence, Burgess Roll, the list of all burgesses entitled to vote. By the turn of

the century, prior to universal adult suffrage in Britain, women could only vote in local elections, providing they were property owners, leaseholders or rate payers. In 1910, Julia Dennis was a rate payer, and was thus entitled to vote in local elections.

[7] Private letter to the author from Douglas Birch.

[8] Goodman, pages 107-108.

Chapter 4
The Police Arrive

[1] Both the police and the prosecution made much of Wallace's demeanour following the murder, claiming he was indifferent and uncaring to his wife's fate. Professor MacFall said Wallace sat and smoked in a callous manner as the police investigated the death; officers reported Wallace having more interest in the family cat. Mrs Johnston obviously saw another side of Wallace's demeanour, and described it during the trial.

[2] In his statement, and in evidence at the trial, PC Williams said he held Mrs Wallace's right hand and wrist. TT, page 102.

Mr Johnston said that Julia was lying on her right arm, which could not be seen. TT, page 81.

Mrs Johnston said the right hand was beneath the body, and that only the left-hand could be seen and touched. TT, page 90.

The police photographs of the scene do show both right and left hands; but the photographs were taken after the body had been moved to facilitate the removal of the mackintosh. It is probable that the policeman confused left with right, and actually touched Julia's left hand.

Jonathan Goodman says that the right arm was visible, but his description of the murder room is confusing: he places the chair holding Wallace's violin case to the right of the fire, close to where Mrs Wallace's feet almost touch the brass fender, and below the right-hand gas bracket. The violin case was on the chair to the left of the fireplace, below the unlit, left-hand gas bracket. Goodman, page 38.

[3] Much criticism has been levelled at the police, particularly by Goodman and Wilkes, over the handling of the investigation. Superintendent Moore is singled out for unjustified criticism, most notably because he was drunk when he arrived on the scene, having just come from a private function. Moore was head of CID and would have been called out to a murder scene, on or off duty. Unless he was expected to sit at home when off duty awaiting such a call, then it is inevitable that at some time or another a call would find him indulging his time off. Goodman, pages 51-53; Wilkes, pages 177-178.

MacFall did secure the crime scene, which had been contaminated by Wallace and Mrs Johnston initially, and Moore's response after his arrival followed standard procedure as he set off the investigation.

By today's standards of investigation, Moore's methods may be open to criticism; but by the standard of the day the investigation was no better, no worse, than that of any other police force in the country, including the Metropolitan Police, which, in 1934, was roundly criticised by an official enquiry for failing in basic procedures when investigating a murder. *Bent Coppers*, by James Morton: Warner Books, 1994, page 66.

[4] A Treasury note was an exceptional currency note issued by the Treasury in addition to those issued usually by the Bank of England. Three issues of Treasury notes were made during the Great War, in August and October 1914, and in January 1917. The first two issues ceased to be legal tender in 1920, while the 1917 issue continued in use until 1933.

[5] There can be no doubt that Wallace clearly identified the mackintosh as his own to Mrs Johnston, PC Williams, Sergeant Breslin, and Moore, before Moore asked him to identify it again in the front parlour. The police and the prosecution made much of what appeared to be Wallace's reluctance to identify the garment, and the police attempted to claim that Wallace was unwilling to identify it because it tied him directly to the murder.

Chapter 5
Investigation and Arrest

[1] The more sensational the murder case, the more false confessions there tend to be. False confessions are the bane of investigating officers. Nevertheless, such confessions have to be checked through and they waste a great deal of valuable investigative time.

Amy Gidson of Blackpool wrote to the police in December 1931 claiming that a Mr G Williams was Julia's killer. MPH file.

In November 1931 an anonymous writer claimed that David Llewellyn Davis, working at the Lyons Bakery in Hanover Street, was the killer. MPH file.

At Prescot Bridewell, William Arthur Ian Forbes confessed to the killing in May 1931. A month earlier, at Walton Bridewell, James Gilmore confessed. MPH file

Colin Wilson says that the false confession, "is obviously closely related to the urge that produces the 'imitative crime': a certain envy of the murderer's experience. It also has some relation to the irrational desire for self-destruction". *Encyclopaedia*, page 32.

Oliver Cyriax says that three types of people are prone to make false confessions: the depressive, animated by a sense of guilt and a desire to be punished; the publicity-seeker and the fantasist, who cannot distinguish between reality and illusion. He adds a fourth category, the involuntary false confessor, citing the example of Hugh Callaghan, one of the Birmingham Six, who succumbed to police pressure and intimidation. *The Penguin*

Encyclopedia of Crime, by Oliver Cyriax: Penguin Books, 1996, pages 175-176. Referred to as Cyriax in the notes.

[2] Official British figures show that while there has been a vast increase in all types of crime since 1900, the comparative rise in murder has been slight. Moreover, there has been very little variation in the types and causes of murder. Ten times as many people die as the result of road accidents than murder.

There were 708 cases of murder in Britain in 1991, 91% of which were solved that year. Cyriax, page 120.

In England and Wales, the majority of murders are committed by people known to the victim: 59% when the victim is male, 78% when the victim is female. Stranger murders, that is, when the killer and the victim are unknown to one another, account for 20% of all homicides. *The Murder Year Book*, by Brian Lane: Headline Books, 1993, pages 18-36.

It is difficult to understand why British commentators, writing about murder rates in Britain, always insist on comparing the murder rates in Britain and America. It is as if they wish to show how good the British are in not killing as many of their own kind as the Americans do. Why they do not accept America, and its statistics, as a huge aberration, and leave the matter at that, without any comparison, is beyond comprehension.

[3] Linea albicans rather than linea albicantes: a white line down the front, centre of the abdomen where groups of muscle fibres meet.

[4] MacFall's post mortem protocol. MPH and DPP files.

[5] Both Wilkes and Goodman say that a fourth youth, Harold Jones, was present when Close told his friends on Wednesday night that he had delivered to the Wallace home at approximately six-forty-five on the night of the murder. There is no mention, whatsoever, of a Harold Jones in the TT, or in the MPH and DPP files. Wilkes, page 63; Goodman, pages 80 and 133.

[6] Qualtrough is an old Isle of Man name, a variant of the Celtic MacWalter. Goodman, page 75; Brophy, page 237.

[7] In 1925 the first coin-operated telephone box, taking two old pence, and having A and B buttons, was introduced. By the summer of 1931, the cost of a local call had risen to three old pence. To make a call, the caller lifted the receiver and was connected to an operator. The caller gave the number he wanted, inserted two pennies, and the operator made the connection. If the call was answered, the caller pressed button A to speak. If the connection was busy, or if there was no reply, the caller pressed button B to return the two pennies.

[8] Rochester Road no longer exists; it is now part of Lower Breck Road.

[9] Spring-heeled Jack first came to the attention of the public and the police in 1837, in London. Wearing a variety of clothing, from a cloak or white gown, to a tight-fitting suit and shining helmet, and of hideous facial appearance, the jumping man, as he was sometimes called, molested men and women

before escaping by prodigious leaps over walls and buildings. Reports of his attacks, gradually moving northwards, continued up to the turn of the century, when, in 1904, he made an appearance in the Liverpool suburb of Everton. *Tales of Liverpool*, by Richard Whittington-Egan: The Gallery Press, 1967, pages 9-13.

Liverpool policemen, among other names, were called Jacks.

[10] Celebrated Liverpool murder case in which Florence Maybrick was found guilty of murdering her husband, James, in 1889. Sentenced to death, she was reprieved and spent fifteen years in prison, before being released and allowed to return America. She died in poverty, a recluse, near the village of South Kent, Gaylordsville, Connecticut in 1941, aged seventy-nine. *Encyclopaedia*, pages 445-446.

Coincidently, James Maybrick met his future wife, Florence Chandler, on board the *SS Baltic*, sailing between New York and Liverpool in March 1880. See note 2, Chapter 1.

Raymond Chandler was asked to write about the case for *American Weekly*. See note 2, Introduction.

Shirley Harrison claims that James Maybrick was Jack the Ripper. *The Diary of Jack the Ripper*, by Shirley Harrison: Smith Gryphon Ltd, 1994.

Part Two

Chapter 6
William Herbert Wallace

[1] Copper mining in Coniston commenced in 1599 under the authority of the Society of Mines Royal. The mines covered four square miles of the Coniston fells. The last mine closed in 1954. *Coniston Copper* by Eric G Holland: Cicerone Press, 1987.

[2] Nathaniel Caine, iron merchant of Liverpool and John Barrat, mine owner of Coniston, opened the Hodbarrow mine in 1855. By 1881, it was one the largest producers in Europe of Haematite, a high-grade, phosphorous-free iron ore, ideal for steel production in the Bessemer Process.

The town of Millom grew out of the necessity for accommodation close to the workings for the miners.

[3] *North Western Daily Mail*, 20 May 1931. Mr Ferguson, who later became a prominent businessman in Barrow, also reported that Wallace had made a one day visit to Barrow in 1921 to see his old friends.

[4] *Plain Tales from the Raj*, edited by Charles Allen: Futura Publications, 1976, pages 95-105.

[5] *Heaven's Command*, by James Morris: Penguin Books, 1979, page 238.

[6] Though Goodman says Wallace returned to the same company in Manchester he had left in 1903, he does not appreciate that it was Whiteway,

Laidlaw and Company. Goodman, page 107.

⁷ Goodman, page 28.

⁸ The diaries of William Wallace disappeared after the trial. However, extracts were published in earlier works on the Wallace case and these are the source of later quotes from the diaries. The DPP file contains a brief summary of the diaries for the years 1927-1930.

⁹ Goodman, page 69.

¹⁰ Superintendent Hubert Moore's report to J R Bishop, pages 2-3. MPH file.

¹¹ Superintendent Moore's report, pages 3-4. MPH file.

¹² Dr Curwen's evidence was taken by Sergeant Bailey. DPP file.

¹³ *John Bull* was a weekly news magazine, founded in 1906 by Horatio Bottomley, patriot, journalist, Member of Parliament, bankrupt (269 times) and fraudster, for whom Dr Samuel Johnson's famous epigram, that the last refuge of the scoundrel is patriotism, would seem to have been coined.

¹⁴ Zeno lectured to his pupils from a porch: the Greek word for a porch is stoa; hence the name stoic to describe Zeno's school of thought.

¹⁵ *Philosophy Made Simple*, by R H Popkin and Avrum Stroll: W H Allen, 1973, page 21.

Chapter 7
Trial, Appeal and Release

¹ According to Goodman, there were 18 mis-statements of fact by Bishop in his rendition of the police case. Goodman, page 127. *The Liverpool Echo* of 3 February 1931.

² Mr W Johnson, MD, FRCP, Honorary Physician and Neurologist, Royal Southern Hospital, of 26 Rodney Street, Liverpool, submitted his report on Wallace's physical and mental condition to the police on 3 February. MPH file.

On 20 January 1843, in Downing Street, Daniel McNaghten, a wood-worker from Glasgow, shot dead Edward Drummond, Secretary to the Prime Minister, Sir Robert Peel, having mistaken Drummond for Peel. *Encyclopaedia*, page 62.

At his trial at the Old Bailey, McNaghten claimed that he was being persecuted by the Tories. The jury found him insane, and he was confined for life to hospital. The verdict was contested in the House of Lords and their Lordships passed the matter on to fourteen learned judges for their opinion.

These opinions are what are known as the McNaghten Rules and can be summarised as follows: an offender is presumed sane and to possess sufficient reason to be responsible for his crimes, until the contrary is proven; to establish a defence of insanity, it must be proven that the offender, at the time of committing the offence, was suffering under such a defect of reason so as not to appreciate the nature and quality of the offence, or, if he did so, that he did not know that the offence was wrong.

[3] In 1931, a person charged with an indictable offence such as murder, appeared at a police court, wherein a magistrate, after listening to the police case, decided whether to remand the accused into custody. If the remand was granted, the accused had then to appear in the police court before a magistrate for committal proceedings. Here, the accused could be represented by a lawyer or a barrister, and evidence was heard of the offence to decide whether the police had a prima facie case against the accused. If there was a case to answer, the magistrate committed the accused for trial at the Assize Court. Today, a similar system applies, but the police court has been replaced by the Magistrates Court, and the Assize Court by the Crown Court.

[4] Wilkes, page 85.

[5] Goodman goes seriously awry in his account of how Wildman's evidence first came to the attention of Munro and the police and he wanders off into the realm of conspiracy theories, alleging that the police tried to exclude witnesses who may have been of help to Wallace's defence. He claims that Munro began to question the integrity of the police and their intentions following his reading of David Jones's statement of 22 January. Goodman quotes Jones as saying that he delivered Julia's *Liverpool Echo* on the night of the murder, "about twenty-five minutes to seven". The newspaper was later found in the kitchen open at the centre pages, which would seem to imply that Julia was alive after twenty-five minutes to seven, thus knocking down the police contention that Wallace killed Julia immediately after the milk was delivered at six-thirty-one. When Munro discovered that Jones was to be excluded from the witnesses at the committal, Goodman has Munro speculating about the intentions of the police.

Later, when Munro heard Wildman's story and saw that he, too, was excluded as a witness, then Goodman has Munro pondering the question of whether the police are purposefully disregarding two important witnesses who can challenge the prosecution's thesis.

In his original statement to the police, Jones said that he had delivered the *Liverpool Echo* at, "about six-thirty", and that was the time Munro would have seen when he read Jones's statement. At Wallace's trial, Jones, who appeared for the defence, changed his testimony, and said he made his delivery five minutes later, at twenty-five to seven. It is this amended time, which Munro could not have known of when the committal began, which Goodman quotes as the starting point for Munro's suspicions against the police. The fact is that the police did not want to call Jones since his appearance at the Wallace house came before that of Allan Close, and so his evidence was superfluous. At the time, Munro, rather than becoming suspicious, agreed with Jones's exclusion from the committal.

The police did not know about Wildman until Munro informed them of him, which was after the committal had begun. Douglas Metcalfe brought Wildman to see Munro: Wildman had not been one of the youths, all interviewed by the police, who had spoken with Allan Close outside the library on the night after the murder. Metcalfe had not mentioned Wildman to the police, and so he had not been interviewed by the police. When Moore heard of Wildman, he immediately interviewed the boy at his home on 2 March, the day before the committal ended. Moore felt that Wildman, some forty days after the event, may not have been too exact with his times, and decided not to call him.

At Wallace's trial it was the decision of Edward Hemmerde KC, prosecuting counsel, not to call Jones and Wildman for the prosecution, but to leave them to the defence to call. And it was the judge, Mr Justice Wright, in his summing up, rather than Hector Munro, who said that both Jones and Wildman should have been called by the prosecution.

There was no conspiracy, as alleged by Goodman, by the police and prosecution to exclude witnesses who may have been of help to Wallace's defence. Goodman, pages 135-36. Correspondence between Bishop and Sefton Cohen during May 1931 in the DPP file.

[6] Joseph Clark, alias Joseph Kennedy, who had been raised in America, preyed upon gullible young women, extorting or stealing their savings from them before disappearing. In the autumn of 1928 he was lodging in Northbrook Street, Liverpool, and courting the daughter of the house, Alice Fontaine. Ordered from the house when Alice discovered a letter from one of his former fiancées, he returned a few weeks later and strangled her mother, also named Alice; he then attempted to strangle Alice, and tried to cut her throat. He confessed to the murder of Mrs Fontaine, and was hanged in March 1929. *Encyclopaedia*, pages 174-175.

[7] *The Murder And The Trial*, by Edgar Lustgarten: Odhams Press, 1960, page 71. Referred to as Lustgarten in the notes.

[8] There was a bloodstain on one of the four Treasury notes in the container in the middle bedroom, which Sergeant Bailey recovered.

[9] Mr Justice Wright's summing up. TT, page 316.

[10] TT, page 333.

[11] TT, pages 333-334.

[12] The first successful appeal to the Court of Criminal Appeal of a capital offence was made by Charles Ellsome, who was convicted of murdering Rose Render, a nineteen-year-old waitress, in Clerkenwell, London, on 21 August 1911. Found guilty in less than half an hour and sentenced to death, the verdict was overturned by the Appeal Court bench on the grounds that the trial judge had misdirected the jury.

The second successful appeal was made during the Great War by the German Consul at Sunderland, HA Ablers. He appealed against his death sentence for treason, and the verdict was overturned on the grounds that his defence had not been correctly presented during the trial.

Neither of these two appeals, however, involved the Appeal Judges declaring that the jury had made a mistake.

[13] Lustgarten, page 86.

[14] JT Ferguson, Wallace's Barrovian friend, quoted in the *North Western Daily Mail*, 20 May 1931.

[15] A telephone conversation with one of the school children, who wishes to remain anonymous, 7 August 1994.

[16] Quote from Wallace's diary. DPP file.

[17] Goodman, page 265.

[18] *North Western Daily Mail*, 22 May 1931.

[19] The postmortem was conducted by Elizabeth Lansdown MRCS. Uraemia and pyelonephritis were noted as the causes of death. Goodman, page 270.

[20] This is different from the one given by Goodman, which is incorrect, and which reads:

In loving and affectionate remembrance of Julia
Beloved wife of WH Wallace
In loving memory of William Herbert Wallace
RIP

Goodman, page 306.

Chapter 8
The Case Against Richard Gordon Parry.

[1] TT, page 69.

[2] Sayers, pages 206-207.

[3] The six *John Bull* articles were published weekly from 16 April 1931 until 21 May 1931.

Parry's riposte in the *Empire News* was published in 1933 under the headline *Wallace Accused Me*.

Following his release, Wallace was interviewed by the *Empire News* for an article on Sunday 24 May 1931 under the headline *The Hell I have Lived in*.

[4] 'But there are a number of further points which, I submit, conclusively prove that Wallace was innocent.' See *Chapter 12*. Goodman, page 272.

[5] For Goodman's account of the case against Parry, see Goodman, pages 296-300.

[6] TT, page 70.

[7] For Wallace's sly finger pointing at Parry, see Wallace's second statement, 22 January 1931. Appendix.

Wilkes wrongly claims that Wallace gave Parry's name to the police on the night of the murder. Wilkes, page 245.

[8] *John Glayde's Honour* by John Sutro: Samuel French, 1907. First performed 8 March 1907, at St James's Theatre, London.

[9] Wilkes, pages 197-198.

[10] Goodman, page 299.

[11] *The Last Sentence* by Jonathan Goodman: Hutchinson, 1978.

[12] For Wilkes's account of the case against Parry, see Wilkes, pages 177-222.

[13] Wilkes, page 177.

[14] *Who Killed Julia?* broadcast by Radio Merseyside on 20 January 1981. Besides Wilkes, those participating in the studio discussion were, Jonathan Goodman; Dr Charles St Hill, retired Home Office Pathologist; RH Montgomery, a Liverpool barrister; Philip Chadwick, a Sheffield solicitor and Ray Jackson, former head of Merseyside CID.

[15] Broadcasted on 26 February 1981.

[16] Wilkes, page 234.

[17] Wilkes, page 235.

[18] Testimony of Inspector Gold. TT, page 263.

[19] Quote from Wallace's diary.

[20] Wilkes, page 209. Members of Parry's family in high places could not prevent him from being charged and publicly branded as a common thief; but they could compromise and manipulate a murder investigation to ensure Parry's guilt was covered up.

[21] Canter, page 92. See also notes 7 and 8, *Chapter 10*.

[22] Canter, page 62.

[23] Canter, pages 48, 58. 'A man who plans his life and thinks things through, who holds down a job which makes some demands on his manual or intellectual skills, will go about the business of murder rather differently from the casual, confused ne'er-do-well.' Canter, page 85.

[24] Wilkes, page 208. Lily Lloyd also tells Wilkes she does not believe Parry killed Julia Wallace. Wilkes, page 201.

[25] Wilkes, page 209. Wilkes claims that Lily Lloyd confirmed to him that she had "assisted Parry to fabricate an alibi". Wilkes, page 201.

[26] Lily Lloyd, statement to the police, given on Monday 26 January 1931. DPP file.

[27] Josephine Lloyd, statement to the police, given on Monday 26 January 1931. DPP file.

[28] Richard Gordon Parry, statement to the police, given on Friday 23 January 1931. DPP file.

[29] Mrs Olivia Brine, statement to the police, given on Monday 26 January 1931. DPP file.

[30] Harold Dennison, statement to the police, given on Monday 26 January 1931. DPP file.

Part Three

Chapter 9
Profiling

[1] Edmond Locard, 1877-1966, was both a lawyer and a doctor of medicine. A student of the pioneering Alexandre Lacassagne, he succeeded him as Professor of Forensic Medicine at Lyons University, France, a post he held until 1910, when he left to set up the Police Laboratory. He lectured in Criminalistics in the Faculty of Law and he founded the Institute of Criminalistics. His classic, *Traité de Criminalistique*, was published in seven volumes from 1912 to 1939.

[2] *Criminal Shadows*, by Professor David Canter: Harper Collins, 1995. Referred to as Canter in the notes. *Mindhunter*, by Jack Douglas and Mark Olshaker: Mandarin, 1996. Referred to as Douglas in the notes. *Whoever Fights Monsters*, by R K Ressler and T Shachtman: Simon and Schuster, 1992.

[3] Canter, page 5.

[4] Canter, page 15. Douglas uses the word signature where Canter would use shadow. Both terms describe, 'something inherent, deep within the criminal's mind and psyche, that compelled him to do things in a certain way'. The signature or shadow is static, and must be differentiated from the criminal's modus operandi, which can, and does, change. Douglas, page 69.

[5] Douglas, pages 33-34.

[6] Within the FBI, profiling was not accepted as an investigative process until after the death of J Edgar Hoover in 1972. Hoover, the Bureau's Director for 48 years, viewed profiling with disdain.

[7] Canter, pages 53-70. Canter's contribution to the arrest and conviction of Duffy must rank as one greatest and most significant pieces of scientific detective work in British criminal history.

Chapter 10
The Killing of Julia Wallace

[1] The police explored the possibility of the killer gaining entrance with a key and Wallace's fourth statement, given on 29 January, reflects their interest. Had the killer done so, and surprised Mrs Wallace, some form of altercation must have occurred, even if she knew him, before he subdued her and took her into the front parlour to kill her. It is not possible to construct such a scenario from the evidence at the crime scene. Wallace's fourth statement is in the Appendix.

[2] The prosecution argued that Wallace wore the mackintosh to prevent contaminating himself with blood; that after the murder he tried to burn it, and later refused to identify the raincoat as his to Superintendent Moore. This is highly implausible. If he wore it, as suggested, then he must have

known it would become stained and if burning it afterwards was part of his plan, then why not burn it in safety of the kitchen fire rather than risk an uncontrollable fire in the parlour, the last thing he would have wanted?

There can be little doubt that Mrs Wallace wore the coat draped over her shoulders against the cold, having come from the warm kitchen along the cold hallway and into the icy front parlour. In the winter in particular, when moving from a warm room to a cold one, elderly people in those days would drape a coat over their shoulders to keep off the cold.

The skirt was burned accidentally when Mrs Wallace fell across the fire.

[3] When lighting such a gas fire, it was necessary to leave the gas full on for a few minutes after ignition, to allow the full flame to heat up the clay bars. It is probable that the gas was still full on when Mrs Wallace collapsed against the fire.

[4] The statements of Professor MacFall and Superintendent Moore. DPP file.

[5] Stating that Mrs Wallace was murdered during a robbery which went wrong simply says what the offender was doing. But it does not say anything about what type of person the offender was, which is far more relevant to the investigation.

[6] See *Chapter 11*, The Qualtrough Plan.

[7] Canter, page 157. Using subterfuge to gain entrance to a house for a criminal purpose is a sign of inexperience, according to Professor Canter. Had there been signs of a struggle, indicating that Mrs Wallace had surprised her attacker, then again this would denote an inexperienced offender: a more experienced criminal, when confronted by a frail, elderly woman, would, more than likely, restrain her, rather than resort to murder. It is reasonable to conclude that if Qualtrough was admitted to the house, then, from the outset, he was intent upon murder. Canter, page 158.

[8] Characteristic criminal behaviour reflects aspects of the criminal's personality. The early profilers such as Howard Teten, Robert Ressler and Jack Douglas developed a typology of violent criminals: they were either organised, or disorganised. The organised offender was one who planned his moves, who did not act impulsively, who would employ risk-reducing strategies, such as wearing gloves. This would in turn be seen in the organised criminal's life: he would be intelligent, socially competent, and have a good work history. In contrast, the disorganised offender was impulsive, acting on the spur of the moment as the opportunity presented itself, without any thought of the consequences, without any attempt to conceal his identity, or avoid arrest. In turn, he would have a poor work history, would tend to be a loner, socially incompetent, possibly shy and uncommunicative.

The organised/disorganised dichotomy is not absolute, nor is it that simple: the boundary between the two categories is extremely broad, flexible, and ambiguous. However, while most investigators recognise this nowadays, the dichotomy is still often employed, mainly as a starting point for an investigation, a convenient peg upon which to hang initial findings. *The Serial Killers*, by Colin Wilson and David Seaman: W H Allen, 1990.

Qualtrough would be initially classed as organised. As one who had planned his crime, who sought to control the situation from the outset, and who had been careful not leave behind any traces of himself, he would be older in the sense of being experienced, and in having lost the impetuosity of youth. He would probably be older than thirty. 'Violent, serious crimes such as … murder come later in a person's developing criminal career.' Canter, page 62.

'An organised crime scene will be produced by an organised criminal. The person who leaves his victim in a hurry … is likely to have left many difficult situations in his life in a hurry and be known for his haphazard ways.' Canter, page 85. Compare the life stories of Wallace and Parry, the former organised and controlled, the latter impulsive and disorganised.

[9] During the hunt for the Railway Rapist, John Duffy, Detective Constable Rupert Heritage, assisting Professor Canter, coined the term 'forensic awareness' to describe, 'the care a criminal has taken to ensure that he is not caught. It embraces not just avoidance of leaving fingerprints, but all other more subtle clues that modern forensic science can make available, such as bodily stains, fibres, facial identity.' That is, the criminal makes purposeful plans to avoid being forensically linked to the crime. Canter, page 373.

It was known that Duffy had combed through the pubic hair of one of his victims following the rape to ensure he left behind no hairs and that he cleaned up his semen with a tissue paper which he then burnt, thereby eliminating the evidence which could have been forensically available from the semen. Canter, page 61.

However, criminals have always been forensically aware. On 30 December 1921, in Melbourne, Australia, the body of twelve-year-old Alma Tirtschke was found in an alleyway in the red light district. She had been raped and strangled. The killer had washed the body to remove all forensic traces. Acting on a tip off from a member of the criminal fraternity, police arrested and charged Colin Ross, the owner of a drinking dive close to the murder scene. Found guilty of murder mainly on the evidence of fellow criminals, he was hanged at Melbourne prison on 24 April 1922, though there may have been a miscarriage of justice. *A Calendar of Killing*, by James Morton: Warner Books, 1997, pages 554-556. Referred to as Morton in the notes.

The case of the 'Black Dahlia', Elizabeth Short, a celebrated dismemberment murder, which occurred in Hollywood, California, in 1947, is another example of a forensically aware criminal. The body had been cut in half, drained of blood, washed clean, and the hair shampooed and hennaed. No forensic traces were found on the body and the killer was never caught. Morton, pages 25-27.

See also the case of Neville Heath, *Chapter 14*.

[10] During the trial Professor MacFall stated that the attack upon Julia Wallace, particularly the assault on the back of her head, had been frenzied. TT, page 138.

'The number of blows struck shows a frenzy of either fear or hate'; Raymond Chandler, in a letter to James Sandoe, critic of the *New York Herald-Tribune*, 21 November 1949.

[11] Canter, page 138.

[12] Douglas, page 178.

[13] John Douglas, profiling a murder case in which excessive force, similar to that used against Mrs Wallace, was employed, concluded that it was a domestic murder: 'This kind of overkill represents rage directed at a particular person, especially since so many blows were directed at the neck. This is not a stranger murder. He did not do what he did simply to kill her. He was making a statement. He was punishing her.' *Journey into Darkness*, by John Douglas and Mark Olshaker: Arrow Books, 1998, page 342. Referred to as Douglas and Olshaker in the notes.

And he adds: 'We know there's premeditation and planning. … The offender selected his weapon of choice. He's got a lot of rage, a lot of hostility, and he wants this to be personal.' Douglas and Olshaker, page 349.

[14] Wilkes, pages 193-198.

The television play, *The Man From The Pru*, portrays Wallace as a suppressed intellectual on the verge of an affair with his sister-in-law, Amy, and Julia turning to Parry for comfort.

[15] Whereas the murder scene was organised, the robbery scene was disorganised. Qualtrough would appear to show organised tendencies for the murder, but disorganised ones for the theft, which was the main purpose of the assault. See note 24 below.

[16] Canter, page 241.

[17] Canter, page 239. See also note 9, *Chapter 11*, The Qualtrough Plan.

[18] Douglas, pages 255, 267-268, 281-293. Canter, page 93.

[19] Canter, page 239. Within an established relationship when one partner plans to kill the other and escape retribution, the murder itself is usually organised. The front parlour was an organised murder scene, and the killer left behind no traces of himself. Canter, page 243.

[20] Douglas, pages 284, 286. Mrs Wallace was losing her hair, and it would appear that what she had was carefully looked after: she kept it well brushed and pulled back in to the chignon, which was false. No doubt she was very sensitive about the matter. The false piece became detached during the assault, and was left in the front parlour after the body was removed. The attack to the back of her head may have been aimed, in part, at detaching the false hair, thereby exposing her partial baldness; or the killer might have tried to pull it free of the head by hand. Either way, the attempted removal of

the false hair-piece was an insulting and degrading gesture on the part of her killer. Such an act would also suggest that her killer knew her very well. Douglas, page 178.

[21] *Written in Blood*, by Colin Wilson: Grafton Books, 1990. The Bamber case is dealt with on pages 275-278.

On 13 November 1974, Ronald De Feo murdered his parents, two sisters and two brothers, at their home at Amityville, Long Island. The murders were staged to resemble a gangland-style execution and De Feo told the police his father had had dealings with various members of the underworld. De Feo later confessed that he hated his family so much that he had to kill them. He was sentenced to life imprisonment. The De Feo family home later acquired an international reputation for horror as the subject of several books, and a film, *The Amityville Horror*. *The New Murderers' Who's Who*, by J H Gaute and Robin Odell: Harrap Ltd, 1989, pages 120-121. Referred to as Gaute and Odell in the notes.

[22] Goodman, page 228.

[23] Douglas, pages 268, 285-287, 290-292.

'We're better at uncovering staging than amateurs are at doing it.' Douglas and Olshaker, page 349.

[24] The possibility exists that there were two criminals engaged in the robbery and murder at Wolverton Street, one organised, the other disorganised. It was the older, calculating organised criminal who planned the enterprise, and sought control by killing Mrs Wallace and it was the younger, disorganised team member who perpetrated the hurried robbery. But if the organised, experienced, killer was in control of the situation, and was determined on robbery, it is highly improbable that he could not control his younger partner and make a success of the robbery. As the robbery was uninterrupted, since their exit was controlled and organised, the organised partner must have been in control throughout the time the two were in the house and so they must have had the opportunity in which to steal. That is, the robbery should have shown more characteristics of being organised: two men searching the house, one directing the other, should have made a better job of the robbery.

The crime scene evidence, and the logic of the situation, indicate that only one man was involved in the crime and that this one man showed characteristics of both an organised and disorganised perpetrator. Organised criminals can, and do, show disorganised characteristics, though the organised features will, by definition, outnumber the disorganised ones. See note 15 above.

[25] PC George Gutteridge was gunned down by Frederick Browne and William Kennedy in the early hours of 27 September 1927, near Brentwood in Essex, when he stopped the two men in the car they had just stolen. The killers were not apprehended until the following year; Browne in London,

Kennedy in Liverpool. Kennedy's arrest was widely reported in the Liverpool press. Browne was hanged at Pentonville on 31 May 1928, Kennedy at Wandsworth on the same day. *Encyclopaedia*, pages 120-123.

The most detailed account of the murder is by Christopher Dee in *The Criminologist*, Autumn, Winter 1987, Spring 1988.

[26] As noted by Amy Wallace, sister-in-law of William Wallace, when interviewed by Inspector Gold in the early hours of Wednesday 21 January. See *Chapter 5*.

Chapter 11
The Qualtrough Plan

[1] Goodman, page 282. Hussey, page 11.

[2] This point was a major contributor to the success of Wallace's appeal.

[3] Each player in the tournament had a number. Wallace was number six. For every round of the tournament, opposite each player's name was another player's number. Thus, on 10 November, Wallace played number three player, Mr E Lampitt. Lampitt lost and had the letter 'L' marked in against his number opposite Wallace's name and Wallace, as the winner, had the letter 'W' marked against his number, opposite Lampitt's name. Two weeks later Wallace was to have played McCartney, but the game was not played; no letters L and W were written by the names, indicating that the game had been played. In the next round, Wallace was to have played Mr Moore but again, no game took place; no L or W by the names. He had a bye, marked as 'X' against his name, in the next round and the game with Walsh was also not played.

It is known now that Wallace did not attend the club for those matches because either he, or Julia, or both, were ill. Wallace might well have attended the club at some time or another, between match dates, for example, but that is not shown on the list. And it is the list, and the information it gives, that is important to Qualtrough. The list states that Wallace had not been at the club since 10 November. Why, after perusing the list, should Qualtrough conclude that Wallace would attend on 19 January?

Goodman reproduces a facsimile of the playing list which is inaccurate, and which does not contain the relevant indicators of Wallace's failure to play his tournament games. Goodman, page 18. Wilkes reproduces a photograph of the list but fails to see its significance.

Wallace did not attend the club regularly, as his record shows. Despite this, both Sayers and Hussey, among others claim that he did. In addition, during the Qualtrough telephone call, both writers put words into Beattie's mouth to the effect that Wallace would attend the club on the Monday night.

'A waitress, Gladys Harley, answered the phone and turned the receiver over to Samuel Beattie, Chess Club Captain, who explained that Wallace was expected at any moment but had not yet arrived.' Hussey, page 18.

'The caller, who spoke in a 'strong, rather gruff voice', asked whether Mr Wallace was in the club. Mr Beattie said no, he was not, but would be there presently.' Sayers, page 164.

See Beattie's own version of the conversation in *Chapter 1*.

Beattie had a very difficult time during the first months of 1931. Not only was he involved in a murder and was a leading witness for the prosecution, but his good friend and fellow cotton-broker, Robert Taylor, committed suicide at his home in Blundellsands, Liverpool, on 15 February, shooting himself in the head in his car parked in the garage.

[4] Hussey, Sayers and Goodman, among others, believe that Wallace was innocent, and that Qualtrough was a thief who killed Mrs Wallace during a robbery which went wrong. They do not examine the crime scenes in their studies of the case, to see if there is support for their contentions therein and they try to squeeze Mr Qualtrough into ridiculous situations and circumstances to promote their unfounded beliefs.

Hussey has Qualtrough following Wallace from home, up Richmond Park to Holy Trinity Church. Wallace turns left into Breck Road and walks to the tram stop at the junction of Belmont Road. Meanwhile, at the church, Qualtrough turns to the right and walks back along Breck Road to the kiosk at the junction with Rochester Road.

Even at a brisk pace, that route would take seven or eight minutes to walk. If Wallace left home about a quarter past seven, then Qualtrough would have arrived at the telephone kiosk just after twenty minutes past seven. The Qualtrough call was timed at seven-fifteen. According to Hussey, Qualtrough arrived too late at the kiosk to make his own telephone call. Hussey, page 62.

Sayers redraws the topography of the Richmond Park area and re-writes Wallace's version of events to support her view. She says that the entry, or lane as she calls it, at the back of Wolverton Street converged with Wolverton Street, approximately four-hundred yards from Wallace's house and that where the entry, or lane, and the street met, stood the telephone box. Outside the telephone box Qualtrough was waiting and Wallace had to pass the box, and hence Qualtrough, to get to his tram stop. Qualtrough therefore knew Wallace was on the way to the chess club. Sayers, pages 166-167.

Goodman has Qualtrough witnessing Wallace leaving home at approximately seven-fifteen, and then hurrying to the telephone box to make his call. The reason Goodman has him hurrying, is that it is a brisk four-minute walk to the kiosk. Thus, in hindsight, Qualtrough must have hurried if he arrived at the kiosk in time to make his own telephone call at seven-fifteen. Goodman, page 293.

[5] The police decided that Wallace must have made the telephone call only after they had concluded that Wallace was the killer because the robbery was staged and there were no signs of forcible entry into the house. Prior to that,

the telephone call was not viewed by the police with any suspicion which could have been attached to Wallace.

[6] Sayers, page 168.

[7] James Allison Wildman, in a conversation with the author in the Childwall Fiveways public house, 4 December 1995. James Allison Wildman is the only surviving member of the cast of the Wallace case. Aged eighty-one, he is very fit and agile of both mind and body. The name Allison is a family name which his Scottish grandfather brought to England. Sayers, pages 170 and 203, says that Wildman is a girl; Wilkes refers to him as Allison Wildman. Wilkes, page 87.

[8] Caird suggested a route via Queen's Drive; McCartney said via Spellow Lane; Wallace said a tram into town and one out again. See *Chapter 1*.

The fourth route was via Wavertree and Picton Roads and Menlove Avenue on the 4A or 4W. See note 3, *Chapter 13*.

Beattie did not know where Wallace lived, and so he did not suggest a route, but a staging point, Penny Lane. See *Chapter 1*.

[9] Canter talks of the logical processes and means which a criminal utilises to escape detection and of how a criminal may establish a pattern of behaviour to avoid detection, behaviour which may become recognisable and identifiable by investigators. Canter, pages 130-136.

Douglas writes of high-risk and low-risk crimes, in terms of risk-level to the perpetrator and of high-risk and low-risk victims, in terms of the way of life of the victims. Thus the murder of a prostitute would be classified as a low-risk crime against a high-risk victim. Mrs Wallace would be a low-risk victim from what is known of her social habits. And with the Richmond Park area alert to the depredations of the 'Anfield Housebreaker', and the fact that Qualtrough was entering a house for a criminal purpose knowing that Mrs Wallace was at home, it can be said that Qualtrough was engaged in a high-risk crime against a low-risk victim, which makes the supposed main motive for the assault, robbery, highly unlikely. Douglas, page 290.

[10] Goodman, page 272.

Chapter 12
Was Wallace Innocent?

[1] Goodman, pages 283-285.

[2] In his statement to the police of 26 January 1931, James Caird said that he saw Wallace enter the chess club at seven-forty-five. Samuel Beattie actually checked with all members of the club who were present on the Monday night, and none of them could remember seeing Wallace in the club until seven-forty-five. "I can now say he was not in the club earlier than 7.45pm on Monday, 19th instant." Beattie's second statement to the police, 24 January 1931. DPP file.

Goodman makes the point that chess games at the club were to start before seven-forty-five, and if they commenced after that time, then penalties would be exacted against the latecomer. Had Wallace arrived just on seven-forty-five or later, then he would have had, argues Goodman, to apologise to his opponent and that his lateness and the apology would have been remembered and passed on to the police during their investigation. Thus Wallace must have arrived before seven-forty-five, since his opponent did not remember an apology.

However, Wallace's opponent on the Monday night should have been Mr Chandler, who did not attend and so Wallace went in search of one of his opponents whom he had not played from previous rounds because of his own failure to attend the club. He turned down Caird's request for a friendly game, and searched out McCartney for a game which should have been played on 24 November. Because the game had not been arranged, or re-arranged, specifically for that night, and was set up there and then, the usual rule about lateness was not a consideration between Wallace and McCartney.

[3] Goodman, page 284.

[4] The first statement by Wallace. Appendix.

Very few writers to date have mentioned the fact that Liverpool had a bus service in 1931. Wilkes also reproduces Wallace's first statement in his book, yet assumes that Wallace always travelled by tram. Wilkes, Appendix 1, pages 273-4. In Hussey, Chapter 2, a chapter surprisingly entitled, *Factual Resumé of the Wallace Case*, Hussey ignores Wallace's first statement, and has him catching a tram on Tuesday evening after finishing work; Hussey, page 19.

During the trial, Sergeant Bailey mentioned, in reply to Mr Justice Wright, that there was a bus route to the chess club. TT, page 205.

Wilkes says the average time of the journey by tram from the kiosk to the chess club was eighteen minutes, as against Goodman's twenty-one minutes. Wilkes, page 264.

[5] The Liverpool Tramways Timetable, in which were carried the timings and routes of all the Liverpool buses, did not print route numbers for the buses as it did for the trams, but simply described their routes and the stops they made. The buses did have route numbers, but with time, changes in ownership, and changes in routes, the 1931 route numbers for the buses have been lost.

The bus routes described herein were actual routes, though their route numbers, 10 and 11, are not, and have been inserted by the author for the sake of clarity.

The Liverpool Corporation tram system began operations in 1869, while its bus service commenced in 1911. By 1931, seven hundred and fifty-seven tramcars, on fifty-seven routes, carried two hundred and fifty-one million passengers, along one hundred and seventy-five miles of lines, and one hundred and seventy-nine buses, carried twenty-four million commuters, on twenty-six routes, totalling one hundred and fifty-three miles. The cost of a bus journey was almost three times that of the equivalent tram trip; but buses were quicker because they reached speeds above those of trams, and were not confined to fixed lines. *Liverpool Red Book*, 1932.

[6] Goodman, page 280.

[7] Brophy, pages 241-42.

In *Mindhunter*, Jack Douglas mentions one of his colleagues, Bob McGonigel, who worked as an undercover agent in various cities of America. McGonigel had a great gift for mimicry, and was able to change his voice and accent as the situation or guise demanded. He particularly utilised his talent over the telephone, on pretext calls, a technique the FBI had developed to catch suspects unaware. He could be a Black Panther, a New York hoodlum, an Irish gangster, or a sophisticated WASP, all within the same call. He was so good that he often hoodwinked his colleagues over the telephone as a joke. Douglas, page 62.

[8] Hussey, page 61.

[9] Canter, page 197.

[10] Annie Robertson's statement to the police, 23 January 1931. DPP file.

[11] Sarah Draper's statement to the police, 21 January 1931. DPP file.

[12] Professor MacFall's post-mortem protocol. DPP file.

[13] Conversation with the author, 20 January 1997.

Sarah Draper said that she had used the iron bar to retrieve a screw from the gas bracket, which had fallen to the hearth and rolled into the gap between the hearth and the front of the gas fire. To manipulate an iron bar in such a confined space, as Draper did, would suggest that the bar was thin, probably no more than an inch in diameter.

[14] Iron has a specific gravity of 7.8. The quarter inch bar, 12 inches long, would weigh 0.66 pounds, the half inch bar 2.65 pounds, and the two inch bar 10.6 pounds.

[15] Sayers, pages 189-190.

[16] Goodman, page 279.

[17] Letter of 2 June 1931, from Samuel Evans to Superintendent Moore. MPH file.

Chapter 13
Menlove Gardens East

[1] Mr Justice Wright's summing up at the trial. TT, page 316.

[2] Goodman, page 294.

[3] See notes 3 and 4, *Chapter 2*. As the number 5 tramcar moved across the Smithdown Lane/Smithdown Road/Tunnel Road/Lodge Lane junction, Ticket Inspector Angus boarded at Earle Road and remained on board until

disembarking at Portman Road, half a mile along Smithdown Road, something he would not have been able to do had he been aboard a number 4 tramcar. The number 4 terminated in Picton Road, some distance from Penny Lane.

Tramcar 4A ran to Menlove Avenue and Calderstones Park via Wavertree and Picton Roads and the 4W travelled to Woolton via Wavertree and Menlove Avenue. Wallace could have used either the 4A or 4W as they both stopped at Menlove Gardens West, but could have boarded neither at the Smithdown Lane stop.

[4] Caird's statement to the police, given on 26 January 1931. DPP file.

[5] Liverpool Tramways Timetable and route map.

[6] Crewe's statement to the police, 26 January 1931. DPP file.

An incorrect version of Crewe's statement in Goodman asserts that Crewe only told Wallace of the number 8 route to his home and that therefore Wallace was a stranger to the Menlove Avenue area. Since Crewe did give Wallace the alternative routes, then Wallace did know them, and could have used them. Goodman, pages 110-111.

[7] To visit his sister-in-law, Wallace used the route described, as it is the only route he could have taken to her home. In his diary for 1930, Wallace records three visits to Amy Wallace, in April, July and November. DPP file.

When visiting Calderstones Park, Wallace himself said that he used the route described. TT, page 256.

Wallace said he went to Calderstones Park twice a year. TT, page 256.

In 1929, the Wallaces went to Calderstones Park twice in three months, recorded in Wallace's diary. DPP file.

Crewe gave Wallace instructions on how to get to his home. Crewe's statement, 26 January 1931. DPP file.

It is significant that Roland Oliver KC for the defence, when examining Wallace, did not question him on his routing to Menlove Gardens, or about his behaviour on the journey. Nor did Edward Hemmerde KC during his cross-examination.

[8] James Evershed Agate (1877-1947), bon vivant, wit, writer and diarist, wrote literary and dramatic criticisms for *The Manchester Guardian*, *The Sunday Times* and BBC Radio. In addition, he wrote several novels, many essays on the theatre and literary criticism, and three anthologies of English Literature. He was not a crime writer, but something about the Wallace case piqued his interest, which was maintained until his death.

He was a close friend of Edgar Lustgarten, and together they spent many hours discussing the Wallace case. His autobiography, *Ego*, was published in nine volumes, and the Wallace case is mentioned and deliberated upon in the sixth. *Ego 6*, by James Agate: George G Harrap and Company Limited, 1944. Referred to as Agate in the notes.

[9] Agate, page 70.

[10] Goodman, pages 273-274.

[11] Nowhere in any of Wallace's statements or outpourings prior to the trial is there even a hint of the type of policy (endowment), the cost (£100), or the amount of commission he could have expected had the Qualtrough offer been genuine. His barrister, Roland Oliver KC, put the words into his mouth. TT, page 235.

If the policy was worth £100 at the time of the trial, why was it not worth £100 on the night he received the Qualtrough message, when he told James Caird he might not go to see Mr Qualtrough?

During the trial, Wallace's Superintendent, Joseph Crewe, made it quite clear, as Wallace did not, that Wallace would receive 20% of the first year's premium, approximately two or three pounds, and not 20% of the value of the £100 policy, that is, £20. TT, page 69.

Sayers, in order to justify Wallace's persistence in attempting to locate Qualtrough, infers that he would have received £20 in commission. Sayers, page 168.

[12] Sayers, page 168.

[13] Goodman, page 289.

[14] 'Now, because of what we've learned, we routinely consider the likelihood that a subject will attempt to insinuate himself into the investigation.' Douglas, page 112.

The case of Leonard Herbert Mills is a classic instance of this tendency. Mills murdered Mrs Mabel Tattershaw near Sherwood Vale, Nottinghamshire, on 9 August 1951. He reported the finding of the body to a reporter for the *News of the World*, led the police to the body, and described a suspicious-looking man he had seen lurking in the vicinity. His story appeared in the newspaper and he continued to prompt the police with ideas and suggestions about the direction of the investigation, and the killer's identity, until he gave himself away. He was hanged at Lincoln Prison on 11 December 1951. *Encyclopaedia*, pages 458-459.

This killing was motiveless in that Mills's motive does not conform to the motives usually ascribed to murderers. See note 14, Conclusion.

Chapter 14
The Murder

[1] Goodman, page 285.

[2] James Allison Wildman's statement to the police, 2 March 1931. DPP file.

[3] James Allison Wildman, conversation with the author, the Childwall Fiveways public house, 4 December 1995.

[4] Mrs Johnston's statement to the police, 21 January 1931. DPP file.

[5] Bertha Holme's statement to the police, 21 January 1931. DPP file.

[6] Allan Close 's statement to the police, 21 January 1931. DPP file.

Close also stated that he usually delivered the milk to the Wallace home between six and six-thirty. Goodman claims that Close usually delivered the milk at about six o'clock, and that the reason he did so at six-thirty on the night of the murder, was because his bicycle was being repaired. Goodman then goes on to try and construct a case for Wallace's innocence, based upon his timing for Close's delivery. But the argument cannot be sustained, because Goodman has his facts wrong. Goodman, pages 294-296.

[7] Jessel, page 891.

[8] Private letter from Dr J Burns MD, Head of Forensic Pathology, Liverpool University.

[9] *The Penney Case*, Jessel, page 888.

The Russel case, Gaute and Odell, pages 107-108.

The Heath Case, Encyclopaedia, pages 312-316. Heath also insinuated himself into the police investigation of both of his murders. See note 14, *Chapter 13*.

[10] But not as far-fetched as the reconstruction suggested by Leslie Walsh, junior to Edward Hemmerde KC, at the trial. In a conversation with Roger Wilkes in October 1980, Walsh said that Wallace was guilty, and that he had killed Julia before Allan Close delivered the milk. When Close did call, Wallace, having forgotten about the milk delivery, quickly disguised himself in one of his wife's dresses, and went to the door to collect the milk, speaking to Close in a falsetto voice. Wilkes, pages 261-262.

[11] How the blood came to be deposited on the rim of the toilet, and to whom it belonged, has never been established. At the trial, no forensic evidence of analysis was cited to say whether the blood was of the same group as that of Mrs Wallace. All that was learnt was that the blood was not menstrual.

Conclusion

[1] *In Cold Blood*, by Truman Capote: Penguin, 1967, pages 304-309. Referred to as Capote in the notes.

Andrews was hanged for the triple slaying on 30 November 1962, at the Kansas State Penitentiary, Lansing.

[2] Lowell Andrews showed more interest in the family dog than in the murders. Wallace apparently was more concerned about his cat than the death of his wife. See note 1, *Chapter 4*.

The author's first appointment to view the Wallace file at Merseyside Police Headquarters in 1992 was cancelled because the file was on loan to Merseyside CID, who were investigating a murder with many similarities to the Wallace case.

[3] Capote, page 308.

[4] Over fifty per cent of Wallace's diary entries refer either to his own, or Julia's illnesses. DPP file.

[5] Goodman, pages 274-276. Reference is made to the possibility that Wallace

became insane as a result of his kidney illness. Goodman rightly points out that the illnesses which caused Wallace's death do not directly produce associated mental illnesses.

[6] Douglas and Olshaker, page 104.

[7] "The suggestion that I murdered my wife is monstrous, that I should attack and kill her is, to all who knew us, unthinkable and unbelievable, all the more so when it must be realised that I could not possibly obtain one advantage by committing such a deed, nor do the police suggest that I gained any advantage." Wallace's statement to the Committal Proceedings, 4 March 1931. DPP file.

[8] Superintendent Moore's report, pages 2-3. DPP file.

Richard Parry, in his article in the *Empire News*, 5 November 1933, rebutting Wallace's accusation of murder, reported that on a visit to the Wallaces's, Mrs Wallace was dirty in appearance and that her clothing was foul-smelling, the house was untidy and uncared for and that when Wallace returned home to find Parry there, he was sneering and resentful towards Parry at his discovery of the state of affairs at his home.

Parry claims that he did not speak of his visit to his colleagues, but word did get out about Mrs Wallace's slovenly appearance, for which Wallace held Parry responsible.

Mrs Wilson, as reported by Superintendent Moore, also mentioned Mrs Wallace's dirty and unkempt appearance. See *Chapter 6*.

Sergeant Bailey reported Mrs Wallace's clothing as being home-made and that she wore a nappy, possibly because she was incontinent. See *Chapter 5*.

There can be no doubt that Julia was eccentric, possibly due to her advanced age and that at times she allowed both her appearance, and the state of her home, to slip into untidiness. Sarah Draper, the char lady, does not report on, though it would appear she was never asked about, the state of the Wallace home, or the appearance of Mrs Wallace.

If Julia Wallace was slovenly and careless at times about her appearance, particularly in front of Wallace's colleagues, then that could have increased Wallace's resentment towards her.

[9] The murder of Ruby May Carter at her home in Penllyn, Glamorgan in 1960 also parallels the Wallace case. George Carter returned home at lunchtime to find his wife dead in bed, her head smashed in by three heavy blows, and their six-year-old son, similarly injured, barely alive. A bureau had been broken into and money stolen.

Carter was tried, convicted and sentenced to life imprisonment for murder, the robbery clearly having been staged, as the bureau was the only place which was searched for cash. No motive for the crime was adduced at the trial.

It is now believed that Carter was in debt at the time of the murder and his car and home furnishings, which he had bought on hire purchase, and of which he was inordinately proud, were in danger of being repossessed. A murderous resentment towards his wife and child, and the financial burden they imposed upon him, is thought to have developed in Carter, who then sought to eliminate his family to safeguard his furnishings and car. *Encyclopaedia*, pages 154-156.

In terms of traditional motives, greed, lust, anger, hatred, this crime may be deemed a senseless or resentment murder. See note 17 below.

[10] Douglas, pages 225-237.

[11] Douglas, page 236.

[12] Diary entry, 29 March 1928. DPP file.

[13] Diary entry, 7 January 1931. DPP file.

There are several entries in the diary wherein Wallace is bent upon educating Julia, and introduces her to various philosophical and scientific theories of interest to himself, but which Julia either has no time for, or cannot comprehend. His attitude towards her in those instances was condescending and dismissive. See Goodman, page 69.

The diary entry of 15 December 1930 records Wallace's visit to the police station.

[14] Diary entry, 18 December 1928. DPP file.

[15] Douglas, page 144.

[16] Chandler, page 169.

[17] In the *Encyclopaedia of Modern Murder*, Colin Wilson, a prolific writer on the subject of murder, discusses the concept of the motiveless murder: 'But in the past, a crime usually brought the criminal some advantage. We call a crime motiveless if it seems to do no one any good.' Wilson is attempting to find an explanation for the explosion of sadistic violence which has afflicted the western world since the fifties, giving rise to the phenomena of spree, serial and thrill killers. Allowing for the activities of the insane, Wilson designates crimes as motiveless which cannot be categorised by the traditional motives of greed, lust, financial gain, etc. A better term would be senseless.

'One interesting clue is that so many of these 'motiveless' killers are of average, or above average intelligence – although the stupidity of their crimes often seems to belie it. It applies to Charles Manson, Ian Brady, ... Ted Bundy, and many others. ... The common factor here is that none made any active use of their intelligence; this, in turn, seems to have been due to the criminal's low opinion of himself – a defective self-image. And this leads again and again to a state of unmotivated resentment. Such men feel – quite incorrectly – that they are as intelligent as many people who have achieved success. So there must be something rotten and corrupt about a society that gives them no opportunity to use their talents. The crimes spring out of this resentment.'

Encyclopaedia of Modern Murder, by Colin Wilson and Donald Seaman: Pan Books, 1989, pages 4-5. Such men strike out against society with what Wilson describes as a definitive act, the act of murder, through which they channel their resentment, by which they make their point and then relish the attendant publicity. Wallace can be placed in this context.

Wilson adds a second explanation. 'There are certain crimes whose only motive seems to be a desire to break beyond the 'indifference threshold' … the Leopold and Loeb murder case; the two teenage students who killed Bobby Franks were bored rich boys who found life dull; … they felt immeasurably superior to their fellow students … But something had to be done to prove it to themselves, something to confirm them in their sense of being … supermen in a society of pygmies … so Leopold and Loeb needed to commit a 'definitive act' to assure them of their status as 'outsiders', as men to be clearly distinguished from the surrounding mediocrity.' *Encyclopaedia*, page 29.

Again Wallace can be placed in this context: he may have rejected the Stoic philosophy which engenders indifference, and struck out to make a niche for himself.

[18] There was no attempt by the police to interrogate Wallace either before, or after, his arrest and at his trial the prosecution did not directly accuse him of having killed his wife. Wallace gave four statements to the police in which he detailed his movements on the Monday and Tuesday nights and that was all that was asked of him. He was never confronted with the suspicions of the police.

Nowadays, as John Douglas writes, the police would develop an interrogation strategy, as would the prosecution, which would involve not only direct questioning but also the application of subtle psychological pressures, in order, for example, to induce remorse or guilt, even horror, in the accused, over the crime he or she had committed. For example, during police interrogations, Douglas has advised having the crime scene photographs within view of the suspect; at trial, another tactic is to get the accused to handle something from the crime scene which is obviously connected to the victim. Douglas and Olshaker, pages 23, 58 and 247.

Bibliography

The Wallace Case

Agate, James. *Ego 6*: Harrap, 1944.

BPC Publishing. *A Mysterious Telephone Call*, 1973.

Bridges, Yseult. *Two Studies in Crime*: Hutchinson, 1959.

Brophy, John. *The Liverpool Classic* in *The Meaning of Murder*: Ronald Whiting and Wheaton, 1966.

Chandler, Raymond. *Raymond Chandler Speaking*: Hamish Hamilton, 1962.

Fido, Martin. *The Wallace Case* in *Murders After Midnight*: Orion Books, 1993.

Gaute, JH and Robin Odell. *The New Murderers' Who's Who*: Headline Books, 1989.

Goodman, Jonathan. *The Killing of Julia Wallace*: Harrap, 1969.

Goodman, Jonathan. *The Last Sentence*: Hutchinson, 1978.

Hussey, Robert. *Murderer Scot-Free*: David and Charles, 1972.

Jessel, David. *Murder Casebook*, Volume 25: Marshal Cavendish, 1990.

Lustgarten, Edgar. *The Murder and the Trial*: Odhams, 1960.

Rowland, John. *The Wallace Case*: Carroll and Nicholson, 1949.

Sayers, Dorothy L. *The Murder of Julia Wallace* in *The Anatomy of Murder*: The Bodley Head, 1936.

Sterling, Jane. *The Murder of Julia Wallace* in *Famous Northern Crimes, Trials and Criminals*: Hesketh, 1983.

Waterhouse, Richard. *The Insurance Man*: Leyburns Designs, 1994.

Whittington-Egan, Richard. *Corpse in the Parlour* in *Tales of Liverpool*: The Gallery Press, 1967.

Wilkes, Roger. *Wallace: The Final Verdict*: Triad/Panther, 1985.

Wilson, Colin. *William Herbert Wallace* in *Unsolved*, edited by John Canning: Futura, 1988.

Wilson, Colin and Pitman, Pat. *Encyclopaedia of Murder*: Pan Books, 1964.

Wilson, Colin and Wilson, Damon. *The Wallace Case* in *World Famous Unsolved Crimes*: Magpie Books, 1992.

References

Allen, Charles, editor. *Plain Tales from the Raj*: Futura, 1976.

Canter, Professor David. *Criminal Shadows*: Harper Collins, 1994.

Capote, Truman. *In Cold Blood*: Penguin Books, 1967.

Cockcroft, William. *From Cutlasses to Computers*: SB Publications, 1991.

Cyriax, Oliver. *The Penguin Encyclopedia of Crime*: Penguin Books, 1996.

Douglas, John and Olshaker, Mark. *Mindhunter*: Mandarin Paperbacks, 1996.

Douglas, John and Olshaker, Mark. *Journey into Darkness*: Arrow Books, 1998.

Harrison, Shirley. *The Diary of Jack the Ripper*: Smith Gryphon, 1994.

Honeycombe, Gordon. *The Murders of the Black Museum*: Arrow Books, 1985.

Lane, Brian. *The Encyclopaedia of Forensic Medicine*: Headline Books, 1992.

Lane, Brian. *The Murder Year Book*: Headline Books, 1993.

Morton, James. *Bent Coppers*: Warner Books, 1994.

Morton, James. *A Calendar of Killing*: Warner Books, 1997.

Morris, James. *Heaven's Command*: Penguin Books, 1979.

Popkin, Richard and Stroll, Avrum. *Philosophy Made Simple*: WH Allen, 1973.

Ressler, Robert and Shachtman, T. *Whoever Fights Monsters*: Simon and Schuster, 1992.

Socialist Research Group. *Genuinely Seeking Work*: Liver Press, 1992.

Stockman, Rocky. *The Hangman's Diary*: Headline Books, 1994.

Wilson, Colin. *Order of Assassins*: Panther Books, 1975.

Wilson, Colin. *Written in Blood*: Grafton Books, 1990.

Wilson, Colin and Seaman, David. *Encyclopaedia of Modern Murder*: Pan Books, 1989.

Wilson, Colin and Seaman, David. *The Serial Killers*: WH Allen, 1990.

Other Sources

Liverpool Echo
The Daily Post
North Western Daily Mail
The Daily Telegraph
Yorkshire Post
Empire News
John Bull
The CPS Journal
The Criminologist
The Police Journal
Merseybeat
Outlook
Liverpool Red Book
Liverpool A-Z
Liverpool Historical and Transport Society(HATS)
Liverpool Record Office
Merseyside Record Office
Thacker's Indian Directory.
Robinson's Harrogate Directory.
The Halifax Building Society.
The Meteorological Office.